AFRICAN STUDIES
HISTORY, POLITICS, ECONOMICS, AND CULTURE

African Studies
History, Politics, Economics, and Culture
Molefi Asante, *General Editor*

AFRICA IN THE 21ST CENTURY

Toward a New Future

Edited by
Ama Mazama

Routledge
New York & London

Routledge
2 Park Square, Milton Park, Abingdon, Oxfordshire OX14 4RN
711 Third Avenue, New York, NY 10017

First issued in paperback 2011

ISBN 978-0-415-95773-1 (hbk)
ISBN 978-0-415-51471-2 (pbk)

Library of Congress Cataloging-in-Publication Data

Africa in the 21st century : toward a new future / edited by Ama Mazama.
    p. cm. -- (African studies: history, politics, economics, and culture)
    Includes bibliographical references and index.
    ISBN 0-415-95773-7
    1. Africa--Social conditions--21st century. 2. Africa--Politics and government--21st century. 3. Africa--Economic conditions--21st century. 4. Africa--Forecasting. I. Mazama, Ama, 1961- II. Title: Africa in the twenty-first century.

HN777.A33 2007
303.496--dc22   2006101834

Visit the Taylor & Francis Web site at
http://www.taylorandfrancis.com

and the Routledge Web site at
http://www.routledge.com

Contents

SECTION II: LANGUAGE, INFORMATION, AND EDUCATION

SECTION III: AFRICAN WOMEN, CHILDREN, AND FAMILIES

SECTION IV: POLITICAL AND ECONOMIC FUTURE OF THE AFRICAN WORLD

List of Tables

Foreword

Dr. Cheikh Tidiane Gadio,
Senior Minister, Foreign Affairs,
Republic of Senegal

African leaders and philosophers have continued to express Pan African sentiments articulated in the 20th century by Kwame Nkrumah, Cheikh Anta Diop, W. E. B. Du Bois and others. In fact, these ideas have crystallized into what President Abdoulaye Wade of Senegal has called "the destiny of Africa." It was not too long ago that the first generation of post colonial leaders of Africa called for the unity of the continent. Such a call for unity can be realized only when scholars such as these who have written for this important book have studied the intricacies of African unity and have given political leaders the kind of advice that is necessary for progressive developments to occur.

Kwame Nkrumah, the first president of Ghana, often maligned during his own lifetime has now become one of the principal icons of the discourse supporting the Federative Union of Africa, also called the United States of Africa. Nkrumah's vision constituted more than a dream; it was a practical and practicable destiny for the continent. Indeed, Julius Nyerere of Tanzania commented late in his life that had the presidents of other nations on the continent had the vision that Nkrumah possessed the continent would have arrived at the point of national unity much earlier.

There is no doubt in mind that the work presented in this book will have a major impact on the way national leaders and scholars in Africa see the future. It is to be expected that there will be detractors who remain trapped in the negative images of the continent. These are the promoters of the myths of primitive, wild, exotic, broken, and dangerous Africa. However, for those who study Africa with an open mind, this book will be an eye-opener, yielding to the readers a wealth of information and analysis of the African situation.

Clearly, the African Union, successor to the Organization of African Unity, has set as its objective the absolute national union of the continent. If this can be achieved, and most of us believe that it can be, then Africa will have a renaissance unlike any that has been seen before. When the fourteen landlocked nations all have outlets to the seas because they are not independent, isolated entities anymore, but regions of a much larger nation that allows free movement of people and goods around the continent, we will have moved to a level of economic, political and cultural integration that could have been only dreamed about a few years ago. Now we know that it will happen and the scholars who have been chosen to write for this significant book will be on the frontlines of African renaissance thinking.

In the coming decades Africa stands to be in the center of global interest in economic, political, and social change. No continent on earth has as many undeveloped resources as Africa. Those resources will either serve the democratic and developmental purposes of the African people or serve as the basis for the continued exploitation of Africa. I am an optimist who believes strongly in the renaissance of Africa. I applaud the scholars who have contributed to this volume because I believe that they, too, have a sense that the African resurgence is real.

Preface
The African Century

Ama Mazama, Temple University

The African triumphalism of the mid-twentieth century has turned once again to hope. One senses that hope is celebrated to hold back the forces of despair. In almost every category of the quality of life, African nations have seen a decline in the past thirty years. Throughout the continent there are wars and rumors of wars as various regional and ethnic communities explode in orgies of violence that shatter all of the idealism that one could conceivably have about the continent. It is as if the lack of triumphalism of the sort that existed when African unity seemed so sure and certain vanished and left in its place the hard-nosed practicality of an entirely new league of Africanists.

Yet there is in Africa, along the corridors of power in the richest countries, and among the university elites, the idea that Africa is on its way to a resurgence. However, all forms of resurgence are based on the people's willingness to devote themselves to something more than their own interest. In the case of Africa it seems now that the ordinary African, as well as the elite, has taken to the idea proposed by Sylvester Williams, W. E. B. Du Bois, Kwame Nkrumah, and Cheikh Anta Diop that Africa must unite.

When we contacted the writers for this volume we indicated that we wanted chapters that reflected Africa's possibilities, not because we sought to overlook the negations that exist on the continent in the form of wars, gender inequality, ethnic conflicts, or class issues, but because Africa's problems are commonplace in the discourses of the West. What if our authors could discover a few silver clouds, a few sunlit places where people have taken hold of hope, and where the human spirit has won out against the negatives? What if the authors could help mold for us a conception of Africa as a center for the next century as Asia has been for the past fifty years?

These questions suggest that we are on the verge of announcing the African century. Already China has increased its trade relations with Africa enormously over the past five years. This has not kept Europe from expanding its base in the continent's oil and energy sector, nor has China's entry kept smaller players, such as Malaysia and the Philippines, from having their own field day in the continent. As one of the last regions of the world to have an abundance of mineral resources, but not an equally robust infrastructure for exploiting the mineral wealth for its people, Africa remains tentative about its future.

We chose some of the most critical thinkers on African affairs for this work, hoping that their remarks might spark debates around the role of national governments in the larger picture of an intracontinental state. As Africans tamed a hostile continent for the benefit of human beings at the dawn of humanity, it seems quite likely that Africans will re-introduce themselves to the world as a proud, determined, and democratic people.

African Unity and Consciousness: Assets and Challenges

Chapter One
The Resurgence of the African World in the 21st Century

Molefi Kete Asante, Temple University

There is a genetic sense in which the African homeland is homeland to the entire human race. According to the latest scientific studies the DNA of all human beings can be traced back to an African woman who lived nearly 250,000 years ago in East Africa. This is the biological reality of all human beings. We know from archaeology and paleontology that skeletal remains of hominids can be dated to 6 million years in Chad and nearly 4 million years in Ethiopia. However, in the continuous human line to the present we have enough evidence to suggest from mitachondrial DNA that all living humans are descended from an African woman, the African mother. However, our current notion of the Diaspora is fairly recent, mainly within the past five hundred years during which time the people of Africa were attacked, victimized, colonized, and enslaved by those who lived outside of the continent. The African Diaspora is vast, encompassing millions of people and many nations.

THE DIASPORA

African intellectuals have used the term Diaspora more prominently since the 1950s when large numbers of African scholars and activists began adopting the term *Diaspora* as a statement of solidarity with the struggles of the African continent. Although there had been from the earliest times a sense of belonging to Africa in the writings of Edward Blyden, Martin Delany, Abdias do Nascimento, Marcus Garvey, and others, it was the

3

liberation of the African continent that brought into existence a new era of pride and dignity. The use of the term "Ethiopia" was prominent in the discourse of *memory* and *return* and there was a sense in which Africans in the Diaspora no longer had to feel that we were motherless children a long way from home.

Despite opposition and criticism from those who have abandoned the idea of homeland, history is richer with universal declarations of solidarity with the African world in the works of Edward Blyden from the Virgin Islands; Marcus Garvey, Leonard Barrett, and Mutabaruka from Jamaica; Sheila Walker, Wade Nobles, and Asa Hilliard from the United States; Arthur Schomberg and Marta Vega from Puerto Rico; Jean Price-Mars from Haiti; George Padmore, C. L. R. James, Kwame Ture, and Khafra Kambon from Trinidad; George James, Norman Cameron, Ivan Van Sertima, and Walter Rodney from Guyana; Aimé Césaire and René Maran from Martinique; George Lamming and Kamau Brathwaite from Barbados; Manuel Zapata-Olivella, Maryse Condé, Ama Mazama, and Simone Schwartz-Bart from Guadeloupe; Nicolas Guillen from Cuba, Abdias do Nascimento and Benedita da Silva from Brazil, and more.

ELEMENTS OF THE DIASPORA

It should be clear now that the African Diaspora has three elements: *concept, process,* and *situation.* At the conceptual level we realize our Pan African potential through the manifestation of a Diasporic interface among all segments of the African population. We must look to each other. The idea of process is a continuation, a becoming, *khepera,* in our classical language, that is not yet complete, but always in motion. When we say *situation* we mean by it the *place* in which we are domiciled, that is, where we live.

The *concept* is political, that is, it contains the potential for influencing economic and social issues. It is also spiritual where the affirmation of our ancestors as philosophers, farmers, metallurgists, scholars, artists, and healers is at the head of our revitalization. Thus, to be in the Diaspora as an African Brazilian or an African Canadian or African Jamaican or African Britisher is to realize similarities and commonalities in memory but also in conquest over obstacles, barriers, and challenges.

As much as the concept is political and spiritual, the *process* of the Diaspora is social. Those of us who voluntarily leave the continent to find education, work, and personal relationships and pursuits constitute an added layer to the Diaspora. In some cases these Diasporas remain essentially distinct; however, within a generation they become a part of the old Diaspora, as the children of the newcomers take on the symbols, language, styles, and ambitions of the older Diaspora while at the same time enriching older the Diaspora with new signs, symbols, art forms, and music. What we must do is to advance the integration of our cultures along the best lines for the advancement of Africa. At the process level we are always becoming.

Africa is not static; one can neither claim Africa as it was one hundred years ago, nor fifty years ago, nor five years ago. The continent is pre-eminent as a dynamic locus for transformation. We are the catalyst for this change. In the Diaspora, it is the same. New Diasporas are being created on the Arabian horn, comprised of Africans from the continent as from other parts of the world. As new people enter the countries of Europe, the Americas, Asia, and the Caribbean, we are forming an inevitable network for international cooperation.

Yet it is true that the Diaspora is also a *situation*. Some of us are in place for a long time. There is the Afro-Asian Diaspora found in the various nations of Asia. There are also Blackfellows of Australia who claim African origins. The Dalits of India, the Siddis of India, the Africans in the United States, Brazil, Mexico, Honduras, Nicaragua, Venezuela, Panama, Colombia, Costa Rica, Ecuador, Guadeloupe, Martinique, Trinidad and Tobago, Cuba, Peru, Surinam, Uruguay, and Guyana must be made to feel a part of this grand movement of consciousness.

African history is replete with creativity, resilience, and nobility. But Africans will have to teach children to share in the respective victories of the continent and the Diaspora as their heritage. None of us is without culture. Indeed, to be without culture is to be without ancestors and we are all the children of our ancestors. Sometimes we do not honor nor respect them and perhaps that is the beginning of Africa's crime against its own history.

Africans were the first, not as a boast but as a fact, to erect monumental architecture as in the Nile Valley and the Axumite Empire. Africans were the first to create a mathematical abacus as with the Isonghee bone calculator nearly thirty thousand years ago. Africans were the first to organize medicine, to create geometry, astronomy, law, politics, kinship customs, theology, art, writing, and sculpture. Indeed, Erastothenes, librarian at Rhacosta, renamed Alexandria to honor the Greek conqueror, reported that Egyptian papyrus ships had sailed as far as Ceylon, now the country of Sri Lanka. In fact, Pliny, the Roman historian in *Historia Naturalis,* says that the Africans had gone as far as the mouth of the Ganges in the Indus Valley. We know, of course, from Herodotus and other sources that Sesostris I of the 12th Dynasty, around 1991 BC, had led his armies into the Black Sea region. We know that Herodotus wrote that Necho, the pharaoh, sent a fleet to circumnavigate the African continent. We know that the mighty king, Ramses II, *user maat re, setep en re,* had his portrait and inscriptions placed in three places on the coastal cliffs of Phoenicia.

Yet the past five hundred years have tested the will of Africa and brought us in contact with an avaricious and aggressive culture that has sought to undermine the very basis of African humanity. It has been African resilience on the continent and in the Diaspora that has kept the flames of renaissance burning. Like the palm that sways in the storm but does not break, Africa has taken the blows, the awful, brutal blows of colonialism and enslavement and survived.

THE EUROPEAN SLAVE TRADE

Africa's record of fighting and resisting invasion, colonization, and enslavement is monumental. In North America, the Native Americans lost an entire continent. This was also the fate of the Blackfellows of Australia. This was to be the end of Africa, but it did not happen. Of course, the devastation of Africa in terms of human and material resources was immense.

Africa was not responsible for its own devastation. The enslavement of Africans was not an initiative of Africans. No African states built ships to transport Africans across the oceans. No African state or kingdom ever insured fleets of ships for the slave trade. No African people ever used slavery as a principal mode of production. It is important to be clear about Europe's role as the initiator of African enslavement. Indeed, there were Africans, some very colorful, who collaborated with the Europeans but they were never the majority nor yet the initiators of this evil business. One cannot blame the collaborators for initiating these horrors. They were in many ways victims themselves.

SETTING AFRICAN TERMS

Africa must examine its own cultures and languages for a revitalization of the continent. This means that Africa must interrogate its own past for values that might be used for renaissance. It must learn from others but it cannot follow in the footsteps of the West as mere imitators. Africa must consider the possibility that its own history contains the seeds for approaching modernization, integration and revitalization. If there must be advantages to scholarship in a material way, let Africa set the terms, let the governments of Africa establish the awards that will attract the best minds to work in the interest of African development. This will mean that the continent must shed its timidity.

There are several steps that Africa might take to dispel the misconceptions about the Diaspora. In the first place, African leaders should assume an Afrocentric stance on everything that affects Africa. This means that ideas promoted by Africans must be evaluated for their consistency with the goal of African renaissance.

AN AFROCENTRIC IDEOLOGY

What is needed is an ideology of success founded upon the principles of an Africa-centered perspective. Afrocentricity is a quality of thought or action that allows the African person to view himself or herself as an agent and actor in human history, not simply as someone who is acted upon. It provides a perspective from the subject place, not from the margins of being victims or being an object in someone else's world. Thus, Africans are seen as creators, originators, and sustainers of ethics, values, and customs. As minimum requirements Africa must accept the idea that:

- Classical African civilizations are necessary references and resources for Afrocentric concept formation and research, and that an adequate understanding cannot take place without reference or organic connections made to classical African cultures.
- The African world is wherever people declare themselves as Africans. This is true whether in Africa, Asia, the Americas, or the Caribbean.
- Africans are people who share the same consciousness (worldview/orientation), culture and physical qualities to those in some region of Africa.
- Afrocentricity establishes a positive approach to all information and data.
- "Absence of evidence" is not necessarily "evidence of absence."
- A necessary goal and outcome of Afrocentric research is emancipatory knowledge.
- "Objective," "objectivity," and "universal" are artificial categories, which have little meaning in the real world because they equate by default to a collective European subjectivity supporting European particularism.

LET US REDEFINE

At a fundamental level, the Atlantic Ocean becomes the West African Sea and the Indian Ocean is the East African Sea. There is no real reason except assertion that the Europeans have called the ocean to the west of Africa, Atlantic, and that they and the Asians have called the ocean to the east of Africa, Indian. The continent of Africa is the largest land mass bordering these two oceans yet the intellectual authority of Africa has been so negligible that Europe has spoken in our name. Never again should Africa or Africans allow that to happen. Just a simple matter like *classical music* must mean Africa's classical music. European concert music must not assume the principal place in Africa's pantheon of music. Africans must act like they are owners ready to claim ancestral birthrights. Loyalty does not imply rubber stamping, but rather an intelligentsia that understands the threat to Africa, and is committed to Africa.

FIVE POINTS TO THIS APPROACH

I believe that there are five important ideas in an Afrocentric approach to the African and Diasporan situation: (1) Africans are subjects, (2) Africans are agents, (3) Africans build on image, (4) Africans claim African interests, and (5) Africans share a consciousness of victory.

1. Subject—the place from which we view the world
2. Agent—self conscious and self-determining causal force
3. Image—ideal form or mode rooted in cultural perspective, perception and values
4. Interest–benefits, rights and just claims shared with other humans (life, freedom, justice, self-determination etc.)
5. A consciousness of victory—the awareness and recognition of African agency and capability; the rejection of collective self doubt, and the ability and courage to overcome challenges and transcend difficulties.

In the Diaspora we are often seen as running toward Africa while in Africa we are often seen as running toward Europe. In this curious activity we shall find each other and there shall be such a happy meeting of the children of Africa. We must not allow those who have for nearly five centuries been the engineers of our despair, the architects of our disorientation, and the designers of our mis-education, to continue their assaults on our ancestors, traditions, morality, ethics, and values. If anything, we must resume a vanguard role in the political and moral leadership of the world. Left to those who have articulated a desire to rule the world through globalization, a new form of white racial supremacy, we will be marginalized in the dust baskets of history by an ethically bankrupt hegemonic culture.

PAN-AFRICANISM AND THE DIASPORA

To claim to be a member of the Diaspora one must demonstrate a Pan African solidarity with the world African community, a desire for the revitalization of Africa, a consciousness of victory, and some accountability to the objectives of African renaissance. Any idea of homeland longing must be seen either in psychological, physical, spiritual, or economic terms. If you cannot return to Africa physically, you can return psychologically and economically. If you cannot return to Africa physically, you can advance Africa's cultural heritage.

ADVANCING AFRICA IN THE WORLD

The Diasporan communities must continue to push for African unity. Ultimately the unity of the continent will benefit the entire African world. The African continent is a vast territory. One could put the United States, China, India, all of Europe, including the United Kingdom inside of Africa. Even taking into account the desert regions Africa has enough arable land to feed the earth. There are forest resources, desert minerals, animals, and oils for all types of industries. There is enough timber in the forests for export and enough land for re-plantation. Thirty percent of the world's useful but underutilized land is in Africa. More types of wood can be found in Africa than all of the rest of the continents combined. Food production in Africa is potentially phenomenal. The continent has the capacity to cultivate oats, maize, onions, peanuts, all manner of fruits, grapes, potatoes, cassava, and yams in great profusion. East Africa alone could produce as much food as is produced in the United States.

Since these facts are true, why aren't the economies of Africa flourishing everywhere? Why do African countries remain at the bottom economically? Of course, these are complex questions with complicated answers. I propose an approach to African unity that is concrete, practical, and inclusive.

We do not believe, nor can we accept on rational grounds, the theories that suggest Africa is unable to organize because of personalities that fail to put Africa's interest before their own personal interests. Thus, African intellectuals from Kwame Nkrumah, Cheikh Anta Diop, Walter Rodney, and

Marcus Garvey to several contemporary African presidents have argued for a United Africa. This has been the vision of most forward thinking African leaders since the 1950s. It is a reasonable and achievable objective which will have far-reaching implications for the continent's ability to feed itself, secure its people, support world stability, and create an expanding economic future for the African people

If you speak of declines in agricultural production in Africa in many instances you are talking about how Western powers prevented or prohibited or reduced exports from Africa. In some cases, African exports have been heavily taxed and consequently in areas such as cotton production (something African nations know about) the European and American nations have supported their own farmers and stifled competition from African farmers. There is no lack of energy, capability, or technical know-how on the part of Africa; it is strictly a lack of organizational and political power to see the continent's economic interests protected. Take the fact that since the 1970s Africa's dependence on wheat has grown each year while locally grown staple crops of Africa can produce enough food to feed all of its people, and the issue is not capability, but the political will to organize for success. By now we all recognize that the major obstacles are the colonial boundaries established by the white colonial powers at the end of the 19th century. Those boundaries have served to exacerbate inadequate communication, ethnocentric worldviews, poor interstate transportation, marginal trade with neighboring countries, lack of crop diversity, and an overemphasis on export crops to maintain connection to the former colonial powers.

In order to project an African ethos on world matters, the unity of Africa is absolutely necessary. There is a continental destiny that must be played out in Africa. Nothing that happens on the continent with one nation can be said to happen in isolation.

I see several areas that are essential as first level steps toward African Unity. Many of these concerns have already been addressed by the African Union and I am merely repeating them in this paper. I think, as a minimum, we need:

1. The African Parliament—This is the legislative body
2. The African President—This is the symbolic head of state
3. The African Foreign Minister—This is the coordinator and interpreter of African policies
4. The African Infrastructural Minister—This is the person responsible for articulating a national vision for the continent
5. The Chief of Military Operations—This is the person who coordinates and operates the security and military sector

6. The Education Minister—The person who fashions a continental-wide curriculum for schools, taking into consideration local and national issues

Other protocols will emerge that will help us formulate a closer connection between the Diaspora and this new rising United States of Africa.

WE HAVE NOT BEGUN TO TAP OUR POWER

While it is true that the largest mass movement of people from one continent to others was the movement of Africans to the Americas and the Caribbean, our struggle has been constant and consistent. We have never acquiesced in the separation from our motherland. More than four hundred million Africans now live in the Diaspora and our population is growing. Africa's population is nearly 900 million. In Brazil, Africans comprise about 110 million people. There are millions of Africans in other South American countries, Peru, Venezuela, and Colombia, have sizable populations. In the United States of America there are 40 million Africans. The Caribbean has some 50 million black people. Mexico has about 100,000 Africans. We know that the combined populations of Africans in countries such as United Kingdom, France, Portugal, Belgium, Italy, Spain, Russia, Germany, Turkey, and Sweden is approximately 1,000,000. Thus, people of African descent, including those scattered in Southwest and Southeast Asia, make up more than a billion Africans.

There are a few ideas that I would like to propose toward the union of the continent and the diaspora.

1. Schools in Africa must include in their curricula information from the Diaspora. There is no reason why every African child should not know Mae Jemison, the first black woman to fly in space, and Guion Bluford, and Arnaldo Tamayo, the first African men to fly in space, one from the United States and the other from Cuba.
2. African nations should have persons in ministries whose job is to interface with the Diaspora on every issue. If there is a need to build a road, a hospital, open a fishery, develop a telecommunication facility, there is no reason why African nations, even if they must deal with Western nations at the level of money, could not understand the issues better by discovering experts of African descent who would take a personal interest in the project.

3. We cannot operate from weakness or the perception of weakness. We must all operate as if we are in charge of our achievement.
4. African leaders should have a precise knowledge of the Diasporan African communities. This would allow them to target these communities for resources, ideas, concepts, and reciprocal political and economic relations.
5. The right of Africans in the Diaspora to return is a legitimate issue for African governments. There is no reason why those who govern the lands of our ancestors should prevent those of us who were taken against our wills from our homeland from returning. This would be a major step in our reconciliation with each other.

Our actions must be based on analysis but we should have no paralysis by analysis. One of the ways ideas are destroyed in the West is by analysis. For example, we know that there may be *a* multiplicity of Diasporas in one nation, as when you have Senegalese, Chadians, Malians, Algerians, and Togolese in France. They may even overlap with each other in different ways because of class, gender, ethnicity, relationship to the West, and ideas of globalization. We can discover similarities and dissimilarities in our cultural and historical experiences knowing that this type of analysis would reveal more similarities than differences. Of course, more dissimilarities mean that we must abandon the comparative model. Most importantly, as we find similarities in cultural forms, we should propose ways that our common political, social, and economic problems can be solved or resolved by looking at various other Diasporas.

EXPOSE FALSE ELEMENTS

We must guard ourselves from false people who grin in our face and take our hospitality for innocence and our grace for stupidity. We must be aware of these lethal people. Our strength must come from an Afrocentric bond, stronger than religion because religion has often been used to divide us. There is nothing stronger than a collective commitment to the rise of the African spirit.

Just as our ethnic experiences on the continent differ so do the Diasporic experiences differ. Our environments are often different and the responses we have made in Brazil may be different from those we made in Jamaica or Cuba or Canada. Yet our similarities are grounded in the way we have sought to maintain our sanity in the face of insanity, by our search for harmony in the middle of political and social chaos. And also by the Pan Africanism and later the Afrocentricity that drives the idea of the Diaspora as a unit for analysis.

Pan-Africanism was a Diasporic innovation. Separated from the continent of origin, unable to control our own destinies, and assaulted on every side, we sought an organizing political instrument for collective action. Thus, Pan Africanism was born to bring us together to struggle for economic, social, and political rights in the Diaspora and on the continent. Pan Africanism allowed us to attack colonialism in Africa and the Caribbean, discrimination in the United States, assimilationism in Brazil, and to promote the unification of black people, particularly those living on the continent.

To the African leaders I make a particular plea. I ask you to give us leadership in the quest for true liberation. With your input, your action, your determination, Africa and the Diaspora will achieve historic successes. We need advocates for our cause and there are no greater advocates than our own African leaders whose collective words, called a preamble might be:

> *The nations, kingdoms, territories, and peoples of Africa with respect to the ancestors dedicate themselves to the united interest of African people.*
>
> *We declare a commitment to freedom, harmony, order, balance, justice, and reciprocity in all our relations with each other.*
>
> *We are a collective people with long traditions in intensifying communal relationships, therefore we obligate ourselves to the African community with a persistent vigilance to hold back chaos.*
>
> *We declare human rights to be universal, irrespective of place of origin, ethnic identity, gender, or religion.*
>
> *There is nothing more important for our unity than a commitment to continental national character, the centerpiece of a constructive advancement toward the fulfillment of our peoples' hopes and desires.*
>
> *We emphasize the common destiny of the African continent, the inculcation of a revolutionary, social and economic transformation based on African principles, and the intent to defend the continent from any colonial domination.*
>
> *We enter this pact with each other willingly, believing that humans are essentially good, that truth and justice are sources of strength, and that our posterity will value the traditions unlocked by our union.*

UP! YOU MIGHTY PEOPLE!

I am ready to see us establish ourselves at the center of the world stage. I am ready to see us create an integrated African world where the ideas, energies, and concepts that have made us creative, resilient, and capable are used for moral and political leadership. I am ready to see us cast aside all neuroses that are associated with the legacy of colonialism, discrimination, and enslavement. I am ready to see us accept our culture, as a heritage to be shaped and molded, rather than baggage to be thrown to the side. I am ready to see us seize the intellectual initiatives for our own destiny. We can do this, we must do this for our children!

REFERENCES

Anselin, A. (1982). *Le Mythe D' Europe*. Paris: Editions Anthropos.

Asante, Molefi Kete (1998) *The Afrocentric Idea*. Philadelphia: Temple University.

Asante, Molefi Kete. (2003). *Afrocentricity*. Chicago: African American Images.

Asante, Molefi Kete. (1990). *Kemet, Afrocentricity, and Knowledge*. Trenton: Africa World Press.

Asante, Molefi Kete. (1994). *Classical Africa*. Maywood, N.J.: The Peoples Publishing Group, Inc.

Ben-Jochannan, Yosef.(1971, 1988) *Africa: Mother of Western Civilization*. Baltimore, MD: Black Classic Press.

Ben-Jochannan, Yosef (1972) *African Origins of the Major Western Religions*. New York: Alkebu-Lan

Bernal, Martin (l987) *Black Athena: the Afro Asiatic Roots of Classical Civilization, Volume I: The Fabrication of Ancient Greece, 1875–1985*. New Brunswick: Rutgers University Press.

Bernal, Martin (1991) *Black Athena: the Afro Asiatic Roots of Classical Civilizwation, Volume II: The Archaeological and Documentary Evidence*. New Brunswick: Rutgers University Press.

Blyden, Edward Wilmot (1887) *Christianity, Islam and the Negro Race*. London: W.B. Whittingham.

Browder, Anthony Y.(1992) *Nile Valley Contributions to Civilization: Exploding the Myths, Vol. 1*. Introduction by John Henrik Clarke. Washington, D.C. Institute of Karmic Guidance.

Carruthers, Jacob H. (1995) *Mdr Ntr: Divine Speech (A Historiographical Reflection on African Deep Thought from the Time of the Pharaohs to the Present)*. Foreword by John Henrik Clarke. London: Karnak House.

Diagne, Pathe (1981). In J. Ki-Zerbo (Ed.), *General History of Africa I: Methodology and African Prehistory*. London: Heinemann Educational Books Ltd.

Diagne, Pathe (2002) *Cheikh Anta Diop et L'Afrique dans L'histoire du Monde*, Paris: Sankore, 2002.

Diop, C. A., (1955) *Nations nègres et culture*. Paris: Présence Africaine.

Diop, Cheikh Anta (1974) *The African Origin of Civilization*. Westport, Ct.: Lawrence Hill

Diop, Cheikh Anta (1991) *Civilization or Barbarism*. Chicago: Lawrence Hill.

Drake, St. Clair, (1987) *Black Folk Here and There: An Essay in History and Anthropology*. Volume I, Los Angeles: Center for Afro American Studies, University of California, Los Angeles.

Drake, St. Clair (1990) *Black Folk Here and There: An Essay in History and Anthropology*. Volume II, Los Angeles: Center for Afro American Studies, University of California, Los Angeles.

DuBois, W. E. B.(1946) *The World and Africa: An Inquiry into the Part Which Africa Has Played in World History.* New York: International Publishers.

Fanon, F. (1967). *Black Skin, White Masks.* New York: Grove Press.

Hansberry, William Leo (1981) *Africa and Africans as Seen by Classical Writers.* Edited by Joseph E. Harris. Washington, DC: Howard University Press.

Harris, Joseph, ed., (1977) *Africa and Afrians as Seen by Classical Writers: The William Leo Hansberry African History Notebook*, Vol II. Washington, DC: Howard University Press.

Herodotus. (1972) *The Histories.* Translated by Aubrey de Selincourt. Rev. ed. Harmondsworth: Penguin.

Hilliard, Asa G. III (2002) "The Myth of the Immaculate Conception of Western Civilization," in Molefi Kete Asante and Ama Mazama, ed., *Egypt vs. Greece and the American Academy: The Debate over the Birth of Civilization.* Chicago: African American Images.

Hilliard, Asa G. III. (1997) *SBA: The Reawakening of the African Mind.* Foreword by Wade W. Nobles. Gainesville: Makare Books.

Hilliard, Asa G. III, Larry Obadele Williams and Nia Damali, eds. *The Teachings of Ptahhotep: The Oldest Book in the World.* Atlanta: Blackwood Press, 1987.

Houston, Drusilla Dunjee. (1985) *Wonderful Ethiopians of the Ancient Cushite Empire.* 1926; rpt. Baltimore: Black Classic Press.

James, George G. M. (1954) *Stolen Legacy: The Greeks Were Not the Authors of Greek Philosophy, but the People of North Africa Commonly Called the Egyptians.* New York: Philosophical Library

Karenga, Maulana, (1978) *Essays on Struggle: Position and Analysis.* San Diego: Kawaida Publications.

Karenga, Maulana (1993) *The Introduction to Black Studies.* Los Angeles: University of Sankore Press.

Karenga, Maulana (2003) *Maat: The Moral Ideal in Ancient Egypt, A Study in Classical African Ethics.* New York: Routledge.

Keita, Maghan (2000) *Race and the Writing of History: Riddling the Sphinx.* New York: Oxford University Press.

King, Leophus Taharka. (2004) *"Philomythy: Ancient Egyptian Correspondences in Greek Creation Myths.* Unpublished dissertation, Temple University, 2004.

Mazama, Ama, (2001) The Afrocentric Paradigm: Contours and Definitions. *Journal of Black Studies,* 31 (4), 387–405.

Mazama, Ama, ed., (2003) *The Afrocentric Paradigm.* Trenton: Africa World Press.

Obenga, T. (1973). *L'Afrique dans l'antiquité-Egypte pharaonique-Afrique noire.* Paris: Presence Africaine.

Obenga, Theophile (1992b) *Ancient Egypt and Black Africa: A Student's Handbook for the Study of Ancient Egypt in Philosophy, Linguistics and Gender Relations.* Edited by Amon Saba Saakana. London: Karnak House.

Obenga, Theophile (1995) *A Lost Tradition: African Philosophy in World History.* Philadelphia: The Source Editions, 1995.

Obenga, T. (1978a). *Africa in Antiquity, Africa Quarterly,* 18, no.1, pp.1–15.

Obenga, T. (1978b). *The genetic relationship between Egyptian (ancient Egyptian and Coptic) and modern African languages.* In UNESCO (Ed.), *The Peopling* of Ancient Egypt and the Deciphering of the Meroitic Script (65–72). Paris: UNESCO.

Obenga, T. (1992a). *Le Chamito-sémitique n'existe pas*, ANKH , no.1, pp.51–58.

Obenga, T. (1993). *Origine commune de l'Egyptien Ancien du Copte et des Langues Négro-Africaines* Modernes. Paris: Editions L'Harmattan.

Rodney, Walter (1969) *How Europe Underdeveloped Africa*. Washington, D.C.: Howard University Press.

Senghor, L.S. (1961). *Negritude and African Socialism, African Affairs*, pp.20–25

Chapter Two
Kwame Nkrumah's Continental Africa: A Dream Deferred but Not Forgotten

John K. Marah, SUNY—Brockport

Compared to his African presidential contemporaries, (Kaunda, Nyerere, Kenyatta, Obote and others) Kwame Nkrumah remains the most outstanding African political figure of the twentieth century (Mazrui, 1993: 13–21); he is also the most outstanding and prolific pan-Africanist politician. In more than ten books, he details his ideas on colonialism, neo-colonialism, the African personality, colonial freedom, pan-Africanism, and the impact of multinational corporations on African politics and development. He is compared to renown world leaders such as Konrad Adenauer of Germany, David Ben-Gurion of Israel, Charles De Gaulle of France, Castro, JFK, and others who have had "resounding impact (s) on world affairs" and "he will go down in history as the first black African leader of the first black African independent country," south of the Sahara (Webb, 1964: 1, 137).

Kwame Nkrumah also remains, among his contemporaries, the one that is most negatively written about, by Africans as well as non-Africans; between his writings and those of others about him, Kwame Nkrumah comes across as a contradiction; those who love him, do so dearly; those who do not, vilify him and point out his most salient shortcomings and attribute to him unfounded cruelties, superior abilities, and other 'peculiar' characteristics. He has been labeled a dictator, a dreamer, a man ahead of his times, a visionary, a showman, and a Marxist-socialist (Omari, 1970). On the one hand, he liberated Ghana; on the other, he appeared more interested in continental African politics; he overforced the issue of continental African unity, which was vehemently rejected by the other African nationalists in 1963; he became the victim of the very forces of colonialism and neo-colonialism that he had resisted the most; he depended on the West's science and technology, yet he devastatingly exposed the destructive forces of Western capitalism in his *Neo-Colonialism: The Last Stage of Imperialism* (1965), a book that partially led to his overthrow in 1966. But President Kwame Nkrumah never gave up his dreams of a continentally united Africa, of an Africa that will be in a position to industrialize and thereby compete effectively in this global village (Marah, 1998: 288).

This paper examines Nkrumahism in the context of the contemporary global village of larger and larger political units, in which Africa must compete for resources within and outside of the African continent. But what is Nkrumahism and what is the global village? What do these two concepts have in common? In the final analysis, what does President Kwame Nkrumah's dream have to do with contemporary Africa's place in the global village? These are some of the issues that this paper attempts to address.

THE CONTEMPORARY GLOBAL VILLAGE

The contemporary global village (global capitalism) is headed by the United States, Canada, Western Europe, and Japan (Huntington, 1993: 22–40). These countries have now firmly set the paradigm of development; as members of the industrialized world, they dictate to the rest of the global village domestic as well as foreign policies. "The West," in particular,

> . . . is now at an extraordinary peak of power in relation to other civilizations. Its superpower opponent has disappeared from the map. Military conflict among Western states is unthinkable, and Western Military power is unrivaled. Apart from Japan, the West faces no economic challenge. It dominates the international political and security institutions and with Japan international economic institutions. Global political and security issues are effectively settled by a directorate of the United States, Britain and France, Germany and Japan, all of which maintain extraordinarily close relations with each other to the exclusion of lesser and largely non-Western countries. Decisions made at the U.N. Security Council or in the International Monetary Fund that reflect the interests of the West are presented to the world as reflecting the desires of the world community. The very phrase "world community" has become the euphemistic collective noun (replacing "the

Free World") to give global legitimacy to actions reflecting the interests of the United States and other Western Powers. Through the IMF and other international economic institutions, the West promotes its economic interests and imposes on other nations the economic policies it thinks appropriate. (39)

Huntington goes on to put African people at the bottom of the global village, by asserting that

Civilization identity will be increasingly important in the future, and the world will be shaped in large measure by the interactions among seven or eight major civilizations. These include Western, Confucian, Japanese, Islamic, Hindu, Slavic-Orthodox, Latin America and *possibly African civilizations*. The most important conflicts of the future will occur along the cultural fault lines separating these civilizations from one another. (25)

In putting Africa as the least important among the civilizations, Huntington echoes the views of most Westerners. Africa's lowly place appears to be enshrined in the social psychology of Westerners as well as others, in the competition to be like the West. Most African people, especially on the continent, are at the bottom of the global village in terms of literacy, health, road construction, science and technology, longevity, and other crucial measures of development, including the number of victims of AIDS.

Africa could rightfully boast of its numerous natural resources, but Kenichi Ohmae (1990: 193) tells us that

. . . natural resources are no longer the key to (development of) wealth. We have to accept that national borders have little to do any longer with the real flows of industrial activity. We have to accept that information and knowledge- a trained and literate population, not military hardware- are the real sources of strength. The better informed people are, the more they know what is going on elsewhere in the world, the more they will want for themselves all those things that make life pleasant and enjoyable. And the more they will want to make their own choices among them.

Whether Africans like it or not, they are now part and parcel of this global village. They cannot go back to their ancient civilizations of Ethiopia, Egypt, Punt, Ghana, Mali, or Songhai; they cannot go back to the days of outright colonialism, nor can they ask the rest of the world to wait for them, until they, too, are ready to get their economic, cultural, social, and political houses in order. In the face of united Western Europe, North American Free Trade Area (NAFTA), Greater China (Hong Kong, Taiwan, and Macao), and other larger and larger economic units, what is the place of fifty-four balkanized African nations? Furthermore, who can today, still refute that Kwame Nkrumah's dream of one African government, one African citizenship, a common currency, a high military command, an integrated pan-African economy, educational system, and a planned industrialization, etc. are not in Africa's interest? In the face of this global capitalism, who can still continue to argue that Nkrumahism is too bombastic for Africa?

NKRUMAHISM: THE BASIS OF THE IDEOLOGY

President Kwame Nkrumah of Ghana, formally the Gold Coast, was right when he submitted in 1963 that *Africa Must Unite;* he stood that ground until his death in 1972.

Dr. Nkrumah, educated in Africa, the United States, and England was a resourceful, charismatic, and dedicated Pan-Africanist. In the Gold Coast, West Africa, Nkrumah quickly showed himself as a hard working young man, becoming a teacher at the tender age of seventeen. As a student at Achimota College, and a teacher at Elmina, in the present day Ghana, West Africa, he organized a student debating society, a literature group, and a teachers' association.

On his way to the United States in October, 1935 to study at Lincoln University in Pennsylvania, he learned that Mussolini's Italy had invaded Ethiopia; the East African nation had defeated that European nation in 1896, in the battle at Adowa. The only African nation that had until then resisted colonization was being gassed and humiliated, in an effort to show that Italy should too not be without African colonies. The other European countries in the League of nations seemed to be in cahoots with Benito Mussolini, the Italian dictator, in his hunger to partake in the scramble for Africa (Esedebe, 1982: 116–121; Padmore, 1972: 123–124).

It was then that Kwame Nkrumah vowed for the liberation of Africa in due time. To all Europeans, including the so-called liberal French, Africans were the junior brothers, who needed to be brought up in the ways of the west; Africans needed to be protected from their cannibalism and child-like innocence. If Africans had not invited the Europeans to come and save them, then the Europeans gave themselves the burden of civilizing Africans whether Africans liked it or not. In the Belgium Congo, Africans who refused to world for Leopold, the Belgium King, simply had their hands cut off. In Kenya and South Africa, Africans became Kaffirs and Shamba boys.

In both World War I and II, Africans had been recruited to fight within and outside Africa, against 'enemies' not of the Africans' making.

From 1885 to 1914, Africa was 'completely' balkanized; pre-existing African nations and groups of people were subdued, separated, and made into French, English, Portuguese, German, Italian, or Spanish. The artificial boundaries that were drawn between European colonial powers in Africa were often ludicrous; there was tiny Gambia in the belly of Senegal; Somalia became French, English and Italian; the Ewe people of West Africa were divided between France and England. When Germany was defeated in World War I, her colonies were mandated to Britain and the then apartheid South Africa, until such time that those mandated African nations were developed enough to stand on their own. As if the Africans in the interior had asked to be 'protectorates' or dependencies, each African region, territory or nation was, by the 1920s and 30s, under the sphere of one European nation or another.

Educated Africans in the colonial service (usually as minor clerks and medical assistants, not medical doctors) were discriminated against. The Englishman saw the educated African as a potential usurper; the Frenchman saw the unlettered African as a cultural throwback. To the extent that the African could not speak French, he was kept at an arm's length; the African was not civilized, had not yet evolved, until he spoke Parisian French and was thoroughly socialized in French culture.

In the United States, Jim Crowism was alive and well, but Kwame Nkrumah worked very hard at his studies in poverty. He preached, lectured, published and organized in the interest of Africa and African people, transcontinentally. In his readings of Lenin, Karl Marx, and especially Marcus Garvey, he formulated his own ideas concerning African redemption and development. He saw that African people, scattered across the globe, belonged to a unified, powerful African nation that he could help create.

NAZISM AND COLONIALISM

If Africans could be recruited to fight against Nazism, why could they also not fight against colonialism? The League of Nations in the 1920s had avowed that the mandated African nations should be sufficiently developed in time to take care of their own affairs; the Atlantic Charter of 1941 explicitly stated that each nation had the right to govern itself; certainly, this pronouncement or document must refer to African nations as well.

By the mid-1940s, another paradigm for development was already on the table. The then USSR and China (Marxism and Maoism) were alternative paths to national development. Furthermore, African ex-servicemen had been to Europe and had duly noted several contradictions within European societies; they had in fact met some Europeans that were against colonialism (Kaggia, 1975: 44–45).

In this zeitgeist, Kwame Nkrumah found himself in London in 1945. In London there was Jomo Kenyatta of Kenya, Ras Makonnen of Guyana, South America, George Padmore, from the West Indies, and other pan-Africanists who saw that Nazism and colonialism were not to be tolerated in Europe and Africa. In 1947, India obtained its independence from Great Britain and Kwame Nkrumah was already in the Gold Coast, actively engaged in liberating that West African nation. The United Gold Coast Convention party (UGCC) that had invited Kwame Nkrumah to be its publicity secretary, proved to be too conservative and elitist for his temperament and Pan-African ideology. He organized his own Convention Peoples Party (CPP) that implemented positive action, the utilization of radio, rallies, newspapers, and other legitimate means to usurp colonial rule. The British were bent on sentencing him. In prison, however, he was elected by the populous to be Minister of Government Business in 1951 (Nkrumah, 1957: 137–146). This was not, however, to deter Kwame Nkrumah from his ultimate goal- the complete liberation of the Gold Coast and the establishment of, at least, the Union of West African States. In 1957, the Gold Coast became Ghana, the first African nation south of the Sahara to obtain its independence from Great Britain.

But Ghana's independence was not enough until the whole African continent was liberated and united politically, economically, monetarily, militarily, with one citizenship and one foreign policy. In 1958, he called two major conferences in Accra, the Ghanaian capital, in which he submitted his own views about the African revolution. He warned his African compatriots that, without a United Africa, the various African nations, some too small to effect massive development programs, others too poor and landlocked, will remain at the mercy of neo-colonialism, a new form of colonialism that gave political independence on the one hand and continued to rule on the other, economically and culturally.

Even though the Ghanaian military and police overthrew Nkrumah in 1966, he stood his ground about African unity until his death in 1972. In 1963, he had compromised with the conservative forces in Addis Ababa, at the founding of the OAU (Organization of African Unity) that made the present (colonial) boundaries in Africa sacrosanct. True to Nkrumah's predictions, by the 1990s, the African continent was the scene of civil wars, coups and counter coups, starvation, malnutrition, food aid, external interventions, and of "the development of underdevelopment" (Davidson, 1974: 28).

KWAME NKRUMAH'S TRANS-AFRICAN NATIONALISM

Kwame Nkrumah states that "the primary aim of his 1958 conferences was to encourage nationalist political movements in colonial areas as a means towards continental unity and a socialist transformation of society" (Nkrumah, 1973: 130). He outlined "the four main stages of Pan-Africanism":

I   National independence
II   National consolidation
III   Transnational unity and community
IV   Economic and social reconstruction on the principles of scientific socialism. (131)

The first of these four stages has been attained, but not the last three. In 1960 alone, seventeen African nations obtained their political independence form their European colonizers. Africans across the globe were jubilant; African leaders espoused African Socialism, Negritude, Authenticity, Marxism, a synthesis of Marxism and capitalism, or other political ideologies that were supposed to propel Africa into the twenty-first century. For a while, Africa's image around the globe was greatly enhanced. African Americans were proud to be African descendents; they positively identified with African cultures, and admired leaders such as Nkrumah, Kenyatta, Lumumba, Nyerere, Kaunda, Senghor, Toure of Guinea and Selassie of Ethiopia. African ambassadors in the United Nations multiplied, and they demanded freedom for the rest of the African nations that were still under colonialism.

But Kwame Nkrumah was not bamboozled by this euphoria of African independence. He urged his contemporaries that Africa Must (indeed) Unite (Nkrumah, 1963). He believed that Ghana's independence in 1957 was simply a stepping stone that the other African nations must follow and even emulate; the independent African nations must surrender their sovereignties to a larger Africa; the inherited artificial boundaries in Africa should not be sacrosanct; African economic integration should be the goal of all the liberation movements on the African continent. One of the enemies of African unity, he declared, was neo-colonialism.

In 1963, at the founding of the Organization of African Unity (OAU), Kwame Nkrumah reiterated his position of a transnational Pan-Africanism, if the continent was ever going to be an active player in the global village. If the African continent did not unite, as it has been evident from the 1960s to the present, balkanization, poverty, neo-colonialism, and underdevelopment will entrench themselves. Nkrumah (1973: 295) believed that

. . . until we in Africa are able to establish our own independent currency and financial institutions, we shall continue to be at the mercy of the financial arrangements imposed by foreign governments in their own, and not in our, interest.

As long as the States of Africa remain divided, as long as we are forced to compete for foreign capital and to accept economic ties to foreign powers because in our separate entities we are too small, weak and unviable to 'go it alone,' we will be unable to break the economic pattern of exploitation established in the days of outright colonialism.

Only if we can unite and carry our coordinated economic planning within the framework of African political unity, will it be possible for us to break the bonds of neo-colonialism and reconstruct our economies for the purpose of achieving real economic independence and higher living standards for all our African States, big or small.

A union African Government will 'demolish' the current African boundaries that have held the continent in economic bondage, from the 1960s to the present. African nations like the Gambia, Guinea-Bissau, and 'countless' others are in no economic positions to develop on their own small economies and powerless currencies. In contemporary global capitalism, large economic units and markets, transnational economies are the most competitive.

"International capital can be attracted to (large) viable economic areas, but it would not be attracted to a divided and balkanized Africa, with each small region engaged in senseless and suicidal economic competition with its neighbours [sic]" (Quoted in Asamoah, 1991: 241).

None of the small African economies has been able to attract large scale investments to jump-start their developments; most of them, as Nkrumah predicted, have become dependent on the World Bank, the International Monetary Fund, and neo-colonialism. "Whether the result of deliberate policy or not the colonially-imposed partition is a political strait jacket for modern Africa. It divides, constraints development, encourages neo-colonialism and helps perpetuate Africa's economic and political weakness in global affairs" (Griffiths, 1995: 3). And in

. . . order to pay for its imports and to service its debts, Africa is forced to sell more and more of its raw materials, the prices of which fall continuously. Africa has hardly any say in the prices of its exports and imports. The volume of its exports is always increasing, while the value is always dropping. Clearly, Africa's trade relations with the West are based on naked exploitation. As a result, more than twenty-sub Saharan countries had debts in excess of their GNP in 1993. Out of the world's twenty poorest nations, sixteen are in Africa. Sub-Saharan Africa's debt is 106 percent of gross domestic product (GDP) compared to 37.4 percent in Latin America. Africa produces 1 percent of the world's manufactured goods. It is also the only region in the world where it is certain that poverty will increase during the next ten years. Essentially, Africa is undergoing a period of negative development. (Chimutengwende, 2000: 31–32)

Kwame Nkrumah was not only against the colonial artificial boundaries in Africa, but also the various regional groupings on the African continent; he therefore was against the French African Community and the East African Federation. These groupings were too far short for his continental African union government. Those African leaders such as Nyerere that preached the step-by-step approach to African unity were selecting "the tortoise paced" developmental approach to African development (Agyeman, 1992: 89), while the rest of the world sped ahead in science, technology, and industrialization. For Kwame Nkrumah, continental Africa must not only unite, but must also be industrialized, if it is ever to be free from the external manipulations of neo-colonialism and exploitation.

In the area of education, in a united Africa " . . . we should nurture our own culture and history, if we are to develop that African personality which must provide the educational and intellectual foundations of our pan-African future" (Nkrumah, 1963: 49). Colonial education had taught Africans that " . . . our culture and traditions (were) barbarous and primitive. Our textbooks were English, telling us about English history, English geography, English ways of living, English customs, English ideas, English weather" (Ibid). Kwame Nkrumah formalized the study of African history, literature, and the other disciplines in African Universities. He established the Institute of African Studies at the University of Ghana at Legon and, for science and technology, the University of Science and Technology at Kumasi. He advanced the idea of Africa's triple heritage (Mazrui, 1985); in his *Consciencism* (1970: 68, 79), he observed that

> African society has one segment which comprises our traditional way of life; it has a second segment which is filled by the presence of Islamic tradition in Africa; it has a final segment which represents the infiltration of Christian tradition and culture of Western Europe into Africa using colonialism as its primary vehicles. These different segments are

animated by competing ideologies. But since society implies a certain dynamic unity, there needs to emerge an ideology which, genuinely catering for the needs of all, will take the place of competing ideologies, and so reflect the dynamic unity of society, and be the guide to society's continual progress.

. . . Philosophical consciencism is the map in intellectual terms of the disposition of forces which will enable African society to digest the Western and the Islamic and the Euro-Christian elements in Africa, and develop them in such a way that they fit into the African personality. The African personality itself is defined by the cluster of humanist principles which underlie the traditional African society. Philosophical consciencism is that philosophical standpoint which, taking its start from the present content of African conscience, indicates the way in which progress is forged out of the conflict in that conscience.

These inherited African cultures, religions, peoples, and consciences must be synthesized to create the renaissant African personality; these new Africans might speak English, Arabic, French, or Portuguese but this would not make them "French or Portuguese" (Nkrumah, 1963: 217). They will be able to view the world from an Africa-centric approach (Ibid, 1973: 206–217); "the African mind must be free from all forms of domination, control and enslavement" (212).

AGAINST NKRUMAHISM

The more Kwame Nkrumah spoke and wrote about his continental Pan-Africanism, the more he attracted enemies from within and outside of Africa; his transnational Pan-Africanism was viewed as too bombastic, unrealistic, too ambitious, even egotistical, and a threat to Western interests. In 1963, at the founding of the Organization of African Unity, the majority of the African leaders in Addis Ababa, the Ethiopian capital, opted for a diluted form of Kwame Nkrumah's radical Pan-Africanism. While Nkrumah vehemently advocated immediate continental unity, the Tanzanians, Nigerians, Liberians, Sierra Leoneans, Kenyans, and the Francophone Africans advocated cooperations between African countries. Mr. Tubman of Liberia, Sir Milton Margai of Sierra Leone, Abubakar Tafawa Balewa of Nigeria, Haile Selassie of Ethiopia, and Julius Nyerere of Tanzania all opposed Kwame Nkrumah's radical Pan-Africanism as unrealistic and too fast-paced.

Kwame Nkrumah's view of Pan-Africanism from a socialist-Marxist perspective did not sit too well with the capitalist West and its multinational corporations in Africa. Nkrumah's alignment with Patrice Lumumba of the minerally wealthy Congo was viewed as a threat to Western capitalism. The myopia of the newly African presidents and prime ministers convinced them that they would rather remain big fishes in small ponds than look at the larger African picture for the benefit of the African masses and an overall Pan-African economic development. Petty jealousies and myopic competitions between giant Nigeria and small Ghana, big Kenya and little Uganda, wealthy Kenya and poorly endowed Tanzania, Francophone, Anglophone, and Lusophone Africans, African socialists and Afro-Marxists, those aligned to the former USSR against those aligned to France, America, China, and elsewhere all came to view each other with suspicion.

Furthermore, the West must not have been too willing to see a powerful Africa emerge out of colonialism, exploitation, and inferiorization to become, all of a sudden, as it were, a formidable competitor in the global village. Western propaganda against Nkrumah was partly responsible for Kwame Nkrumah's political downfall. Agyeman (1992:183) tells us that

> Nkrumah's efforts to move Africa forward along the road of Pan-Africanist nationalism met with many formidable impediments. Within Ghana, the people's party he led, which was the organizational motor of the Pan-African movement, was largely demobilized by a colonial fiat of 1951 which debilitated and corrupted it, making it difficult for Nkrumah's government to effectively contain and neutralize the depredations of an opposition which had a history of resorting to violence, and which was linked to external enemies of the goals of Africa's total liberation and unification that Nkrumah championed. In the wider African world, the other newly independent states were, but for one or two exceptions, immersed in a suffocating neocolonial order that made a virtue of Africa's continued servile attachment to the purposes of the West. In the broader global environment, the historic antithesis between Africa's underdevelopment and Europe's development continue to play itself out in a Western policy of sustained hostility to, and outright sabotage of, the Nkrumah regime, capped off by CIA plots of assassination and overthrow.

Some African political leaders and military men, including Colonel A.A. Afrifa, began to accuse Nkrumah of plotting to be the leader "of the entire African continent" (Essedebe, 1982: 207; Afrifa, 1966: 113).

In the midst of these oppositions, Kwame Nkrumah continued his plans for continental African unity, but the more adamant he became the more the opposition's scales were turned against him. "When Nkrumah dismissed Gbedemah from his cabinet following the interception by the Ghanaian security discussions of the CIA plot by Americans speaking on an open transatlantic telephone line, he fled to Togo, the base of terrorist operations against the Nkrumah regime, where he joined other CIA-sponsered opposition exiles" (Agyeman, 1992: 49). Other conflicts between Ghana and the United States ensued, over the CIA's interference in Ghanaian affairs (Ibid). When Kwame Nkrumah published his *Neo-Colonialism: The Last Stage of Imperialism* in 1965, in which he depicted Western multinational corporations as neo-colonists exploiting Africa's minerals, the United States was outraged by the Ghanaian President's "unacceptable affront to American interest" (Ibid, 49).

Thus, with internal Ghanaian, Pan-African, and external Western opposition to Kwame Nkrumah's continental Pan-Africanism, it appeared inevitable that his demise was only minutes away. The various unsuccessful attempts at his life were merely the tip of the iceberg. In February 1966, Kwame Nkrumah of Africa was couped out of office and later accepted exile in Guinea, West Africa.

THE DEFERMENT OF NKRUMAH'S TRANSNATIONAL PAN-AFRICAN DREAM

The deferment of Nkrumahism has had disastrous effects on Africa's political economic developments. Nkrumah's fear of neo-colonialism, balkanization, lack in unity, the retention of the artificial boundaries erected during colonial times, the competing African currencies and foreign policies, the absence of a high military command and one African citizenship (just to mention a few), have left Africans as the hewers of wood and drawers of water for the other world regions; Africa remains the epitome of poverty, monopolizing " . . . the bottom places in (the) quality of life rating(s) released . . . by the United Nations" (*Democrat and Chronicle*, 2000: 8A) and remains a dumping ground for excess Western goods and more 'welfare' packages, in the form of World Bank loans and International Monetary fund's recommendations for African development. Yet all the loans in the world have not improved the lives of the African masses. Instead, a new form of colonialism has spread its tentacles over Africa from the 1970s to the present. A Western form of democracy is now being preached to Africans to emulate, if they ever want those loans and financial exhortations.

In the absence of an African high military command to prevent military take-overs of civilian governments, Africa has seen the Amins, Siad Barries, Samuel Does, and the Foday Sankohs inflict havoc on the very people they claim to represent in numerous African countries. Instead of one African currency, the Cedis, the Leones, the Nairas and other power-less African currencies have continued to be devalued while competing with each other against the Dollar or Euro (Kibazo, 2000: 32). Instead of one African citizenship, Sierra Leoneans in Guinea, Liberians in Sierra Leone, Ghanaians in Nigeria and the Ivory Coast are considered foreigners, and are often expelled, for good measure, to their countries of birth.

As President Kwame Nkrumah used to say, until we in Africa have one independent African currency, one foreign policy, one citizenship, an overall Pan-African economic and industrial plan, and a unified Africa, we will continue to be the hewers of wood and the drawers of water in this global economy; for what will individual African nations, with their pow-erless currencies, do against a united Western Europe, the large economic units of Canada, USA and Mexico, East Asian countries, North and South Korea and Greater China?

Indeed, a disunited Africa equals Africans sitting on the banks of a river while they wash their hands with spittle (Achebe, 1959: 154). But the more African people remain far behind others in our twenty-first global village, the more Kwame Nkrumah's dream of united Africa explodes for attention and positive action.

ETHIOPIA SHALL SOON STRETCH FORTH HER HANDS UNTO GOD

In cognizance of Greater China, North America, and a United Western Europe, it will be foolish and suicidal for African countries to remain bal-kanized. Africans must not expect outsiders to tell them what to do about their own development; they should have appreciated Kwame Nkrumah, Toussaint L'Ouverture, Marcus Garvey, George Padmore, W. E. B. DuBois, and other Pan-Africanists who believed, and those who still believe, that in African unity lies African people's salvation, positive image, political and economic power, and the respect that comes with socio-economic develop-ment (Marah, 1998: 13A).

Furthermore, we submit that, the 2001 African Union (AU) that has replaced the 1963 Organization of African Unity (OAU) must, in addition to planning "its own parliament, central bank and court of justice" (Cole-man, 2001: 28), also establish a central Pan-African University and other institutions of higher learning all over the continent for the express purpose of institutionalizing continental African integration. The centrally located "Pan-African University as supported by Haile Selassie in 1963" should educate Africans to be citizens of continental Africa (Marah, 1989: 259); we also insist that, in this Pan-African University,

. . . Africans be trained and educated to the economic, social, political, cultural and international realities of Africans and the African continent; that African schools, especially at the levels of Higher learning, establish departments of Black American studies, Caribbean Studies, Latin America Studies, West European Studies, North American studies, Asian Studies, East European Studies, and that these various departments be conducted with a Pan-African, or Afro-Centric perspective. The curriculum in Pan-African education must be Pan-African centered, not European or narrowly nationalistic-centered. (259).

Finally, we aver that Pan-African integration—continental or sub-Saharan Africa—will decidedly be more positive than the current African 'diseconomies' of scale, that have repeatedly shown themselves to be weak, fragile, and powerless against the smallest of European nations and most multinational corporations. Those who opposed Nkrumah in the 1950s and 60s must now accept the aphorism that conventionality is not morality, that Kwame Nkrumah of Africa was right, and the majority that opposed him were apparently wrong.

REFERENCES

Achebe, Chinua. 1959. *Things Fall Apart*. Greenwich, Connecticut. Fawcett Publications, Inc.

Afrifa, A.A. 1966. *The Ghana Coup, 24th February 1966*. New York: Humanities Press.

Agyeman, Opoku. 1992. *Nkrumah's Ghana and East Africa: Pan-Africanism and African Interstate Relations*. London and Toronto: Associated University Presses.

Asamoah, Obed. 1991. "Nkrumah's Foreign Policy 1951–1966," pp. 236–253, in Kwame Arhin, (ed). *The Life and Work of Kwame Nkrumah*. Accra, Ghana: Sedo Publishing Limited.

Chimutengwende, Chen. 2000. "Africa Should Resist Foreign Economic Exploitation," pp. 28–37, in David L. Bender's *What Economic Development Strategies are Best for Africa?* San Diego, CA: Greenhaven Press, Inc.

Coleman, Sarah. 2001. "The African Union." *World Press Review*, vol. 48, V010 October: 28–29.

Davidson, Basil. 1974. *How Can Africa Survive: Arguments against Growth without Development*. New York: Little, Brown & Company.

Democrat and Chronicle, "African Nations at the Bottom as U.N. Rates Quality of Life." Rochester, NY: June 30, 2000: 8A.

Esedebe, P. Olisanwuche. 1982. *Pan-Africanism: The Idea and the Movement 1776–1963*. Washington, D.C.: Howard University Press.

Griffiths, Ieuan LL. 1995. *The African Inheritance*. London and New York: Routledge.

Huntington, Samuel P. 1993. "The Clash of Civilizations," *Foreign Affairs*. Vol. 72, No. 3 (Summer), pp. 22–49.

Kaggia, Bildad. 1975. *Roots of African Freedom 1921–1962*. Nairobi, Kenya: East African Publishing House.

Kibazo, Joel. 2000. "No More Naira," *BBC Focus on Africa*. Vol. 11, (July-September): 32.

Marah, John K. 1989. *Pan-African Education: The Last Stage of Education Development In Africa*. Lewiston, NY.: The Edwin Mellen Press.

———. 1998. *African People in the Global Village: An Introduction to Pan-African Studies*. Lanham, Maryland: University Press of America, Inc.

———. 1998. "In Unity Lies Africa's Key to Power," *Democrat and Chronicle*, Rochester, NY. April 29, 2000: 13A.

Mazrui, Ali A. 1992. "Introduction," pp. 11–21, in Opoku Agyeman, *Nkrumah's Ghana And East Africa: . . .* London and Toronto: Associated University Presses.

———. 1986. *The Africans: A Triple Heritage*. New York: Little Brown & Company.

Nkrumah, Kwame. 1957. *Ghana: An Autobiography of Kwame Nkrumah*. London: T.H. Nelson.

———. 1963. *Africa Must Unite*. New York: International Publishers.

———. 1965. *Neo-Colonialism: The Last Stage of Imperialism*. New York: International Publishers.

———. 1970. *Consciencism: Philosophy and Ideology for De-Colonization*. New York: Monthly Review Press.

———. 1973. *Revolutionary Path*. London: Panaf Books. Ltd.

Ohmae, Kenichi. 1995. *The End of the Nation State: The Rise of Regional Economies*. New York: The Free Press.

Omari, T. Peter. 1970. *Kwame Nkrumah: The Anatomy of an African Dictatorship*. Accra, Ghana: Moxon Paperbacks Ltd.

Padmore, George. 1972. *Pan-Africanism or Communism*. New York: Anchor Books.

Webb, Robert N. 1964. *Leaders of Our Time*. New York, New York: Franklin Watts, Inc.

Chapter Three
The Philosophical Challenges for Africans in the 21st Century

Daryl Zizwe Poe, Lincoln University

Kwame Nkrumah, the single most important African philosopher of state of the 20th century, declared that:

> The critical study of the philosophies of the past should lead to the study of modern theories, for these latter, born of the fire of contemporary struggles, are militant and alive. It is not only the study of philosophy that can become perverted. The study of history too can become warped. The colonized African student, whose roots in his own society are systematically starved of sustenance, is introduced to Greek and Roman history, the cradle history of modern Europe, and he is encouraged to treat this portion of the story of man together with the subsequent history of Europe as the only worthwhile portion. This history is anointed with a universalist flavoring which titillates the palate of certain African intellectuals so agreeably that they become alienated from their own immediate society. (Nkrumah, *Consciencism*. 1970, 5)

INTRODUCTION

The 21st century is an era characterized by the relatively recent nation-state liberation movement from colonialism juxtaposed with neo-colonial retrogression. For the Africans domiciled outside of Africa the recent experience has been one of rising African consciousness and nationalism juxtaposed to reactionary backlashes of neo-enslavement in the social environments in which they find themselves. The protracted battle of Africans fighting to regain their personal and collective agency is registered in these ups and downs.

The last half of the 20th century was a time marked by a baby-boom of so-called independent African states. They were "so-called" because many of them were not independent and few were African in character. Historical assessments reveal that the narrow interpretation of independence was quite fragile. Where states sought to consolidate the control of resources and use them toward the betterment of the African masses, intrigue and conspiracies bedeviled the ruling elites. Former colonial masters united to orchestrate both financial policies and public opinion against authentic African agency. That, however, should have been expected. The disappointing factor was the self-defeating worldview of many African intellectuals and trained experts.

At the outset of reading this chapter the reader deserves notice that this chapter evaluates movements and the philosophies that inform them with an Afrocentric criterion. While academic literature and orature reveals debates that question the very existence of African philosophies there is no debate on the existence of a vibrant Afrocentric movement filling contested intellectual space with African culture. This author begins with the minimal assumption that Africa produced the first philosophies known to humanity. The existence of African philosophies is not questioned here but an expose of the tension within African philosophies and the ideologies that they support is sought after.

To offer a set of philosophical challenges that will affect Africa in this, the 21st century according to the Euro-Christian calendar, this chapter requires the reader to peer through the lens of "historical consciousness." The Afrocentric approach to this topic calls for the African voice at the appropriate level of agency. Since the chapter is on African philosophy the voice must be Pan-African in space, time, and volume. Therefore, the voice of the African masses will be enlivened in its ancestral, social, and yet unborn realms. The general themes that underlie the Pan-African ethos provide the philosophic blueprint for the maturing of the African personality. The qualification of that personality remains Africa's perennial exigency of the 21st century.

THE CULTURAL–IDEOLOGICAL EXIGENCY

In an effort to move the reader from broad parameters to a narrow focus the term; "culture" is explicated here. Discomfort sometimes surrounds the use of the term, "culture," which has come to speak to the identity, beliefs, practices, and artifacts of a collective in its efforts to flourish against natural and social challenges. The term was initially made popular in the discipline of anthropology and traces its etymological roots to the Latin term: "colare," meaning to cultivate. It had evolved, however, to take on a pejorative sense reminiscent of a cult, or more succinctly, a group of heathens. Rather than wallow in the confusion of this latter use of the term this chapter builds on the description of culture presented by Sékou Touré in his landmark work titled, "Dialectical Approach to Culture."

According to Touré, culture should be understood as,

> all of the material and immaterial works of art and science, plus knowledge, manners, education, a mode of thought, behavior and attitudes accumulated by the people both through and by virtue of their struggle for freedom from the hold and dominion of nature; we also include the result of their efforts to destroy the deviationist politics—social systems of domination and exploitation through the productive process of social life.
>
> [*Black Scholar*, November 1969, page 12]

THE THREE CONSCIOUSNESSES

Additional insight into the philosophical challenges for Africans in the 21st century will hinge not only on the absorption and filtering of cultural consciousnesses but also on the introspective prioritization of the "three consciousnesses" asserted by Sékou Touré in his ideological work. In this work he elucidates the concepts of "historical consciousness," "social consciousness," and "individual consciousness" and explains their ordered relationship. The overriding and overarching consciousness advocated in Touré's model was the *historical consciousness,* which included the wisdom of the ancestors and the common senses of the masses. Ranked as second was *social consciousness,* which reflected the awareness of a contemporary collective. Finally, ranked as third, was the *individual consciousness,* which is often referred to as a microcosm of the *social consciousness.*

The utility of Touré's 3-Consciousnesses model is its map for resolving the lethargy that too often accompanies tautological social analyses, be they of European, African, or other origin. When the description of the universe is dependent on the scope of the individual's lens the multilateral nature of reality can be overlooked. While society and social organizations, with their spatial advantage, stand a better chance than individuals of uncovering truths they still lack an expanded temporal vision. Wisdom resides in the historical vision, which is characterized by African ancestors. When employing these visions in the prioritized order recommended by the model, the individual, the point of ideological implementation, is empowered with the common sense of the collective and the collective consciousness of the ancestors. Wisdom, knowledge and intellect can then impact the individual's productive behavior.

Touré's 3-Consciousnesses model offers relief from the bloated individualism that runs rampant among African intelligentsia suffering from the philosophic infection of "Western Liberalism." It also offers a model of consideration which serves more persons than the flat concept representative democracy which only speaks to contemporary majority.

NKRUMAHISM AND PHILOSOPHIC CONSCIENCISM

The situation was not reversed until the traditional values were enriched with updated strategies, tactics, techniques and methods. New philosophies emerged to challenge debilitating ideologies. The ideologies that gained power were the ones that fit into the value-matrix of the mass culture and gained popularity amongst the intelligentsia.

One of the most popular ideologues of this time was Kwame Nkrumah (1909–1972). He provided a philosophy and strategy for a viable African nation. He and a cadre of African revolutionaries used the resources of newly independent Ghana to support freedom fighters and independent states throughout the African continent (Poe, 2003). Nkrumah's philosophy and strategy advocated the qualification of African agency.

In his book, *Africa Must Unite*, (1970) Nkrumah stated,

> Under arbitrary rule, people are apt to become lethargic; their senses are dulled. Fear becomes the dominant force in their lives; fear of breaking the law, fear of the punitive measures which might result from an unsuccessful attempt to break loose from their shackles. Those who lead the struggle for freedom must break through this apathy and fear. They must give active expression to the universal longing to be free. They must strengthen the peoples' faith in themselves, and encourage them to take part in the freedom struggle. (50)

Prior to Nkrumah's ideological declarations Marxist and Maoist ideologies dominated intellectual space within the Pan-African movement. Invoking the spirit of Blyden and Garvey, Nkrumah re-Africanized the discussion concerning the uplift of the African masses. Nkrumah was attempting to develop Africa toward Pan-Africanism, which he defined as the total liberation and unification of Africa under a Socialist Union Government.

Nkrumah's "Philosophical Consciencism" built upon regenerative ideas. These ideas prominently included the African Personality[1], the African Genius[2], and the African Community[3]. The core text describing Philosophic Consciencism refers to the philosophy as "a philosophy for decolonization."

"Philosophical Consciencism" employed a formulaic synthesis with the intent of resolving the inherent conflicts between earlier African experiences and later exploitative cultural intrusions. Nkrumah sought to harmonize these experiences by filtering them through the cauldron of African revolution. The difficulty of such a task did not escape Nkrumah but capitulation was not considered an option.

In his model, *traditional*[4] African experience operates as a foundation for the African Personality and African Genius. The Islamic and Euro-Christian experiences were identified as secondary and tertiary experiences respectively. The latter experiences were to be culled for positive characteristics helpful to the well being of Africans. Some have argued that an Asian element should be incorporated to include the experiences of the Dhalit of India, the Aborigines of Australia, and like populations within the same region. These latter additions are still being researched and debated and have not as yet been ideologically incorporated into the Nkrumah formula. The key to the formula is that the philosophical filter is based in the historical memory of the African People. Unlike the modified model produced by Mazrui, the other experiences are *not* equal to the traditional base.

THE DYNAMISM OF AFRICAN CULTURE

The dialectical relationship between culture and time requires abandoning the earlier notion that African culture was static. The fact that new "traditions" were created within African culture reveals that there was a vital dynamism between old, and sometimes useless, traditions and cultural innovations. Seemingly successful innovations became the new traditions. Given this obvious process of cultural evolution our understanding of "traditional Africa" must allow for dynamism. The prevalent view that social change in African cultural was always undesirable is overly simplistic and inaccurate.

The classification of pre-colonial experience as uniformly communal may be at the root of this error.

Before the existence of European imperialism and Islamic influence, Africa had experienced internal organizations controlling expansive geographical areas and populations. Contrary to the dogmatic edicts of unilinear models of development, Africa experienced centralized societies co-existing with relatively decentralized societies, sometimes sharing symbiotic relationships. Ancient Nile Valley civilizations, Sahara-Sahel and Mediterranean civilizations, Western-Central African civilizations, and the Eastern-Central-Southern corridor civilizations, shows that Africa's cultural diversity included the social and political-economic areas. This diversity adds conceptual depth to the term "traditional Africa."

If we accept the declaration that traditional Africa was predominantly communaucratic then communalism itself must be viewed as a general set of values operating under a diverse array of organizational types. The philosopher is also forced to realize that the seed of counter-communalism was omnipresent in traditional Africa. It was a seed that was kept to a negligible impact until it was strengthened by counter-communal forces from outside of Africa.

Nkrumah's attraction to basic Marxian ethics of rejecting economic exploitation of persons by persons, and its analytical tool of dialectical materialism, was deemed to be digestible and healthy for the African personality. Nkrumah sought to employ the economic policies reflecting the formulas of scientific socialism, as they were then understood. In political philosophy, however, Nkrumah followed the models that were culturally idiosyncratic to the Pan-African movement. It is doubtful that any European Marxist would have initiated a call for an economically sound and politically valid African Union, which is exactly what Nkrumah called for.

Nkrumah agreed with the perspective of seeking the *social contention* in phenomena and applied that perspective to the philosophical systems he explicated. For Nkrumah, this contention was a sign of the life within philosophy. He was aware of traditional academic ways to examine philosophy, which he often saw as lifeless and abstract. "When philosophy is regarded in the light of a series of abstract systems, it can be said to concern itself with two fundamental questions: first, the question 'what there is'; second, the question how 'what there is' may be explained" (Nkrumah, *Consciencism* 1970, 6).

While standing firm on the African assertion of the essential nature of humans as spiritual, Nkrumah also accepted the explanation of the natural cosmic raw material as "matter" which he defined as a plenum of forces in tension. Nkrumah's description of spirit was that it could be explained as a surrogate of critically organized matter.

ANALYTICAL FOCUS

Chuba Okadigbo criticized Nkrumah in his text titled, *Consciencism in African Political Philosophy* (1985), for capitulating to oppressive influences facing Africa. Okadigbo claimed that Nkrumah erred in not categorizing Marxism as a separate and equal "invasion" into Africa. Okadigbo's assessment was not precise. Nkrumah saw the Marxian analytic concepts of dialectical and historical materialism as salvageable aspects of the Euro-Christian impact but he did not dismiss any aspect of African people's experience. Okadigbo may have disregarded or disagreed with Nkrumah's declarations on the role of the social milieu in regards to philosophy. This may have led Okadigbo to dismiss the power of synthesis offered by Nkrumah's analysis.

Nkrumah had no problem using the analytical tools of dialectical and historical materialism after some required fine-tuning. He used these tools to assist with the liberation of Africa. In fine-tuning these tools, he added the concepts *categorial conversion* and *cosmic contrast,* which assisted in explaining the vitality of the cosmic raw material. They were also necessary to resolve the 'outside-inside' contradiction suffered mostly by the Eurocentrically trained African intelligentsia.

Nkrumah addressed the *cosmic raw material* and the academic preoccupation with its origin. In doing so he exposed the incipient tautology that resulted therein. Nkrumah showed the impact of the philosopher's social milieu on their consciousnesses and their subsequent postulations. Finally, he warned "non-Western" students to search for their philosophic tools within their own culture and social milieu. On this point Nkrumah is in agreement with African centered thinkers and Afrocentric scholars from Blyden through Asante. Nkrumah spoke not only from academic speculation but from his real experiences and initiatives.

"Cosmic contrast" was a conceptual contribution based in African historical memory that sought to resolve the contradiction of the relationship between "inside" and "outside" which bogged the foreign philosophers and clergy down. These foreign philosophers and clergy often found themselves bogged down in a quagmire of seeking "first-ness" and "universality" when addressing "creation" questions. Nkrumah's offered the following:

> Many African societies in fact forestalled this kind of perversion. Making the visible world continuous with the invisible world reduced the dialectical contradiction between 'inside and outside.' For them heaven was not outside the world but inside it. These African societies did not accept transcendentalism, and may indeed be regarded as having attempted to synthesize the dialectical opposites 'outside' and 'inside' by making them continuous, that is, by abolishing them.
>
> (Nkrumah *Consciencism,* 12)

Nkrumah was an ardent struggler for African redemption and was out to remove any impetus toward escapism and lethargy, both of which led to avoidance of necessary struggle. Thus, he philosophically removed external deterministic control and asserted the agency of the People. In fact, Nkrumah exposed the European clergy's use of the "outside" assertion in order to shore up their social-political power among the European masses.

Nkrumah's application of Philosophical Consciencism to historical materialism, preempted the social determining force of production modes, so often referred to by Marxist philosophers, and replaced it with the determining force of the "condition of the consciousness." Nkrumah did not allow these different positions to become logically "either-or" debates. He understood both concepts to be needed to secure the accomplishment of African liberty, unity and social revolution. Nkrumah advocated scientific socialism and understood the need for socialists that were ideologically convicted to its establishment. Ideological training, therefore, was seen as the only safeguard for the establishment of a socialist mode of production. The ideology proposed by Nkrumah was defended by the philosophy of Philosophical Consciencism.

Nkrumah added socialism to the definition of Pan-Africanism. He attributed its appeal to the communal values deeply resident in the historical memory of the Revolutionary African Personality. Nkrumah's qualifying statement concerning the term "African Personality" is useful for Africa's 21st century philosophers so it is quoted below:

> An important aspect of Pan-Africanism is the revival and development of the "African Personality," temporarily submerged during the colonial period. It finds expression in a re-awakening consciousness among Africans and peoples of African descent of the bonds which unite us—our historical past, our culture, our common experience, and our aspirations. . . .
>
> The spirit of a people can only flourish in freedom. When the liberation and unification of Africa is completed, the African Personality will find full expression and be meaningfully projected in the international community. In the meantime, while Africa remains divided, oppressed and exploited, the African Personality is merely a term expressing cultural and social bonds which unite Africans and people of African descent. It is a concept of the African nation, and is not associated with a particular state, language, religion, political system, or colour of the skin. For those who project it, it expresses identification not only with Africa's historical past, but with the struggle of the African people in the African Revolution to liberate and unify the continent and to build a just society. (Nkrumah, *Revolutionary Path* 1973. 205–6)

The "Principle of Sufficient Reason" cannot be applied to the existence of a cosmic raw material that is "self-caused," which logically means it is "uncaused." This logical fact implies a basic unity of matter. This concept, when converted into social behavior, provides a supportive environment for the principle of egalitarianism. The connection between spirit and matter was explainable through "categorial conversion." Traditional African societies accepted the vitality of matter. He asserted that this concept was an African one that added vitality to matter as reflected through matter's internal motion. Nkrumah accepted the "ordinal primacy" of matter, while asserting the 'exigency primacy' of ideology.

NKRUMAHISM'S CARDINAL ETHICAL PRINCIPLES

Nkrumah advocated a core of cardinal principles. The principles were: "humanism," "egalitarianism" and "collectivism." Nkrumah posited that these principles were related to the concept of "unity" through matter's oneness. He insisted that these principles were consistent with Africa's communalist tradition that imbued matter with life. These are principles of a living conscience and therefore require constant "refinement and clarification." Nkrumah explains the base and definition of these principles in depth in his work *Consciencism*.

Simply speaking their definitions are as follows:

- **Humanism:** recognizes human beings as an end within themselves not *merely* as a means to an end.
- **Egalitarianism:** the equal and fair opportunity for all and each in society to develop to their fullest capacity.
- **Collectivism:** the assertion of the paramount interest of the collective over the alien individual. That is to say that the individual that chooses to serve the collective at the same time chooses him or her self. However those that remain self-absorbed have chosen themselves without the collective.

According to Nkrumah, these values could only be advanced with the organization of a continental-wide nation that supports this ideological exigency with material resources.

THE PEOPLE'S CLASS AS A PHILOSOPHICAL CONCEPT

Another powerful concept that aided in the African liberation movement was Touré's "People's Class" and his prioritization of the 3 consciousnesses (historical, social, and individual). The concept of the "People's Class" added a dimension of agency to the paradigm of class struggle. Prior to the use of this concept the dogmatic Marxist dominated the discussion on class struggle with a historical materialism saturated with a moribund determinism. It reduced human behavior to a proscribed formula rooted in a person's place in the relations of production and distribution. Thus, capitalist collaboration among the poor or African nationalism among the wealthy professionals was difficult to account for. Touré and his organization, the Parti Démocratique du Guinée (PDG), articulated the "People's class" and added it the ideological tool chest of African revolutionaries. It provided a classification system locating the political position, initiative, and intent of political activity. Touré's concept of class descriptions, centered on the position of the People's happiness, strengthened and broadened the support for the liberation of the African masses.

The arch nemesis in the Touré class model was the Counter-People's class, often called counter-revolutionary elements. Between that consciously selfish and greedy class and the People's class was the Anti-People's class which was categorized by its lack of commitment to the masses of Africans in their quest for regained liberty and dignity. Belonging to the People's class, therefore, was a conscious initiative on the part of a member. Your mere relation to production did not automatically make you on the side of the masses or against them. The operatives, guided by the ideology of the African revolution, were evaluated by their work and were classified by their fidelity to the organization of revolutionaries and their proximity to the needs of the African masses.

The political and intellectual revolution launched during the era of Africa's liberation decades renewed the agency latent in the African masses. The courage and genius of African liberation movements forced the corrupted elites to muffle their interests and the foreign oppressors to reassess their fragile relationship with Africa. Some of these latter forces were made to vacate under the pressure of "positive action" campaigns, votes of "non," and/or military actions.

The battle against colonialism and enslavement was articulated as a battle to eradicate the African homeland of economic parasites and hostile foreigners. Africans abroad sought an opportunity to regain dignity and end the life-deteriorating depredations of marginalization. Africans everywhere were engaged in struggles to reclaim their human rights as persons and as peoples. Nearly all segments of African society blurred their distinctions and united to seek power through the machinery of the state (their own or others).

The farmers, peasants, and workers have shown their willingness to unite and revive Africa in its cultural renaissance. The students stay militant and appear willing to support radical change, even if they are not sure about the direction of the change they support. All that remains is for the African intelligentsia, who dominated the leadership of the liberation movements, to unite their efforts and reintroduce the African Personality on to the world stage. This, however, has not happened for the intelligentsia has more often than not been corrupted with a "mind's eye" provided by the former colonial institutions. The African intelligentsia often sought the mentorship of their European and US educational institutions and those institutions welcomed the role. At this point the term intelligentsia seems misplaced in light of this group's apparent ignorance toward the previous attitude and malicious intent of the former colonial institutions.

Had the requested mentorship from the colonial powers come only in the form of technical support, the damage might not have been as bad. It came, however, in the form of visions of future planning and reflected the unadulterated interests of the former parasitic overlords. The formulaic trap went as follows: "development" required "capital investment" and that required "structural adjustment." Adjustment to structures meant removing the coordination of resource flows from the governments that used such flows to improve the lives of the African masses. Without that coordination, capital investment came to mean unruly debt and economic misery for the society invested into, as well as profane profits for the investors. Sapped of resources by structures adjusted to facilitate capital flight, the African masses suffered worse than during the era of Euro-Christian colonialism.

To remain fair to the African intelligentsia, one must mention the factor of the socialist camp that played a significant role in the struggle for African liberation. This camp seemed to be a viable alternative to the imperialism of capitalists from Europe. Many of the African intelligentsia had total hope in receiving support from the USSR and China. Some, however, knew of the experience of George Padmore during Stalin's rule and the USSR's abandonment of the African liberation movement in light of the USSR's perceived national interests. In the face of this disappointment, Padmore remained committed to socialism but broke his ties with the USSR. For Padmore it was Africa's interest first and other interests after.

In a sense, Padmore's experience provides a key to the challenges that still face the African intelligentsia. In order for this intelligentsia to serve the African masses and complete the African journey toward liberation, unity, and renaissance it must rediscover the African Mind and African Personality. African agency must first be self-aware in order to become self-reliant. The African intelligentsia has a crucial role to play in the continued efforts to resurrect the African Personality. Its first discovery, however, must be Africa's historical consciousness. In a word, it must rediscover the African People!

Salvation through self-reliance is an obvious idiom and seems to reflect common sense. The problem is that a considerable portion of the African intelligentsia suffers from common sense deficiency syndrome (CSDS). Without this basic sense rooted in the common experiences of the African People the collective consciousness required for rehabilitation of the African Personality is unobtainable. The initiatives that Africans need are sidelined for unworkable formulas that benefit foreign and often hostile interests.

To mature into the "Era of the Masses" the African Personality has to respond to certain exigencies. Arriving at this era will require the African People to overcome downpressing classes while catapulting itself to new heights of effectiveness. This goal requires the freedom of the African Personality and the African People from economic exploitation, political manipulation, and social degradation. In general, Human cultures proactively respond to *ideas of reality* and this is the important point about ideology in the quest to guide collective agency. It is the particular role of the intelligentsias to review and select the appropriate ideology depending on the interest groups that they pledge allegiance to.

THE CURRENT SITUATION

To restate this chapter's focus, philosophy addresses the process of elucidating basic beliefs. In that light, there are but two philosophies competing for African space, a conservative one and a revolutionary one. The conservative seeks to maintain the colonial relations established in the second half of the previous millennium. The revolutionary one seeks to bring about the "Era of the African Masses." The conservative philosophy supports ideologies and practices that ease the way for economic, political, and cultural interventions into the African hearts, minds, and continent. The revolutionary philosophy seeks Africa's salvation and resurrection through the self-reliant evolution of the collective agency of the African masses.

Ideology serves as culture's consciousness and conscience. Ideology is both a cultural product and a culture generator. The integral relationship between ideology and culture explains why each ideology insists on a cultural identity to be accepted as a pivotal anchor for a collective personality. Ideologies actively defend the cultures that they give rise to. The ideologies that surface on behalf of Africans in the 21st century will advocate two conditions at minimum: the direct political control of the African masses over the collective self and African homeland as well as the establishment of a non-capitalist unified governing apparatus. The functional unity of

Africa and the self-empowerment of the African masses were the cultural exigencies of the 20th century and remain the cultural and ideological exigencies of the 21st century.

THE PHILOSOPHIC EXIGENCY

Social milieu affects the content of philosophy, and the content of philosophy seeks to affect social milieu, either by confirming it or by opposing it. In either case, philosophy implies something of the nature of an ideology. In the case where the philosophy confirms a social milieu, it implies something of the ideology of that society. In the other case in which philosophy opposes a social milieu, it implies something of the ideology of a revolution against that social milieu. Philosophy in its social aspect can therefore be regarded as pointing up an ideology. (Nkrumah, *Consciencism*, 56)

The contemporary African opinion makers—the intelligentsia, are in need of a philosophy that advances the effectiveness of African agency. Put in another way, they need a philosophy that defends the African Revolution. The term "Afro-pessimism" describes a breed of African thinkers that have accepted defeat and have lost the ability to imagine a resurrected African Personality. Worst still, some among this group have lost the desire to work toward such a noble goal. Some of these 'thinkers' have gone so far to as to advocate for a return to colonialism. It is precisely in such utterances that the lethal impact of European cultural intrusion and its ideology of dominance shines through.

Ideologies of dependency foster policies of compromise with neo-colonial organizations and consortiums. Deeper still, it is the philosophy of capitulation that supports these retrogressive ideologies.

The ultimate philosophy for Africa in the 21st century will support optimizing ideologies. It has to bolster the collective agency of the African People. This collective agency, performing optimally, is the only guarantor of cultural renaissance and stability. Without this cultural renaissance and stability there will be no "growth and development." "Growth and development" as it is used in this chapter, is not meant to indicate a mere vulgar economic accumulation or global economic integration but insinuates a higher valued human self-consciousness, a more humane social order, and a socially responsible individual. These are indicators of "growth and development" for Africa in the 21st century.

This century will witness the maturing of the African Genius and a Redemptive African Personality. That maturity will lead to the fortification of the African nation and a renaissance of African spirituality. All and each of these accomplishments will contribute to peace among the subgroups of the Human species.

It is the violation of the spirits on the micro and macro level that stand in the way of African redemption. Enslavement, colonization, and neo-colonization all involve the mutilation of African agency such that the material world offers very little relief regardless of its potential abundance. Organized volition, right ordering, and collective self-confidence are prerequisites to the next phase of African emancipation and elevation. The next statement may sound rhetorical but it is not: the African without collective and personal agency, will remain a poor subject in a sea of material wealth. Herein lies the conundrum. Herein lies the challenge. Herein lies the clue.

African People, in the twenty-first century, embody the paramount exigency of constructing viable programs and machinery that facilitate optimal collective agency. Only this optimal collective agency will make possible the achievement of Pan-African power. History has shown that power is required to enable the redemption and maturing of the African Personality in the face of the global "new world order."

Collective agency operates within parameters laid down by the wisdom and logic of ideology as a guiding force. It is simple folly to imagine any human endeavor that does not recognize the determining factor of ideology in encouraging agential options.

THE DELIVERY OF PHILOSOPHIC MESSAGES AND THE CHALLENGES TO AFRICA

In the 21st century, ideological statements will be delivered through three main media:

- mass media,
- educational institutions, and
- organized religion.

Each of these media will have to be vigilantly scrutinized and modified to be of service to the African masses and to prevent the neocolonization of African culture and the recolonization of our homeland. Moreover, these media may have to be reconstructed to fortify the African personality in such a way that the collective agency of the African masses is philosophically enriched.

The vanguard penetration into the hearts and minds of our population during the area of European colonialism was similar in tactic to the

Northeast penetration centuries earlier. It was the religious believer that came in small-organized groups to carry the message of piety. This work was done by the big "M," the missionary. The missionaries were accompanied with shadowy rear guards of trading businesses (the second big "M" for money) and state gendarmes (the third big "M" for military). In the 21st century, the vanguard penetrations are not done through missionaries but MTV-type programs from abroad and their shadowy sponsors like McDonalds' and other multinational merchants of culture. These forces are both dangerous and effective for their ability to modify the self-image of African youth. They cannot simply be stopped through outlawing the watching of television; in fact this will give rise to a rebellious movement that will cause chaos in our societies.

Only an African counteroffensive, utilizing this medium as a staging ground, will neutralize this force and possibly infect the medium on a global level with a cultural alternative that will be of service to humanity in general. In this area, African artists from throughout the world, armed with ideological clarity and ample resources of a united Africa, will have to be employed with the logistical support of a military operation. It is the hearts and minds of our youth, thus it is our future, which is at stake. The philosophic concepts of life-appreciation, collectivism, and an elevated value in communicratic behavior should flow through the performances delivered over this medium. Beauty and goodness should be defined within the parameters of the African cultural renaissance. Life reducing behaviors and philosophies should not be ignored or hidden, they should be amply dismantled and displayed as the monsters that they are. To hide them will be to build an aura around them that will tempt our youth to engage them without the protection of elders. The negative portrayals should be periodically displayed and collectively devalued then publicly destroyed. Like all vaccines, the poison will have to be introduced in a controlled amount and overcome through an African philosophical regimen.

The situation with educational institutions is just as severe as mass media. This is particularly true because of the near dogmatic belief of African populations in the liberty producing power of organized education. Only careful reflection reveals that educational institutions are merely vessels of ideology and technique. They operate with the goals of producing cadres in the service of their sponsors—or at least that is how they should operate. During the colonial era it was the money taken from the colonial subject that paid for the establishment of whatever meager schools that were provided by the governments. Nevertheless, the curricula of these schools were designed to produce caricatures of Europe. A quote from Nkrumah need not be paraphrased but simply repeated as its succinct message clarifies this point:

Our pattern of education has been aligned hitherto to the demands of British examination councils. Above all, it was formulated and administered by an alien administration desirous of extending its dominant ideas and thought processes to us. We were trained to be inferior copies of Englishmen, caricatures to be laughed at with our pretensions to British bourgeois gentility, our grammatical faultiness and distorted standards betraying us at every turn. We were neither fish nor fowl. We were denied the knowledge of our African past and informed that we had no present. What future could there be for us? We were taught to regard our culture and traditions as barbarous and primitive. Our text books were English text-books, telling us about English history, English geography, English ways of living, English customs, English ideas, English weather. (*Africa Must Unite*, 49)

The onslaught of arrogance from abroad may have changed somewhat since the era of the African Liberation Movement (though this is not a given) but in most cases it has been made more subtle in approach while remaining consistent in the philosophy that is imparted. Education in Africa still points to the USA and Europe as examples of "development." The magnificent achievements of the African masses across time and space is still absent in many of our educational institution's curricula. In the 21st century these cultural attainments will have to be established as the historical anchor of our curricula throughout the length and breadth of the African continent. It is only this mental and spiritual legacy that will safeguard the faith in the present and future capacity of the African masses. This is the first step in countering the "brain-drain" taking place at present.

Of course the author wants to avoid the appearance of naiveté and will therefore acknowledge that the reversal of "brain-drain" hemorrhaging will require significant redirection of resources to African educational institutions. The current level of funding for such institutions is dangerously insufficient. Since this is not a chapter on the technique of governance there is no recommendation on where funds should be shifted from. It is sufficient to say in this intellectual space that an area in which the population is properly educated to its self interests, its collective goals, and trained sufficiently in the science and techniques to reach those goals can provide more security than a military utilizing an equivalent amount of resources. In sum, African educational institutions that were invaded by foreign philosophies and related ideologies will have to be evaluated and adjusted through thorough re-Africanization. Where these institutions were never constructed they will have to be built before opportunistic foreign interests take advantage of the African faith in "education" to penetrate African hearts and minds.

While the missionary movements of Northeastern Islam and Euro-Christianity are not in the "point-guard" space at present, their legacies still wreak havoc and instability in the mental space of Africa. African agency has too often been supplanted by the explanations of these breeds. Even the creator has been recruited through these religious presentations to represent non-Africans. The ancestors have been purged and not allowed to support the African masses in their effort to negotiate their environment and challenge social situations. This is a serious challenge for African philosophy in the 21st century.

It is painful to state this but it is an unavoidable assessment: new religions will have to surface in the 21st century. Sin and servitude cannot continue to drive the African believer. The celebration of life and the reintroduction of African ancestors must be part of any religious formations that arise on the African continent. All older religious forms, including Judaism, Islam, and Christianity, that can shake off solo-theistic attitudes might contribute concepts that have utility but the fundamental factor will be the concepts' ability to revive the African personality and deliver faith to the African masses as Africans.

NOTES

1. A composite reflection of the African People across space and time motivated and illuminated by African cultural unity. Like other 'personalities' it is texturized through categorial idiosynchrasies.
2. The 'mental-physical' discoveries of the African mind, the life-inspired morality expressed in African spirituality, the technical acuity and aesthetic mastery of African art, the scientific success of African architecture, and other splendors that African culture donates to human civilization are aspects of this concept.
3. This concept refers to the community of large (region or nation-state) level organizations of African governments. At the time of its origin as a term it was used by Nkrumah to designate the Independent African States of the 1960s.
4. This speaks to a period of pre-Islamic and pre-Euro-Christian interactions.

Chapter Four

Neo-Pan-Africanism and Presidents William Clinton and George W. Bush's Images in the Nigerian Press

Minabere Ibelema, University of Alabama at Birmingham

President William Clinton of the United States of America made an official visit to Nigeria in August 2000, and the visit generated considerable coverage by the Nigerian press. President George W. Bush did the same about three years later and also received considerable coverage. However, the extent and especially the theme of coverage were markedly different and seem to mirror the perception of both presidents among the African American populace. This paper analyzes the themes of the coverage and suggests how they might reflect a neo-Pan-African solidarity. Of particular interest is the portrayal of President Clinton as a friend of African Americans, with the implication that he would probably help another member of the extended African family, Nigeria. Issues and coverage of the visits are also analyzed within the framework of the African tradition of the extended family and related values.

Data for the analysis are drawn from Nigeria's major newspapers and magazines and the dominant television network, Nigeria Television (NTV). Particular attention was paid to: *The Guardian, The Punch,* the *Vanguard,* and the *Daily Independent* (all major Nigerian dailies); *Tell* and *Newswatch* (both leading weekly newsmagazines); NTV Port Harcourt, the federal government-sponsored station in the capital of Rivers State, and RSTV, the state- government sponsored television station in Port Harcourt.

For Clinton's visit the primary period of coverage was from August 19 to September 7, 2000. This is the period of significant coverage, before, during and after the visit. For Bush's visit, primary period of examination was July 1 to July 21, 2003. Although coverage of Bush's visit was neither as extended nor intensive as Clinton's, an equivalent period around his visit was monitored to ensure comparability.

CONTESTED NOTION OF PAN-AFRICANISM

Pan-Africanism, a concept that encompasses matters of identity, solidarity, and values in Africa and the Diaspora has been a contested notion as far back as the times of Marcus Garvey. Though pan-Africanism within Africa itself has been problematic in the political sphere (Adeleke, 1998a; Agyeman, 2003), its basis is more readily presumed. Moreover, its political structure has long been formalized through the Organization of African Unity, now the African Union, and other avenues of social and cultural synchronization such as the Pan-African News Agency and modalities for exchange of television programs (Eko, 2001). The transcontinental or Diasporan dimension of pan-Africanism has been more seriously contested.

There are questions as to whether, indeed, Africans and the African Diaspora have enough in common to make pan-Africanism a meaningful ideology or basis for policy and action. Disagreements that have abounded since the times of Marcus Garvey came into even sharper focus in the 1990s when two African Americans—Eddy L. Harris and Keith B. Richburg—wrote scathing accounts of their experience in Africa (Harris, 1992; Richburg, 1997). In a concurring review, Bracey (2003, pp. 66–67) thus sums up the "striking and obvious" similarities in the claims of both authors: "Blacks in America are not 'native-born' Africans, nor does the African continent have much to do with American blacks living the Diaspora. . . . More specifically, Africans in Africa do not necessarily see blacks in America as brothers." Of course, in the primary thrust of their reflections, Harris and Richburg bluntly disavow any such feelings toward Africans.

Such disavowal is not new, though its pungency might be distinctly contemporary. Adeleke (1998a, 1998b), for instance, has taken the broader stance that African-American ideological interests have been historically different from those of Africans. "A critical examination of the history of Pan-Africanism, particularly of the strategies devised by leading black American nationalists for implementing the Pan-African ideal, reveals a deep cultural distance and alienation from Africa consequence, no doubt, of the acculturation process in the New World" (Adeleke, 1998a, p. 45). Moreover, he argued, a lack of ethnic and national unity within and between African countries makes implausible any notion of solidarity between Africans and the African Diaspora.

Responding to such arguments, Asante (1988, p. 67) has written that, "This is not merely an error, it is nonsense." Indeed, arguments that dismiss pan-Africanism seem to suggest that any condition that hinders or detracts from an ideology, principle, or relational orientation consequently negates it. But in human affairs, there are no ideal conditions. All orientations of ideology and even principles must contend with countervailing realities, or else their very existence is of little significance.

It is the assumption of this study then that pan-Africanism in the 21st Century, that is neo-pan-Africanism, has to be conceptualized not just to transcend geographical and cultural distances but also to accommodate ideological differences. The focus has to be what Bauman (2001, p. 471) would call "experiential grounds" and, one might add, perceptual parallels. For instance, between Africa and the Diaspora, respectively, there are parallels in the experience and perception of colonialism and slavery, struggles for economic development and racial equity (Chinweizu, 1975), and the challenges of cultural re-assertion and identity development (Ferkiss, 1966; Ngugi, 1993; Mudimbe; 1988; Ibelema, 2003). These realities are extant in their implications and weigh in the construction of identities. However, as Bauman (2001, p. 482) has written in describing the general trend, "instead of talking of identities . . . it would be more in keeping with the realities of the globalizing world to speak of identification, a never-ending, always incomplete, unfinished and open-ended activity in which we all, by necessity or by choice, are engaged."

In effect, the nature of identities or identification is evolving. For the study of pan-Africanism, this suggests the need to ascertain its contemporary manifestations. It is in this context then that this study examines the pan-Africanist implications of the image of Presidents Clinton and Bush in the Nigerian press.

FRAMING, SIGNIFICATION, AND THE AFRICAN VALUE OF THE EXTENDED FAMILY

Underlying this study are the related concepts of framing and signification in the analysis of news coverage, especially as developed by Entman and Hall. Entman (1993, p, 52) has written that "Framing essentially involves selection and salience." And in explaining the concept of signification, Hall (1982, p. 64) has argued that what the press does is "not merely the transmitting of an already-existing meaning, but the more active labour of making things mean." In effect, news is always reported within a political, social and even cognitive framework that gives them meaning through selection, emphasis, and interpretation (Galtung, 1965; Gans, 1979).

For instance, in a framing analysis of the coverage of Bush's visit to Botswana and South Africa (on the same mission as the visit to Nigeria), St. Clair (2004) compares the predominant orientation of two newspapers with different ideological interests. She concludes that Botswana's government-owned *Daily News* and South Africa's independent *Mail & Guardian* both reflected the tenor of their respective government's stance on the implications of the visit. The *Daily News* was more obliging in its coverage and commentary, reflecting the cozier relations between the United States and Botswana; in contrast, the *Mail & Guardian* was more skeptical and critical, reflecting the rather tense relations between the Bush administration and that of South Africa's Thabo Mbeki.

This study goes beyond an analysis of news coverage in relations to inter-government relations. It examines news framing in the context of the broader socio-political context. Specifically, it examines the ideology of pan-Africanism using the metaphor of the extended African family and related values.

In the African tradition, in-laws are an important part of the extended family, and often the marriage of a member of the family to a wealthy man is seen as an opportunity for higher standards of living not just for the betrothed but for the extended family. This is consistent with African communal values by which individuality is de-emphasized and members of the family are seen as a part of the whole (Gbadegesin, 1998). When such an in-law is visiting there is great expectation, often unrealistic. The nature of the relations between the couple and the wife's extended family often depends on success in managing the unrealistic expectations given the inherent limits of an in-law's capacity for charity.

To complete the analogy, one could think of Nigeria as the family, African Americans as the betrothed, and the United States as the wealthy in-law, embodied in Presidents Clinton and Bush. The metaphor is further facilitated by the fact that each president was accompanied by at least one African American in a prominent role in the administration. President Clinton was accompanied by Susan Rice, the Assistant Secretary of State for African Affairs. In that position she was a frequent spokeswoman during the visit and as such may be said to represent the betrothed (African Americans). President Bush was accompanied by Secretary of State Colin Powell and National Security Adviser Condoleezza Rice, though neither featured as prominently in the press as did Susan Rice. (Incidentally, that the two African American women share the same last name seems only a fortuitous coincidence for purposes of this analysis.)

It should be noted at this point that the African news media have been criticized for their manifestation of Euro-American values (Golding, 1979; Jimada, 1991; Bourgault, 1995). Jimada has called instead for an Afrocentric approach that puts African interests and values at the core of news judgment. The coverage of the Presidents Clinton and Bush seems to reflect some aspects of this perspective.

CONTEXTS OF VISITS

President Clinton visited Nigeria about two years after the installation of an elected president following nearly 13 years of military rule. During the military dictatorship, U.S.–Nigeria relations were severely strained. That ended in 1998, when the Nigerian dictator, General Sani Abacha, died and his successor instituted a rapid transition to electoral democracy. President Clinton's visit was intended, in part, to underscore the changed relations and to demonstrate U.S. support of the new administration.

President Bush's visit in July 2003 took place in the context of the already cordial relationship between Nigeria and the United States. However, it was also in the additional context of the post-September 11 war on terrorism and the U.S. invasion of Iraq. These contexts of the visits provided the backdrop for press coverage and this analysis.

COVERAGE OF PRESIDENT CLINTON

President Clinton arrived on a Saturday morning, August 26 and left on Monday, August 28, 2000. As a Nigerian news magazine reported:

> The [Nigerian] media blitz which started on August 18 did not end even days after he left. All the electronic and print media tried very hard to outdo one another in the coverage of the historic event. On a daily basis, journalists searched for exclusive reports about the preparations and expectations of the visit. Radio and television stations had all kinds of programmes to analyze the visit" (Mba-Afolabi, 2000, Sept. 11, p. 46).

President Bush arrived on July 11, 2003 and left the following day. Again the press covered Bush's visit as befitting such an august occasion. However, the coverage lacked the exuberance of the coverage of President Clinton and the framing of the visit was significantly different. To a considerable degree, coverage by the Nigerian press of the presidents' visits reflected variations in expectations as would be predicted by the norms of the metaphor of the extended family and a visiting in-law.

For President Clinton's visit, the norm was actually breached some-what in the direction of over-exuberance. By traditional values, families receiving wealthy in-laws engage in a balancing act between maintaining their dignity on the one hand, and, on the other hand, making it be known that the guest's generosity would be appreciated. This is in keeping with the African value of dignity even in poverty and, in fact, the ethic that a family may be needy but not poor. Indeed, irrespective of the disparity in wealth, there is supposed to be parity in dignity between a family and the visit-ing in-law. The Nigerian press's coverage of President Clinton's visit tilted heavily in the direction of expressing needs. In this regard, there was an element of national diminution, that is, the surrendering of aspects of one's sovereignty, or, in this case dignity, for purposes of advancing economic development (Onwudiwe, 1993).

The dominant theme of the coverage was what President Clinton could and would do to alleviate Nigeria's economic difficulties, includ-ing especially with regard to the country's external debt burden. In stating Nigeria's need for debt forgiveness, the press was quite blunt in contrasting U.S. political stability and economic prosperity with Nigeria's instability and moribund economy. There was no trace of jingoism in what some ana-lysts characterized as a "beggarly posture." On the other hand, the United States was portrayed as the epitome of national accomplishment.

To suggest what President Clinton could and, perhaps, would do for Nigeria, the press detailed his accomplishments in the United States and especially his record of inclusiveness of African Americans. This latter theme seems to have created an affinity toward Clinton, who was also lauded as "the most powerful man in the world" and "the world's foremost citizen." Maya Angelou's description of Clinton as "the first black president" of the United States was cited to substantiate the affinity and justify hope in the visit. This factor of Clinton's perception was further underscored by the prominence of Susan Rice as a frequent spokeswoman in connection with the visit. Rice appeared several times on both federal and state television stations, though most of the appearances were replays or excerpts from the same extended interview.

The factor of affinity was further emphasized on the day of Presi-dent Clinton's arrival with a two-page-spread article in *The Guardian* by the banner headline: "Over land, across seas, a mission to re-unite a divided house" (Nwosu, 2000, Aug. 26, pp. 16–17). The article, which featured a photo of Jesse Jackson—identified as one of the most influential African Americans—discussed the assimilation movement to grant Afri-can Americans citizen rights in African countries, including rights to own lands. The Akran of Badagry, a traditional leader who is actively involved in the movement, said of its benefit: "You know many African Americans are doing very well now in different fields side by side with the Europeans. There is no doubt that [their] greater presence here will help us in the advancement of the policy, in the modernisation of the economy and maybe move forward from under-development to development" (Badagry, 2000, Sept. 26, p. 17).

Other issues arose and were covered with respect to the visit, among them the massive U.S. security apparatus and the uncertainties of the itinerary (even the exact date of the President's arrival was not publicly confirmed until the day before). But the substantive coverage focused on the theme of probable delivery from difficulties by a prodigious visitor with whom there is a familial bond of sorts. In this sense, President Clinton's visit may be seen in the context of Africa's extended family tradition. It is analogous to the visit of a wealthy in-law to the wife's impoverished family. Much was expected, even if only hopefully.

The Nigerian press was effusive in praising President Clinton. He was consistently described as intellectual, competent, astute, caring, and, above all, a most capable leader. Full-page ads sponsored by various businesses and organizations appeared in several Nigerian newspapers welcoming President Clinton, lauding his achievements, and expressing hopes for beneficial relations between Nigeria and the United States. Similar commercials and announcements also ran on television, many of them presumably sponsored by the government, given that the government-owned stations did not identify their sponsors.

In a two-page spread four days before President Clinton's arrival, the *Guardian* wrote of President Clinton's "extraordinary accomplishments" and "superlative performance;" it described his presidency as an "untrammeled service to America and the rest of mankind," and it credited him with "the longest ever economic expansion in the history of their country" (Dakolo, 2000, Aug. 23, pp. 16–17). The writer claimed further that, "The [U.S.] citizenry, in all strata of society and across the racial divide, thinks and dreams Clinton, for the miracles he has performed in a world where despondency and cynicism hold sway." There was little reference to the scandals that engulfed much of Clinton's presidency, especially the second term. One apparent reference to the Monica Lewinsky affair described it as "Clinton's single moral slip" (Dakolo, 2000, Aug. 23, p. 17).

Of particular relevance to the theme of this paper, the press described President Clinton's relationship with African Americans in effusively laudatory terms. As already noted, a writer quoted Maya Angelou's characterization of Clinton as "the first black president of the United States" (Dakolo, 2000, Aug. 23, p. 17). The writer added that Angelou, "is, like a vast majority of her African America kinsmen, eternally bound to him" (p. 17). The article stated that "among the African American community, [Clinton] became and has remained an icon, . . . an embodiment of all they had hoped for in the New World of their dream." Furthermore:

> It's right in the sub-conscious of every African American that Bill Clinton is it, the one whose aura alone diminishes the reality of a scheming Abraham Lincoln; the one that symbolises equality and harmony, the one who embodies the philosophy [that] "Discrimination against an American is un-American" (Dakolo, pp. 16–17).

Though this characterization of the bond between Clinton and African Americans may seem unduly superlative, it approximates the portrayal of the relationship even in the U.S. press. In their study of public support for President Clinton, Brooks and Rada (2002, p. 146) write that: "The homogenization of the African American population was consistent throughout the sample of stories. Media texts framed the discussion in a manner whereby virtually all Blacks supported the President."

Critics have questioned both the substance of President Clinton's policies toward African Americans and the universality of their positive perception of him. Robinson (2000, p. 100) writes, for instance, that, "Beyond cabinet and other job appointments that have little impact on the general black community, Bill Clinton did discernibly little for black people." Brooks and Rada (2002, p. 146) write also that, "While polls clearly indicated that a vast majority of African Americans supported the President, such support was not universal among Blacks."

There is little chance, of course, that anyone would receive 100 percent approval from any segment of the population, when people have any semblance of freedom to express themselves. Robinson's claim is itself debatable. But even if it were conceded, there remains the reality that Clinton's perception among African Americans not only corresponds with but actually contributed to his positive portrayal in the Nigerian press. The Nigerian press portrayed Clinton as having an interest in African countries that paralleled his affinity for African Americans. In an edition in circulation during Clinton's visit, for instance, *Newswatch* declares that, "Unlike his predecessors, President Clinton's African policy has promoted greater US–Africa partnership, co-operation and development" (Akpaekong, 2000, Aug. 28, p. 16).

Given these encomiums, expectations were high. A story in *Newswatch* on Clinton's imminent visit bore the theme summary: "Nigerians expect President Bill Clinton's three-day visit to the country to usher in a regime of economic, political and socio-cultural benefits" (Sowunmi, 2000, Aug. 28, p. 15). The economic issues were especially emphasized. The *Newswatch* article states that "A similar visit by Clinton to Ghana opened substantial in-flow of American investment into that country" (p. 19). And an industrialist was quoted by the *Guardian* as saying: "Clinton's visit should demonstrate confidence in the Nigerian economy, in Nigerian democracy, in the return of investment and in the protection of assets" (Industrialists, 2000, Aug. 24, p. 27). In an article following the visit, *Tell* magazine offers the theme summary: "United States president, Bill Clinton, concludes a historic visit to Nigeria raising the glimmer of hope for economic revival for a nation in distress" (Okolo, 2000, Sept. 11, p. 44).

Debt relief was a particularly pressing economic concern, and here too there was considerable optimism. *Newswatch* quotes a fellow of the Nigerian Institute of International Affairs as saying:

> Clinton's visit to Nigeria will provide [Nigerian President Olusegun] Obasanjo the opportunity to discuss the issue more extensively with the American president. Obasanjo will be able to convince Clinton that Nigeria will not just be a stronger economy but also have a stronger democracy with debt relief (Sowunmi, 2000, Aug. 28, p. 19).

Similarly, the president of the Nigeria-America Chamber of Commerce is quoted as saying: "I am sure something positive will come regarding relief for Nigeria. I am optimistic that there will be debt relief" (Sowunmi, 2000, Aug. 28, p. 20). U.S. Congresswoman Maxine Waters was also quoted as supporting such aid: "Nigeria needs a lot of support and is lacking resources to execute its democratic agenda" (Sowunmi, 2000, Aug. 28, p. 20).

Actually, the payoff with regard to Nigeria's democracy was reported to be hinged not just on what Clinton did to help the country, but on the reality of the visit per se. On the day Clinton arrived in Nigeria, a two-page headline in the *Guardian* declares: "Clinton's visit: A triumph for democracy" (Jolayemi, 2000, Aug. 26, pp. 18–19). Before then, a contributing columnist has declared that: "The visit of United States President Bill Clinton to Nigeria further underscores the reality of our country's re-emergence into international respectability" (Fadun, 2000, Aug. 24, p. 49).

The importance of this aspect of the visit was evident in the government's heavy promotion of the visit in radio and television announcements several days before Clinton's arrival. Time and again broadcasts on the state-owned radio and TV stations fervently urged Nigerians to prepare to welcome Clinton. The promos typically included a summary of U.S. and Clinton's stature in the world and the significance of the visit to Nigeria. In one version, the announcer then stated: "No wonder the Nigerian President Olusegun Obasanjo has asked all Nigerians to join hands to welcome our august visitor to Nigeria." This was followed in this and other versions of the promos by the chorus: "Welcome, welcome, welcome to Nigeria. Welcome, welcome, welcome to Nigeria." Given that Clinton's itinerary severely limited his exposure to the country and the populace, the heavy promotion can only be significant as an orchestration of the symbolic import of the visit.

Several other benefits were expected and requests made. One contributing columnist, who described himself as American educated, married to an American, and is "an artiste, a television presenter and producer," even urged Clinton to help get the U.S. media industry interested in Nigerian productions and to tighten copyrights laws in Nigeria.

COVERAGE OF PRESIDENT BUSH

In comparison to the exuberant coverage Clinton, the coverage of Bush's visit was much more subdued. There was little of the elation that preceded Clinton's visit and none of the affinity. Even the government was less enthused in promoting the visit to the general public. And though Bush was accompanied on the visit by at least two high-level African Americans in his administration—Secretary of State Colin Powell and National Security Adviser Condoleezza Rice—there was little of the visiting in-law effect as described above in the analytical metaphor. Neither Powell nor Condoleezza Rice got the scope of media exposure accorded Susan Rice during Clinton's visit.

Moreover, there was somewhat of a reversal in the expectations. Whereas the Nigerian news media, as will be discussed later, were criticized for taking a prostrate stance with regard to President Clinton, they portrayed President Bush more as a favor seeker, even if Nigeria also needed his favors. This parallels the coverage of Bush's visit to South Africa by that country's press (St. Clair, 2004).

In an editorial a week before President Bush's arrival in Nigeria, the *Vanguard* notes that he was the first Republican president to visit Nigeria, then adds:

> We believe that Bush would not visit Nigeria if he does not consider
> Nigeria as being strategic to American interest. After all, Nigeria apart

from being [the] black world's most populous country with strong economic ties with the United States, is the sixth largest exporter of crude oil in the world (Welcoming George Bush, 2003, p. 16).

The editorial urges reciprocity and summarizes what the United States can do for Nigeria, most of which were on the shopping list presented to President Clinton three years earlier.

On the second day of President Bush's visit, an analyst for the *Punch* further discussed the mutual needs between the two countries, noting especially that the United States had an increasing need to reduce its dependence on Middle Eastern crude oil and sees African countries, including Nigeria, as potential alternatives. The analyst underscored the equivalence in needs by noting the parallel between the controversy attending to President Bush's election in 2000 with the accusations of rigging that faced his Nigerian host, President Olusegun Obasanjo, after he was re-elected in March 2003. (The Bush Visit, 2003).

Even on the point of economic support, the former president of the Nigerian Senate, Wada Nas, notes that Nigerians pump hundreds of millions of dollars of investment into the U.S. economy. In an article in the *Daily Independent* addressed to President Bush, Nas (2003, July 10) writes as follows:

> In a recent interview Mr. Andrew Young, former US Ambassador to the UN estimated that Nigerians have up to about USD700 million investment in your country and I believe yours too have as much here. This fruitful economic ties are very vital in strengthening international friendship and human brotherhood.

More central to the thesis of this paper is the criticism directed at President Bush as a representative of Washington's, especially the Republican Party's, policies toward Africa. Whereas much of the same policies existed during President Clinton's administration, he was portrayed overall and in specific terms as an agent of change. In contrast, President Bush was portrayed as an embodiment of those policies.

In the article in the *Daily Independent,* Nas addresses President Bush thus: "Your excellency, we feel that Africa, or more specific the Black race, is sidelined to the back bench of the foreign policy of your country." Another analyst, writing for the daily newspaper *Champion*, specifies President Bush's continuation of the policy of neglect. Noting that Bush "is not a widely popular man across the African continent" for the most part because of his policies in the Middle East, especially the invasion of Iraq, the analyst for the Champion writes:

But also [R]epublican presidents, unlike their Democratic Party coun-
terparts, are not generally regarded by Africans because of what is being
perceived as their lack of commitment to the continent. George Bush
Junior had in fact begun to [toe] the very same line of his [R]epublican
predecessors when in one of the early declarations of his presidency,
he stated that Africa was not a priority. But since the tragedy of September 11, 2001, Bush has virtually taken a U-turn. He now recognizes—it seems—Africa's prominent role and relevance in the U.S.-led
war against international terrorism" (Okerafor, 2003, p. 38).

One of the more optimistic coverages of Bush's visit appears in the
Daily Independent of July 11 (Jolayemi, 2003, pp. A1 & A5). The paper
concedes that:

> President George Walker Bush is not popular in Africa. Not many see
> him as a friend of the continent. In fact, when the news of his visit was
> first broken, it was received with mixed feelings.

In contrast, the paper states:

> When Mr. Bill Clinton met the crowds in Nigeria, South Africa and
> Ghana towards the end of his tenure, the mutual affection was unmis-
> taken. They were charmed by his style, carriage and more importantly
> his passion for Africans.

The "Cover Story," though tucked merely three inches at the bottom right
of the front page (and continued more extensively on p. A5), asserts nevertheless that "Africa cannot afford to give the American president the cold
shoulder" because "Mr. Bush's visit may turn out to be more significant
and more rewarding for Africa despite the low expectations."
    The paper discusses various indications of President Bush's commit-
ment to Africa, including passage of the African Growth and Opportunity
Act and continuation of the diversity immigration visa program. A separate story in the same issue reports a "gift" from Bush of $58.9 billion,
approved by the U.S. House of Representative to assist Nigeria in air traffic
control and other aviation-related projects (Alo, 2003, July 11, p, A2).
    Still, in the "Cover Story" of July 11, the *Daily Independent* was
careful to note the reciprocity in U.S.–Africa relations: "Beyond all these,
President Bush's visit presents both America and Africa an opportunity to
reappraise each other, re-examine the options before them as countries and
as individuals."

BEGGARLY POSTURE AND ITS REVERSAL

The element of reciprocity is significant in this comparative analysis. During Clinton's visit, there was criticism that Nigeria, as represented in the press, was overly beggarly in its reception of Clinton. The coverage of Bush's visit reflects a reversal of the beggarly posture.

As suggested before, a beggarly posture is inconsistent with the value of relational parity and dignity in welcoming an in-law. In framing Clinton's visit this way, the Nigerian press deviated from this custom. Of course, the framing reflected some social realities and general expectations, but the scope was not inevitable. A political analyst and lecturer at the University of Lagos, Dr. Ayo Akinbobola, is quoted as saying, for instance, with regard to Clinton's coverage: "Nigeria is a regional power, and the voice of Nigeria echoes as the voice of Africa. Outsiders regard [us] more than we regard ourselves" (Nwosu, 2000, Aug. 25, p. 11). Akinbobola was paraphrased further as saying that: "[I]t would be belittling Nigeria and dampening expectations of Americans if Nigerians opt for the beggarly posture instead of rubbing minds at all levels—business, civil society and government to so tap the magic round (sic) with which God's own country was able to get where it is today."

Incidentally, the reference to the United States as "God's own country" was a common one, heard even on news programs on government-owned television stations. In contrast, a contributor to the *Guardian* during Clinton's visit described Nigeria as "the land that has promised so much but has delivered so little to its citizens" (Oputa, 2000, Aug. 26, p. 18).

A few months after President Clinton's visit, a columnist for the *Vanguard,* returns to the theme: "Although former President of the United States of America, Bill Clinton made some promises to speak with those creditors of ours especially the Paris Club to whom 70 percent of our indebtedness stands, we must not continue to deceive ourselves, our destiny lies in our hands" (Farukanmi, 2001, Feb. 1).

Concerns about the beggarly posture were also expressed by the African American woman Susan Rice. The *Guardian* reports that "Rice could not hide her disgust at the apparent [Nigerian] myopic view of the U.S. leader's visit instead of embracing it from a wider spectrum of a meeting of two nations and peoples of shared aspirations trying to look at what they could do together for themselves, the region, the international community and humanity" (Nwosu, 2000, Aug. 25, p. 11). In the televised interviews, Rice took pains to emphasize that the United States also stood to benefit from close relations with Nigeria. She also warned against "exaggerated expectations" regarding debt relief and articulated the paradox that though

Nigeria was too poor for its debt burden, it was too rich for debt relief. She noted also that of the $30 billion Nigeria owed foreign lenders, less than 4 percent was to the United States.

Rice's statements parallel the sentiments an African woman would express to her natal family regarding her wealthy husband's pending visit. Just as Rice was reportedly disgusted with Nigeria's beggarly posture, the wife of a visiting in-law would be similarly dismayed if her family prostrates for charity. A family's beggarly posture toward an in-law is demeaning to the wife. Rice's statement that the U.S. also stood to benefit indicates some relational parity, which is consistent with the family's dignity. The statement that Nigeria is too rich to merit debt relief serves also to enhance Nigeria's stature. Moreover, Rice's explanation that the U.S. could only do so much is parallel to a wife's attempt to create realistic expectations of her husband by her natal family. The balance in portraying Bush as both a seeker and potential giver of favors evidently addresses this concern.

CONCLUSIONS

This paper has examined the Nigerian press coverage of Presidents Clintons and Bush's visits to Nigeria to suggest what it conveys about Africans' solidarity with African Americans. The paper employs the metaphor of a visiting wealthy in-law to the family of his wife to illustrate how the pan-Africanist ideology in the coverages mesh with Africa's extended family values.

It seems evident that press coverage of Clinton's visit suggests considerable perceived common bond and destiny of Africans and African Americans. His good relations with African Americans were an important element in the positive way Nigerians perceived him and the high expectations they had of him. The metaphor of a visiting in-law illuminates this element of Clinton's reception and even sheds some light on the general relations between Africans and African Americans. Even when a member of the family is in union with another family, the natal familial solidarity remains though that member may bring new perspectives to family discourse.

The paper also applies the metaphor to the notion of national diminution. In this regard, the Nigerian press coverage of Clinton deviated from some norms of the metaphor to the extent that the ethics of relational parity and dignity in poverty were substantially absent. Ironically, the reason for the ethics is to inspire confidence and respect, attributes that are helpful when seeking economic aid. The African American woman, Susan Rice, joined some Nigerians—perhaps unwittingly, definitely significantly—in calling for the exemplification of this ethic. Perhaps, there is a lesson here about the relevance of African values in contemporary affairs and their manifestation (and sometimes breach) in Africa as well as in the Diaspora.

The breach in the coverage of Clinton was rectified in the coverage of Bush, possibly because of the criticism of the coverage of Clinton, but more likely because of the changed circumstances. There was lowered expectation of Bush, which makes the projection of relational parity more cogent.

It is important to note that the lowered expectation of Bush parallels lowered expectations when a disapproved son-in-law is visiting. Not much is expected from an in-law who is perceived to be indifferent to his wife's family, especially if he is also perceived to be uncharitable to the wife.

It must be reiterated that a number of factors are involved in Bush's unpopularity in Africa and his image in the Nigerian press. Among them are his invasion of Iraq, U.S. policies in the Israeli/Palestinian conflict, the general image of the Republicans, and Bush's own stated initial indifference to Africans and other foreign policy matters. In all this, there is a consonance in his perception by Africans and African Americans.

More pointedly, there is the solidarity factor, whereby the presidents' images in the Nigerian press mirror their perceived relations to African Americans. Clinton's image clearly benefits from this factor. In contrast, though no explicit report was found of a discordant relationship between Bush and African Americans, there appears to be a presumption that if he was indifferent to Africans he was probably indifferent to African Americans.

REFERENCES

Adeleke, T. (1998a). Black Americans and Africa: A critique of the Pan-African and identity paradigms. *International Journal of African Historical Studies, 31,* 505–536.

Adeleke, T. (1998b). *UnAfrican Americans: Nineteenth-century Black nationalists and the civilizing mission.* Lexington, KY: The University Press of Kentucky.

Agyeman, O. (2003). *The failure of grassroots pan-Africanism: The case of the All-African Trade Union Federation.* Lanham, MD: Lexington Books.

Akpaekong, O. (2000, Aug. 28). America's new thinking. *Newswatch,* p. 16

Alo, Dan. (2003, July 11). Bush offers N7.7 trillion gift. *Daily Independent,* p, A2.

Asante, M. K. (1988). *Afrocentricity.* Trenton, NJ: Africa World Press.

Atiku hopeful of fruitful Nigeria-US relations (2001, Jan. 23). *The Guardian* http://ngrguardiannews.com .

Badagry is ready to assimilate African-Americans—Akran (2000, Sept. 26). *The Guardian,* p. 17.

Bauman, Z. (2001). Identity in the globalizing world. In Ben-Rafael & Sternberg (Eds.), *Identity, Culture and Globalization* (pp. 471–482). Leiden, The Netherlands: Brill.

Bourgault, M. (1996). *Mass media in sub-Saharan Africa*. Bloomington, IN: Indiana University Press.

Bracey, E. N. (2003). *On racism: Essays on black popular culture, African American politics, and the new aesthetics*. Lanham, MD: University Press of America.

Brooks, D. E. & Rada, J. A. (2002). Constructing race in black and whiteness: Media coverage of public support for President Clinton. *Journalism & Communication Monographs*, 4, 115–156.

Chinweizu (1975). *The west and the rest of us: White predators, black slavers and the African elite*. New York: Vintage.

Dakolo, D. (2000, Aug. 23). William Jefferson Clinton: The Journey to Nigeria. *The Guardian*, pp. 16–17.

Eko, L. (2001). Steps toward pan-African exchange: Translation and distribution of TV programs across Africa's linguistic regions. *Journal of Black Studies*, 31, 365–379.

Entman, R. M. (1993). Framing: Toward clarification of a fractured paradigm. *Journal of Communication*, 43 (4), 51–58.

Esedebe, P. O. (1994). *Pan-Africanism: The idea and movement, 1776–1991*. Washington: Howard University Press.

Fadun, B. (2000, Aug. 24). Clinton's visit: Matters arising. *The Guardian*, p. 49.

Farukanmi, O. (2001, Feb. 1). Debt relief and poverty alleviation. *Vanguard* http://allafrica.com/stories.

Ferkiss, V. C. (1966). *Africa's Search for Identity*. Cleveland, OH: Meridian Books.

Galtung, J. & Ruge, M.H. (1965). The structure of foreign news. *Journal of Peace Research*, 2 (1), 64–91.

Gans, H. J. (1979). *Deciding what's news: A study of CBS Evening News, NBC Nightly News, Newsweek, and Time*. New York: Pantheon.

Gbadegesin, S. (1998). Individuality, community, and the moral order. In P. H. Coetzee & A. P. J. Roux (Eds.), *The African philosopher reader* (pp. 292–305). London & New York: Routledge.

Golding, P. (1979). Media professionalism in the Third World: The transfer of an ideology. In J. Curan, M. Gurevitch, & J. Woollacott (Eds.), *Mass communication and society* (pp. 291–308). Beverly Hills, CA: Sage.

Hall, S. (1982). The rediscovery of 'ideology': Return of the repressed in media studies. In M. Gurevitch et. al. (Eds.), *Culture, society, and the media*. London: Routledge.

Harris, E. L. (1992). *Native stranger: A Black American's journey into the heart of Africa*. New York: Simon & Schuster.

Ibelema, M. (2003). Tradition and modernity: The triumph of African culture. In E. Onwudiwe & M. Ibelema (Eds.), *Afro-optimism: Perspectives on Africa's Advances* (pp. 21–38). Westport, CT: Praeger.

Industrialists see image boost from Clinton visit (2000, Aug. 24). *The Guardian*, p. 27.

Jolayemi, M. A. (2000, Aug. 26). Clinton's visit: A triumph for democracy. *The Guardian*, pp. 18–19.

Jolayemi, Moses Ayo. (2003, July 11). Bush and the African challenge. *Daily Independent*, pp. A1 & A5.

Jimada, U. (1992). Eurocentric media training in Nigeria: What alternative? *Journal of Black Studies*, 22, 366–379.

Mba-Afolabi, J. (2000, Sept. 11). Stop! Don't Move Any Nearer. *Tell*, p. 46.

Mudimbe, V.Y. (1988). *The invention of Africa*. Bloomington: Indiana University Press.

Nas, Wada. (2003, July 10). *Daily Independent*, p. C7.

Ngugi, T. wa (1993). *Moving the centre: The struggle for cultural freedoms*. Portsmouth: Heineman.

Nwosu, N. (2000, Aug. 25). Analysts query beggarly posture as Clinton visits. *The Guardian*, p. 11.

Nwosu, N. (2000, Aug. 26). Over land, across seas, a mission to re-unite a divided house. *The Guardian*, pp. 16–17.

Ogbodo, J., Obayuwana, O. and Abuh, A., (2001, March 13). U.S. votes $110 million yearly aid to Nigeria. *The Guardian* http://ngrguardiannews.com.

Okerafor, Tony. (2003). The ramifications of Bush's African Safari. *Saturday Champion*, July 12, 2003, p. 38.

Okolo, A. (2000, Sept. 11). New vistas of hope. *Tell*, p. 44–47.

Onwudiwe, E. (1993). Sovereignty diminution: A new path to Africa's development. *BOCTOC: A Journal of Russian Academy of Sciences*, #3 pp. 73–80.

Oputa, C. (2000, Aug. 26). For President Clinton's eyes only. *The Guardian*, p. 18)

Richburg, K. B. (1997). *Out of America: A Black man confronts Africa*. New York: Basic Books.

Robinson, R. (2000). *The debt: What America owes blacks*. New York: Dutton

St. Clair, D. (2004). President Bush visits Africa: An analysis of Botswana's Daily News and South Africa's Mail & Guardian. Paper presented at the annual meeting of the Association for Education in Journalism and Mass Communication, Toronto, Ont., Aug. 4–7.

Sowunmi, A. (2000, Aug. 28). Waiting for Bill Clinton. *Newswatch*, pp. 15–20.

The Bush visit: What he will discuss with Obasanjo. (2003, July 12). *The Punch*, p. 11.

Thompson, V. B. (1970). *Africa and unity: The evolution of Pan-Africanism*. New York: Humanities Press.

Welcoming George Bush to Africa. (2003, July 4). *Vanguard*, p. 16.

Section II
Language, Information, and Education

Chapter Five

African Betrayals and African Recovery for a New Future

Molefi Kete Asante, Temple University

Clearly, the structure of knowledge in the West has created a situation where the betrayal of Africa has been quite common. Few African scholars have completely escaped the vise of Europe in the analysis of the past, present, or future prospects of Africa. Thus, a web of betrayal of the continent occurs in the language and education of African children in such a way that one generation passes it to the next with little or no question. It is the purpose of this paper to explore the various ways the betrayal of Africa has undermined the continent and to suggest ways forward.

TWO BETRAYAL AREAS

The betrayal of Africa appears in two general areas. One I have called the *ordinary* areas of commerce and culture and the other I have called the *extraordinary* areas of thought and knowledge. They are interconnected, but distinct in how they function in the marginalizing of Africans. Both betrayals have been set in motion to disinherit Africans and to dislocate Africans in the context of human history.

ORDINARY AREAS

Let us see how this has worked.

Africa has been betrayed by the Western nations' use of the instruments of international commerce and trade. Recently it has been reported that fake medicines have been sold to Botswana, Haiti, and Ghana. European companies involved in pharmaceuticals have distributed empty capsules to African nations. Thus people in Botswana who thought they were getting treatment for tuberculosis discovered that they were taking empty shells. And in Haiti, instead of glycerin to be mixed with active ingredients for cold medicines the country was supplied with anti-freeze fluid and many children died. Ghana has had to deal with non-African pharmaceutical companies willing to sell drugs with less than the required amount of anti-malarial medicine.

Africa has been betrayed by the genetics of food, and the unequal distribution of resources. We have been told that fast food chains are now requiring that their food suppliers stop using Monsanto potatoes because they have been genetically altered. What do you think they have been selling to Africa? I am of the opinion that Africa is in more danger of poverty and hunger than of AIDS. This is not to say that AIDS is not an issue, it is rather to say that poverty is killing more people than AIDS. We have been betrayed in the area of food distribution.

Africa has been betrayed by missionaries and imams who have called our own priests and priestesses false while presenting us with non-African alternatives.

Africa has been betrayed by education, the Academy, and the structure of knowledge imposed by the Western world. It is this betrayal that has set us up to become victims in the world of thought.

EXTRAORDINARY AREAS

A people so often betrayed must take a serious look at its own approach to phenomena, to life, to existence, to knowledge and the structure of knowledge. Where there have been others, our thoughts must now become our own thoughts. Where we have forgotten our own traditions of knowledge and information we must remember. New forms of thinking and new ways of asserting ourselves in our own history must be invented. This means that African scholars must think beyond Europe. Why cannot we research the relationship between Ethiopia and China without going to Britain. We already know the relationship of Britain to China and Britain to Ethiopia, but in a Eurocentric world we are not allowed to discover the relationship between China and Ethiopia before Europe.

Of course we know that African thought in World History takes us to the very beginning of human history.

Africans have thought about the universe longer than any other people.

In fact philosophy itself originated in Africa and the first philosophers in the world were Africans. Scientists know that the Khoisan people have the oldest DNA of any humans, thus showing a contemporary relationship to the ancient Africans of the Great Rift Valley.

Our tradition is intertwined with the earliest thought. The European writers referred to the ancient African works as "Wisdom Literature," in an effort to distinguish African thinking from European thinking. They could not conceive of Africans as having philosophy.

Philosophy was meant, in their minds, to indicate a kind of reflection that was possible only with the Greeks. They constructed a Greece that was miraculous, built on the foundation of a racial imagination that established a white European superiority in everything.

Since philosophy was seen as the source of all other arts and sciences, philosophy was the chief discipline. This place was left to philosophy, not history or politics or grammar. In the mind of Europeans, philosophy was the epitome of thought.

Numerous Western writers glorified the achievements of the mind of the Greeks. A Greek stood at the door of every science in the European mind. There were no secrets that had not been discovered by the Greeks. They owed allegiances to no one. They were immaculate, without blemish, isolated from every other people as the standard by which the world was to be judged. Even today when the European scholar speaks of art, poetry, theater, rhetoric, or politics, the names of the Greeks are invoked.

Whether in art or science, in sculptor or mathematics, in astronomy or literature, they had no equal and were without antecedents.

However, according to the tradition of Western thought, it was in philosophy that the Greeks excelled. As Theophile Obenga says, others may have had religion, stories, wise sayings, and wisdom literature but the Greeks had philosophy. This was the highest of all disciplines and it was only through the minds of whites that philosophy came to the world.

Yet we know that the word philosophy is not Greek, although it came through the Greeks to English and other European languages. Seba, wisdom, the ancient Mdw Ntr word is the earliest example of reflective thinking. In fact, on the tomb of Antef I, 2052 BC we see the first mention of wisdom.

The word *sophia*, wisdom in Greek, is derived from the more ancient word *seba*, wisdom, an African word. To say "philo" is to say brother or lover. One normally says that a philosopher is "a lover of wisdom." But the ancient Africans had come to this understanding long before there was even a nation of Greeks.

Indeed the first serious thinkers or philosophers were not Greeks. This means that not only is the word philosophy not Greek, the practice of philosophy is not Greek, but African.

Thales who lived around 600 BC is usually thought of as the first Greek philosopher. Some claim that it was Pythagoras, who was a younger contemporary of Thales, but I claim, with most Greek scholars that it was Thales since he is said to have told a young Pythagoras "You must do as I have done and go to Egypt to learn philosophy from the Egyptians." This is advice that Pythagoras followed and went to Egypt, spending twenty three years at the feet of such venerable teachers as Wennofer.

There were several select places where various aspects of philosophy such as social ethics, natural laws, metaphysics, and medicine were taught. One could study at the Temple of Ptah at Men-nefer, at the Temple of Bast at Bubastis, at the Temple of Hatheru at Dendera, at the Ausarion at Abydos, at the Temple of Amen at Waset, at the Temple of Heru at Edfu, at the Temple of Ra at ON, and the Temple of Auset at Philae. Indeed, scholars and others could assemble at scores of other sites from Siwa to Esna for intellectual discussion and discourse. Kemet, the ancient name of Egypt, was not without a considerable body of thought that had been amassed over many centuries.

Here along the Nile River Africans thought about the nature of the universe, the condition of good and evil, human relations, beauty and the nature of the divine. I am not here interested on the impact Africa had on Europe or the influence that Kemet had on Greece. In fact I believe that it is time we wrest the study of Africa from any comparison with Europe. We will become far more insightful about our own cultures as we gain deeper knowledge of our own societies in relationship to continuities, migrations, land tenure philosophy, governance, writing styles and techniques, and the nature of morality in African terms.

Perhaps one day the names of the earliest philosophers will be as familiar to African children as the names of the Greek philosophers are to us today. Why shouldn't our children know the names of the philosophers?

Imhotep, 2700 BC, earliest personality recorded in history. Like the later personalities of Socrates and Jesus nothing of his writing remains, but we know that he understood volume and space, because he was the builder of the first pyramid, the Sakkara pyramid. He was the first philosopher, the first physician, the first architect, and the first counselor to a king recorded in history.

Ptahhotep, 2414 BC, was the first ethical philosopher. He believed that life consisted of making harmony and peace with nature.

Kagemni, 2300 BC, was the first teacher of right action for the sake of goodness rather than personal advantage.

Merikare, 1990 BC, valued the art of good speech. His classical teachings on good speech were recorded and passed down from generation to generation.

Sehotepibre, 1991 BC, was the first philosopher who espoused a sort of nationalism based in allegiance and loyalty to a political leader.

Amenemhat, 19991 BC, was the world's first cynic. He expressed a cynical view of intimates and friends, warning that one must not trust those who are close to you.

Amenhotep, son of Hapu, 1400 BC, was the most revered of the ancient Kemetic philosophers. Next to Imhotep, he was the epitome of the philosopher. The people deified him as a god, as they had deified Imhotep, long before Jesus. He was called the most knowledgeable thinker of his day.

Duauf, 1340 BC, was seen as the master of protocols. He is concerned with reading books for wisdom, the first intellectual in philosophical history. Reading, he said, was the best way to train the mind.

Amenemope 1290 BC promoted the philosophy of manners, etiquette, and success.

Akhenaten, 1300 BC, promoted Aton as the Almighty One God. He has been erroneously called the Father of Monotheism.

All these philosophers were hundreds of years before any Greek philosopher. Indeed, Homer, the first Greek to write something that was intelligible, lived around 800 BC. But he was not a philosopher. Thales, 600 BC, is usually referred to as the first Greek philosopher. Isocrates was the second major philosopher of the Greeks.

Kung Fu Tzu, 551 BC, the great Chinese philosopher, who believed that humans could make the Way great, lived much later than the African philosophers. But Kung Fu Tzu was a contemporary of the Greek philosophers and of Buddha.

Siddartha Buddha, 563 BC, the Indian philosopher lived about the same time as Isocrates who lived around 550 BC. Both were much later than the early African philosophers.

Now as an Afrocentrist I approach the construction of knowledge from the standpoint of Africans as agents in the world, actors, not simply spectators to Europe. This allows me to examine the characteristics that would create a new vision for African people. I believe that a critical Afrocentricity could unleash an era of exceptional progress in the African world.

Afrocentricity is a paradigm that takes Africans as agents and subjects. Therefore, theories related to Afrocentricity ask the question of centrality of subject, location of actor, and orientation of text or phenomena. In order to grasp the potentiality of Afrocentricity I have identified characteristics, general areas of inquiry, and principles of intellectual creativity.

CHARACTERISTICS

As a cultural configuration the Afrocentric idea is distinguished by five characteristics:

(1)   an intense interest in *psychological location* as determined by symbols, motifs, rituals, and signs.

(2)   a commitment to finding the *subject-place of Africans* in any social, political, economic, or religious phenomenon with implications for questions of sex, gender, and class.

(3)   a *defense of African cultural elements* as historically valid in the context of art, music, and literature.

(4)   a *celebration of "centeredness" and agency* and a commitment to lexical refinement that eliminates pejoratives about Africans or other people.

(5)   a powerful imperative from historical sources *to revise the collective text* of African people.

FOUR GENERAL AREAS OF INQUIRY

I am convinced that the constituent elements are rooted in four general areas of inquiry:

- Cosmology—nature of beingness, ontology, mythology
- Axiology—nature of ethical values

- Epistemology—nature of knowledge, proofs, methods
- Aesthetics—nature of creative motifs

I have dealt with these elements in my book, *Kemet, Afrocentricity, and Knowledge,* as keys to a fundamental inquiry into language, society, culture, and politics.

PRINCIPLES OF INTELLECTUAL CREATIVITY

Classical Foundations
> The foundation of human origin and the role of classical Africa

Tradition and Innovation
> Preservation and generation are instruments of the interplay of change and continuity

Location in Time and Space
> Discovering chronology and geography as keys to interpretation

Creation and Exchange
> Investigation into principles of production, distribution, and consumption of goods and services

Politics and Power
> The study of participation in the use of power and authority

Scientific Applications
> Application of science and technology to create and enrich community

Ethics and Values
> Enhancing and promoting critical thinking in the area of affective human behavior

The Afrocentrist seeks to redirect the study of Africa away from the interest of Europe into a study of Africa for itself. This is a major task that will become a neo classical revival rooted in the study of Kemet. In the end, Afrocentricity is not about self congratulations or self esteem, it is about the proper way to assess African experiences and behaviors. Thus, as an African thought or an Afrocentric idea it is a positive element in human understanding. We seek nothing more than a proper orientation to truth and the restructuring of knowledge away from a hierarchical framework.

Chapter Six

The Legacy of Colonialism on Language in 21st Century Africa

Adisa A. Alkebulan, San Diego State University

Colonialism in Africa has left its mark in a number of ways. Language seems to be one of the most profound indicators that reveal its legacy. In most postcolonial African countries, the "official" language remains the language of the former colonial power. This paper will explore the colonial language policies of Britain and France in order to explain the current language situation in their former colonies. Both colonial administrations had different methods, but both have had lasting effects on the current linguistic circumstances. The debate between African writers of literature will help us put the discussion into proper context. Furthermore, the linguistic reality of Africa will also be discussed. Who actually speaks European languages is crucial to this discussion.

Missionaries played a tremendous role in both the British and the French's colonial aspirations but to a greater extent, the British. The missionaries preceded the colonial forces and laid the groundwork for them. It is important to point out that missionaries, and not colonial forces, initiated Western education in Africa. The missionaries were enthusiastic about spreading Christianity throughout Africa and converting its people. To this end, the missionaries attempted to teach Africans how to read scriptures in their own languages. The missionaries' first charge, then, was to learn the indigenous languages of the communities in which they settled. Gerda Mansour writes:

[It] was their first task to learn their language. Furthermore, since the
Christian message, particularly in its protestant form, relies heavily on
literacy, it was part of the missionaries task to analyze the phonology
and grammar of the African language in order to devise a writing system, and ultimately, to translate the Bible, the catechism and hymns.
This practical goal of their linguistic analysis was always foremost in
their minds rather than the development of a scientific methodology
(Mansour 1993: 12).

Bamgbose (1976: 9) points out that "the first school in Senegal
opened in 1817, experimented with the teaching of Wolof and French . . .
An intensive study by missionaries of selected African languages accompanied the attempts at winning converts through literacy in the mother
tongue." Thus, early western education in Africa was strictly intended for
religious instruction. Through missionary schools, particularly in what
were to become British colonies, the tradition of early education in the
native language got its start. This is an educational policy that still persists
today. Bamgbose further reveals that the missionaries did not have "free
hand in the control of the system of education for long (9)." The colonial governments seized control of missionary schools and implemented
their own policies. Moreover, the British government found it economical
for missionaries to continue to control the day-to-day functions of these
new colonial schools. In some cases, it is reported, the colonial government provided missionaries with grants-in-aid for their educational programs (Awoniyi 1976: 35). Colonial governments and missionaries were
often seen as one in the same because the colonial administrators and the
missionaries not only sprang from the same culture but they also shared
the same worldview. In addition, colonial administrations often funded
mission schools. Furthermore, colonial governments protected the mission
schools (Bohaen 1985: 525).

The Missionaries' responsibility was to provide a Western education
to the indigenous population, who were considered "ignorant savages,"
as a means of spreading Christianity and later to facilitate the economic
exploitation of Africa for the benefit of the colonial power. In 1816, the
Church Missionary Society was established and its aim was to teach African children in its missions to read the Bible in their own languages. The
British and Foreign Bible Society published 36 Bibles and 83 New Testa-
ments in African languages (An African Survey Revised 1956: 80). In contrast, in French colonies, in 1829, the governor-general issued instruction
that teaching must concentrate exclusively on the use of French (Fishman
1974: 163). The distinction between the British and the French policies will

be discussed later. In order to ensure the teaching of each colonial language, language policies were created to meet this end.

COLONIAL LANGUAGE POLICY AND LANGUAGE PLANNING

Colonial language policy and education were inextricably linked. The policy determined how language would be used in education, mass communication and in legislation. To this end, colonial administrators devised language plans to determine how their language would be implemented into their colonial scheme. Of course, the multiplicity of languages in Africa was a potential problem for colonial administrators. How would the diversity of language impact with the colonial objective? How would these languages coincide with the colonial language? Which languages, if any, would serve as "national languages"? The process of answering these questions is commonly referred to as language planning. Rubin explains that language planning is:

> . . . deliberate language change, this is, changes in the systems of a language code or speaking or both that are planned by organizations established for such purposes of given a mandate to fulfill such purposes . . . It might also be defined as the modification of a language code to certain preferred specification, namely, the modernization and standardization of the lexicon, grammar, pronunciation or discourse. (Kennedy 1983: 4)."

Eastman (1983: 12) provides four aspects to language planning: 1) The formulation of the policy by setting its goals; 2) codification of the policy by setting out strategies for the practical achievement of the goals; 3) elaboration of the policy by seeing that the languages involved may be extended into the arenas specified by the policy goals and; 4) implementation of the policy by providing the authoritative backbone to achieve the goals and the motivation for the use of the language of the policy by the people affected. It is legislators, implementers of policy, government agencies, language academy personnel, and language specialists in private industry, etc., who primarily concern themselves with language planning (Fishman 1974: 15). In regards to language use and function, Kingsley Andoh-Kumi offers us this:

> There are three main types of language policies—official, educational and general. The official language policy relates to the languages that are recognized by the government, and the determination of the functions or purposes for which they have been recognized. The educational

language policy relates to the languages that are recognized by the government and educational authorities and agencies for use as media of instruction and subjects of study at the various levels of education, both public and private. The general language policy encompasses unofficial state recognition or tolerance of languages that are used in the mass media, business and contacts with foreigners (Andoh-Kumi 1997:14).

There are also two types of language policy decisions: explicit and implicit. An explicit language policy, he observes, is the type that is expressly stated or embodied in a document. He also notes that the absence of explicit language policies does not mean the absence of a policy. The policy can be inferred from the practices of the people or government bodies or other agencies. This, he asserts, may be referred to as an implicit language policy (Andoh-Kumi 1997:15). Language policies give advantages to those who speak a particular language, while excluding those who do not.

In essence, language planning entails the belief that social change can be "engineered and directed, produced at will (Sachs 1995: 132)." In this vein, Arturo Escobar maintains that there is an assumption that through planning, poor countries can "move smoothly along the path of progress (Sachs 1995: 132)." To further illustrate this point, Ama Mazama writes:

> Language planning . . . was simply the more recent application to the domain of language techniques and practices of social control intricately linked to the rise of Western modernity. Two of the major assumptions of such activities are that human beings and nature are tools that can be manipulated, and that through appropriate manipulation and planning 'social change can be engineered . . . One major effect of planning in the West has undoubtedly been the homogenization and standardization of life, which in turn entails injustice and the erasure of difference and diversity.' . . . In the 19th and 20th centuries it was [called] civilization. Since 1949 it has been development (1994: 3–4).

Language planning was seen as a necessity by colonial powers. Only through planning could their aspirations of "progress," and "development" be met. Of course we can look at African nations today and see that the use of European languages does not automatically give access to wealth and power on a global scale. African countries are still among the poorest in the world in spite of European languages and their "official language" status. We can easily see that the linguistic heritage of colonialism reveals the inequity of the economic relations between the colonizer and the colonized. As Coulmas puts it: "while the Europeans exported their language wholesale, they only took a few words from their *trading partners,* colonial goods, as it were (1992: 42)." There was no emphasis placed on public servants in the colonial regime to learn any of the indigenous languages. For example, in South Africa, "recruits for the public service are not required to give any proof of knowledge of an African language, and no preference is given to those candidates for the Native Affairs Department who may have taken the course of Bantu Studies at one of the universities (An African Survey Revised 1957: 90)." And in French colonies, "it does not appear that the local Administrations attach in practice any great importance to a knowledge of the vernacular by their officers (An African Survey Revised 1957: 91)." Indigenous languages had little significance or importance for colonial governments on a large scale.

In *Language Repertoire and State Construction in Africa,* David Laitin contends that *language rationalization* was an attempt at consolidating the modern state. In other words, it was the primary linguistic aim of colonial administrators to establish linguistic hegemony as a means of controlling or consolidating the mother country's international resources. He defines *language rationalization* as "the territorial specification of a common language for purposes of efficient administration and rule (1992: 9). When colonial rule is established and language acquisition occurs, the colonizer can easily encourage members of the dominated speech community to translate documents from their native language to the language of the colonizer. He further maintains that:

> To the extent that political rule is stable, more and more members of the newly incorporated speech community will find it useful to learn the language of the ruling elite. Language rationalization is successful when there is a sufficient number of bilinguals among linguistically distinct communities so that the business of rule can be transacted in a single language. (1992: 10)

Here we can see that the colonial language was more of an institutional link than a community language (Bokamba 1991: 493). However, this "institutional link" has cultural implications as well. State rationalization seeks cultural change. The ruling class attempts to maintain their rule within their arbitrarily constructed boundaries. The masses of people will then encounter a new world created for them by the ruling class. "Newly installed religious authorities may be banned from practice. And new languages may be required for petitions, licenses, or simply for bargaining with the tax collector. In light of state-building processes, people may alter their sense of national identity, their religion, and their language" (1992: 24).

BRITISH COLONIAL POLICY

The British, who were said to be the most "voracious" of all coloniz-ers, occupied Ghana, Nigeria, West Cameroon, Zambia, Zimbabwe, Botswana, South Africa, Uganda, Lesotho, Swaziland, Madagascar, Kenya, Tanzania, Malawi, and Sudan (Adegbija 1994: 17–18). Britain passed its first colonial education ordinance on May 6, 1882 (Bokamba 1991: 497). It was intended to regulate the educational practices in its colonial territories. Bokamba further reveals that this ordinance pro-vided for grants-in-aids to voluntary agency schools where English was used as a medium of instruction (1991: 497). As a result of the so-called "educational reforms" of the Phelps-Stokes Commission on African edu-cation in West Africa in 1920–21 and in East Africa in 1924, Bokamba also maintains: "the introduction of public education by the colonial administration, strengthened considerably the English language policy (Bokamba 1991: 497)." Partly because of the work of this commission, the British Secretary of State for the colonies set up the Advisory Com-mittee on Native Education in 1924 and it was made permanent in 1929 (Fishman 1974: 165). Their first report in 1925 recommended the use of so-called "vernacular languages" or indigenous languages as well as Eng-lish in primary education. The second report submitted two years later underscored the previous one. Spencer writes:

> [Colonialists admit] that one of the major incentives for Africans in sending their children to school was to enable them to acquire knowl-edge of English. Any overall attempt to delay the introduction of Eng-lish, the report claimed, would be interpreted by Africans as 'an attempt of the government to hold back the African from legitimate advance in civilisation.' [This] represented the general policy of British colonial administrations . . . (Fishman 1974: 165)

This would remain the British colonial policy until the independence of their territories. The 1943 Memorandum on Language in African School Education reemphasized the need to use indigenous languages in the early stages of education. Under this policy, however, a small number of indige-nous languages were used and "they were selected based on their usefulness as instruments of control (Akinnaso 1998: 20)." Akinnaso asserts that the use of the indigenous language was only meant to facilitate the acquisition of English increasing the children's' use of it while decreasing the use of the indigenous language until the latter language was completely omitted as a medium of instruction. In 1951 at the Unesco meeting of specialists, the importance of indigenous language instruction was reemphasized. These "experts" concluded that:

> Ideally, the medium of instruction for a child living in its own language environment should be the mother tongue and that children should be educated in the mother tongue for as long as possible. The meeting of the Unesco advisory group of consultants . . . reiterated the basic position of the . . . report and went on to assert that 'teaching at least initial literacy in the mother tongue may be advisable even in situation where the scanty number of speakers appears not to warrant the large-scale production of educational materials (Bamgbose 1976: 11–12).

FRENCH COLONIAL POLICY

The French language policy developed through several official documents and proclamations by colonial administrators. The initial policy was the Metropolitan Ordinance of Villers-Cottteret, in 1539 by King Francois I. This ordinance made French the sole official language of the French empire and prohibited the use of any other language (Bokamba 1993: 178). This ordinance was established in all French colonies. It first appeared in Africa in 1826 at the establishment of a girls' school in Senegal. A French decree outlining proposals for teaching French in Africa was signed in 1903 and in 1944, the Brazzaville Conference modeled Africa's educational system on that of France (Lafage 1991: 222). The French government also deemed it necessary to develop the Ordinance of February 14, 1922. This policy addressed private education and sought to draw a clear distinction between these schools and public schools. The ordinance read:

> General Education must be carried in French . . . The Coranic schools and catechist schools are authorized to provide exclusively a religious education in the vernaculars. Such schools are not considered as institutions of public education (Kotey & Der Houssikman 1977: 35)

The French colonies in Africa included: Benin, Burkina-Faso, the Central African Republic, the Congo, the Ivory Coast, Gabon, Guinea, Mali, Niger, Senegal, Togo and Zaire.

Unlike the British policy that advocated the use of indigenous languages, with some limitations, as a means of acquiring English, the French actively discouraged the use of African languages and mandated that all instructions were to be carried out in French at all levels. Thus, France adopted an assimilationist philosophy in that "education for the colonized people was not an end in itself, but rather a means through which acculturation and servitude were to be achieved (Bokamba 1993: 182)." Perhaps in their own words we can better understand France's colonial "missions." The following is an application for an increased subsidy for a colonial school where the administrators state the aims of their school. The application reads:

> Our general aim is the religious—regeneration of the Negroes of Africa; the means to this will be our holy religion, and next to religious knowledge, work. Literary and scientific work for those who have the capacity to engage in it; manual work supplemented by a certain cultivation of the intelligence for those whose vocation is more humble. Our particular aim is to provide the French possessions with intelligent and loyal servants. (Hargraves 1969: 102–3).

Under the French policy of assimilation, all under her dominion were granted French citizenship (An African Survey 1968: 207). France's policy reflected their colonial philosophy and belief that it was on a civilizing mission in Africa. So convinced of this belief, Bokamba writes:

> They felt that their civilization was superior to that of the Africans, and that the best way to bring them to par was through an active policy of cultural assimilation. Education a la francaise, initially aimed at the sons of chiefs and subsequently extended to a highly selected youth population, was the medium through which the policy was implemented (1993: 183).

This policy of assimilation was viewed as the correct approach to eliminate the cultural differences between the French and their African subjects "so as to develop a common culture—a French way of life (Bokamba 1993: 184)." Spencer holds that civilization, for the French, meant the extension of the French language and culture (Fishaman 1974: 170). As a result, French was used as the medium of instruction throughout colonial education from start to finish. There was, in essence, an official neglect of indigenous languages. Spencer asserts:

> There was less pressure upon French colonial officials, as compared with the British . . . to learn the local languages, and more reliance was placed upon African interpreters. Very little positive action was

taken to encourage vernacular literatures or to standardise and extend 'dominant' languages. Yet it is fair to recognise that while French cultural and linguistic policy in Africa was aggressively imperialist, its imperialism in this respect was based upon the majestic belief that the language, thought and culture of France represented the highest form of civilisation (Fishman 1974: 171).

The French viewed their language as the highest linguistic form. The French academy attempted to establish the language as being "pure" and bestow upon it prestige "so that others would aspire to its use, thereby bringing about political integration and linguistic homogeneity (Eastman 1983: 207)." Furthermore, the teaching of African languages was seen as obstacles in the path of cultural assimilation. Thus, the study of African languages in schools was prohibited. Even in Senegal where Wolof was spoken by 80 percent of its population it was discouraged in the colonial school system (Fishman 1993: 305). Unlike the British and their use of Hausa in Northern Nigeria, the French's assimilationist policy prevented them from taking a similar position in spite of the fact that Wolof was spoken by a far greater percentage of the territory than was Hausa. As a result of their policy, colonial administrators completely ignored indigenous languages. Attempts were made, however, to incorporate indigenous languages into the school system early on, but were promptly discouraged, and French would be the sole medium of instruction (Fishman 1993: 6).

Much like British colonial policy, access to education was highly restricted. A small percentage of the population was selected for admission into colonial elementary and secondary schools and an even smaller percentage managed to complete that education (Bokamba 1993: 191). Proficiency in French was just as important, if not more, as in the British colonies. While admission to school was available to all eligible children, the elevation from one level to the next was solely dependent on the students' performance in French as well as other subjects all taught in French (Bokamba 1993: 192). Bokamba points out that as a result of this French only policy, the failure rate in schools in former French colonies is far greater than other African nations after independence. He maintains that: "A consequence of this system of education is the disproportionately high wastage rates found in [former French colonies] (Bokamba 1993: 192)." In fact, students who fail the secondary school admission examination are still primary school graduates. These students are prevented from advancing because they fail to pass French or mathematics (Bokamba 198: 198).

LANGUAGE AFTER INDEPENDENCE

Perhaps amidst the discussion of language and colonialism, the issue of the multiplicity of languages in Africa has been missed and warrants a brief discussion. Rather than guesstimate a total number of languages spoken in Africa, let us survey several countries. This way, we can better understand the multiplicity of languages spoken in various countries. Kenya, for example, has 35 languages; the Sudan has 133; Tanzania, 113; Zaire, 206; Ethiopia, 92; and Nigeria, 400 (Bamgbose 1991: 2)! Imagine the concerns of administrators charged with dealing with language diversity in the newly independent African nations.

In most of postcolonial African countries, no single indigenous language is dominant in terms of the number of speakers. This has often been an excuse for continuing the worship of European languages in "official" functions. As a result of the colonial language being supreme in these independent countries, there has been a gross neglect of indigenous languages. According to Adegbija, this position has hindered the "development" of indigenous languages. He holds that the "minds of the elites seem to have been colonised and many of them now seem to regard everything European, including the languages and cultures, as inherently superior to African languages and cultures (Adegbija 1994 : 22)." Until recently, most indigenous languages were considered unworthy of official use and were believed to be inadequate for articulating ideas in official functions. This is evident in French colonial policy and its "civilizing mission." In Senegal, for example, even though 80% of the population speaks Wolof, the language serves no official purpose. Remember that the French maintained that African languages stood in the way of cultural assimilation. Consequently, "indigenous African languages and cultures were deliberately trampled on as if they did not exist (Adegbija 1994: 20)." It is not surprising that the attitudes towards African languages were negative considering the official neglect of them by postcolonial and colonial governments. In former British colonies, English remains at the top of the language hierarchy with carefully selected indigenous languages coming after it. In former French colonies, French remains the only language worthy of any serious attention.

Beginning with Ghana in 1957, each new African nation "was forced to consider all the problems impeding their survival;" namely "the areas of concern were national policies regarding official and national language status, and the teaching of these languages (Richmond 1983: 1)." Richmond writes:

> One of the highest priorities of the new governments was to render policy regarding the status of the colonial language as well as the recognition of indigenous languages as an important and natural means of

communication. The formation of these language policies determined which would become official and national languages (1983: 1–2)

Language and education in independent Africa go hand in hand. These governments were also responsible for educating those within their European drawn borders. One cannot survive with out the other. Therefore, without a language policy or plan, there could be no education.

The language policies in Africa after independence reflect an "unsevered colonial umbilical cord (Adegbija 1994: 22)." In fact, many former British colonies in West Africa in the 1960s and 70s mandated the use of English as the sole medium of instruction at all levels (Bokamba 1991: 496). During the colonial era, education in Africa took the form of the colonial government. However, the educational philosophies have continued through the transitional period in to African school systems today (Richmond 1983: 3). So pervasive was this language problem, Bokamba asserts:

> At the beginning of the 1960s, the newly liberated countries inherited this policy and its consequences in education, both formal and informal. Almost a quarter of a century after the advent of political independence in the region, the policy has remained largely unchanged, and its negative effects are increasingly being felt in education, language development, and the psychosocial behavior of the children. While a few educators and linguists in the region are advocating a change in the language policy, those in power want to and have succeeded in maintaining the status quo for various reasons (1993: 208).

Furthermore, as Lafage asserts: "[French] . . . appears to have survived the crisis of independence and there does not appear to be any challenge in the foreseeable future to the role of French in the functions for which it is used—administration, international relations, teaching, the media, trade, transport, science and technology, literature and so on . . ." (Lafage 1993: 216). These policies perpetuate the dominance of European languages. In most former colonies, they are still using the former colonial language either with one or more indigenous languages either as "official" or "national" language (Fishman, et al 1968: 121). According to Laitin, European languages will not lose official status in most African states because "bureaucratic elites have invested heavily in European languages and do not want to lose the benefits of that investment (Laitin 1992: 104)." Adegbija further articulates the claims of colonial language dominance while he analyzes Phillipson. He writes:

> Phillipson, . . . speaking specifically with regard to the dominance
> of French and English in Africa, aptly summarises the dominance of
> European languages in Africa thus . . . 'The continued dominance
> of French and English in independent African countries indicates that
> these countries have inherited the same type of legacy. This is a legacy
> . . . in which the colonised people have internalised the language and
> many of the attitudes of their masters . . . (Adegbija 1994: 17–18).'

In spite of the fact that all African states are multilingual, the use of
European languages is still dominant. Noted historian, anthropologist
and linguist, Cheikh Anta Diop, accurately asserts that: "The influence
of language is so great that the various European mother countries feel
they can afford to withdraw politically from Africa without great loss as
long as their (linguistic) presence remains in the economic, spiritual and
cultural spheres (1978: 13)." In other words, Europeans need not be present in post colonial Africa because the institutions they created have been
perfectly maintained by Western trained Africans to continue European
domination. Mansour rightly concludes that the legacy of the colonial language policy is so extensive that it affected and in some cases paralyzed
any subsequent policy decisions (1993: 77). She further states "Any examination of language policy therefore has to begin with the policy of the
colonial administration. One of the functions of colonial education was
to create the lower ranks of colonial administrators among the indigenous
population. In some cases, no written policy exists. However, as Bamgbose
informs us, an "absence of a statement (on language policy) does not, however, mean absence of a policy. What tends to happen is that such absence
indicates the continuation of an inherited policy, such as the policy on an
official language. (1991: 112)." In the case of Sierra Leone, for example,
she reveals: "No officially documented statement or national language policy appears to exist, but convention and practice have formed themselves
into an operative yet elusive language policy (1991: 112)." There are two
kinds of language policies—explicit and implicit. An implicit policy can
be inferred from the practices of the people, governmet or other agencies
(Kumi-Andoh 1997: 15). Bamgbose writes:

> Since language policies often have political repercussions, it is not sur-
> prising that they are often vaguely indicated. This situation could be a
> blessing in disguise in the sense that it means that no rigid rules are laid
> down in matters of detail. For example, in a country or state where the
> use of the mother tongue is allowed in literacy and/or primary educa-
> tion, it is advantageous that such a policy does not go on to indicate

which languages are to be used and which are not. On the other hand, where there is vagueness or indecision concerning fundamental aspects of policy (for instance, whether the mother tongue is to be used and if so, at what level), serious problems could arise leading to lack of uniformity, frustration on the part of the teachers and lack of direction. Perhaps the best way of pin pointing the language policy of a state or country is to observe what actually goes on in the system (1976: 17).

THE LANGUAGE LEGACY AND THE GOVERNING ELITE

"It was obviously in the best interest of all the colonial powers to produce a small body of Africans . . . educated . . . to serve as minor functionaries and interpreters . . ." (Fishman 1974: 164). This group eventually replaced the colonial administrators and obtained positions that were afforded them because of their knowledge of European languages and a European style education. These Western-educated elite, who under colonial rule were, for the most part, excluded from government, was actually being groomed for the positions they would soon assume. Language would, therefore, become one of the key criteria for certain positions one would assume following independence. Access to education meant access to European languages. In Kenya, for example, if one does not speak English, that usually implies that his or her primary education did not pass the primary level (Kennedy 1983: 124). Furthermore, access to a European language almost guaranteed a place in the colonial and postcolonial administration or other "well paying" jobs." Mansour asserts that "the ultimate goal of education appears to be the same in most of the countries included in this study: mastery of the European official language is considered to be the only way to personal economic and social advance and, ostensibly, the only hope for development and modernization for the country as a whole (Mansour 1993: 78)." This can be said for all of the former colonies. Komarek agrees and writes:

> The influence of power politics on African linguistic policy is most clearly evident in the retention by the power elite of the colonial languages, of which only they are masters, as official languages. In so doing, the elite ensures its exclusive access to information, prevents self-determination and thus sharing of power by others. Decipherable information, on the other hand, would mean giving others the chance to make a claim to power for themselves. Incumbent African governments have absolutely no willingness—beyond the strict minimum demanded by domestic politics—to support national languages as the official, media or instructional languages (Komarek 1997: 30).

Further, the ruling elite views "the promotion of any African language to serve as a subject of instruction or a national language for the purpose of radio and television services . . . as a divisive undertaking (Bokamba 1993: 202)."

The obvious remaining ties to the former colonial government speak volumes about Africa's language inheritance. The economies of former colonies have been integrated into and made dependent upon the former colonizer's economy (Bokamba 1993: 184). Of former French colonies, and it certainly applies to colonies of other European powers, Bokamba writes:

> French colonies provided cheap labor and the raw material that made the French economy prosper. The economic infrastructure developed in the colonies was oriented towards the export of raw materials to France and other Western European countries . . . economic "assimilation" worked so well during the colonial period that the leaders of pre-independence . . . Africa saw no need to change it. In fact, they approved . . . the formation of a French economic community and a common monetary zone under the French franc (1993:190).

Since former colonies were dependent upon their former masters, individuals who spoke "the master's" language, constituted the elite class who had access to the job market and held limited power. Moreover, when people are required to learn a new language to have access to education and higher paying jobs, language is a factor in creating and sustaining social and economic division (Tollefson 1991: 8–9). Civil servants and educational officials have vested interests in European languages because their jobs, in large part, are dependent upon their proficiency in the colonial language. Tollefson further explores the notion of language and class structure when he writes:

> Hierarchical social systems are associated with exploitative language policies . . . policies which give advantage to groups speaking particular languages varieties. Exploitative polices are evident in educational systems that impose disadvantages on minority students, and in restrictions on bilingualism among both subordinate and dominant populations (1991: 17).

Laitin contends that "elite closure" or when the language of the elite class is preferred over the languages of the lower strata is a common practice in Africa. It fosters the class divide created by colonialism's linguistic barriers. In *Languages and Language in Black Africa*, Pierre Alexandre reveals that " . . . the kind of class structure which seems to be emerging [in Africa] is based on linguistic factors . . . (1972: 86)." Laitin maintains that the elite class relies on a language for intra-elite communication, usually French or English, but relies on a different form of communication with the masses. (1992: 57)." In Kenya, for example:

> There is no question that in the capital city of Kenya the language of prestige is English. English is used, not only for the more complex technical type of discussion, but also 'as a means of everyday communication' between . . . the middle and upper-middle classes. The higher in the scale of employment or activity, the more they speak English . . . In some elite families, where the parents do not have the same source language, effective communication is only in English. . . . It will be a sad day when a section of [the] African population cannot express themselves except in a European language . . . (Kennedy 1983:123–24).

Although the elite class *can* effectively communicate with the masses (for now), the power still resides among the elite because the business of government, education and all other official functions are negotiated in a European language, prohibiting the participation of the masses. Coulmas accurately identifies that the "co-opted elites" were easily convinced of European superiority and without hesitation, and in their own best interest, adopted the colonial language thereby allowing the former colonial power to maintain easy access to the African market (1992: 43). It is hard to imagine how independent African nations can truly achieve independence while so passionately holding on to their colonial language. Part of the problem lies in the assumption that many Africans "consider themselves the proud recipients of the Cambridge certificates of education and are in many cases direct beneficiaries of British education, do not perceive their English to be different from that of their mentors (Bokamba 1991: 498)." Bokamba and Tlou further maintain that there is a danger in duplicating the former colonizers' style of education. Perhaps they can explain better than I, they assert:

> [We] argue that as long as formal education a la European remains the main avenue through which personal upward mobility and national development can be achieved, the continuation of the use of foreign languages such as English, French, and Portuguese as the media of instruction will restrict access to post-considerable waste of potential human resources. The consequences of such language policies vis-à-vis education will be to considerably slow down, if not make impossible, the achievement of self-reliance that many African states have been striving

for, and thereby perpetuate African dependency on foreign 'experts' for
the survival of Black Africa (1977: 35)

In most African countries, the knowledge of a European language is
viewed as a symbol of power, prestige and status. Not only do the governing elite place value on these foreign languages, but non-speakers also
view it as an emblem of "making it," "being up there," and "being able
to achieve (Adegbija 1994: 20)." Therefore, it is not only government and
educational officials who have negative attitudes towards their native languages. Bokamba reveals:

> The teaching of African languages in elementary and secondary schools
> is viewed by both students and parents as a waste of time, because the
> languages do not have a market value; that is, they do not enhance the
> chances of the learner to secure employment (1993: 202)

This view is undoubtedly a result of years of colonial domination. For a
people to aspire to the use of an alien language and abandon the language
of their ancestors speaks volumes of the impact of colonialism on African
culture.

There does not appear to be any change in the near future of promoting indigenous languages to the status of official or national. Mansour
(1993: 78) maintains, "in some particularly heterogeneous countries the
official language has been proclaimed as the language of "national unity."
Consequently a number of changes were made in the educational policy of
Nigeria and Ghana which, in the name of national unity, in fact reduce the
extent to which African languages were used." Moreover, he asserts, the
policy of promoting a single indigenous language to official status has been
"vociferously attacked." He further explains why:

> European authors . . . have an interest in defending the cultural domi-
> nation of Europe over Africa, but more often [the idea is attacked] by
> Africans themselves. Such a policy has been labeled 'imperialist' and
> described as an attempt by certain African ethnolinguistic groups to
> impose their language on others in order to usurp power over the state
> and exclude or sideline other groups. The irony here lies in the use of
> the word "imperialist" referring to what amounts to official recogni-
> tion of a sociolinguistic fact: namely the widespread use of a lingua
> franca (spoken by more than 80% of the population) while the mainte-
> nance of the foreign language spoken by at most 15% is seen as a more
> sensible solution (26).

Bokamba and Tlou (1977:38–41) suggest three motivating factors for the retention of colonial languages: efficiency and expediency; national unity or political considerations; and national progress. The efficiency and expediency argument holds that development is only possible through the ability to communicate with industrialized or modern societies. The second, national unity, argues in favor of the colonial language retention because the selection of an indigenous language can be a "highly divisive undertaking." To elaborate, it is argued that in a multilingual society, as in most of Africa, the choice of one language can be viewed as a rejection of other languages destroying the "the delicate national unity that African nations have tried to forge." The third factor, national progress, holds that only through education can development take place. In this regard, if the medium of instruction is in an African language, then this will "impede the progress of the African people and retard their integration into the modern world." In response to these arguments, Bokamba and Tlou write:

> [The] conclusion that English or other European languages must therefore serve as the medium of instruction is unwarranted . . . While it is undeniable that strong language loyalties exist in Africa as they do elsewhere, the fears associated with the adoption of a single national language can be alleviated by adopting a comprehensive language policy which recognizes the functions that each language objectively deserves . . . [And] the claim that the use of selected African languages as media and/or subjects of instruction constitutes a barrier to progress, regardless of how this term is defined, is, in our opinion, pedagogically unfounded and unsupported by the case histories of language planning in countries such as China, Norway, etc . . . A sound language policy would call for the assignment of specific functions to each [African] language according to the realities of the society concerned. This is the type of language policy that we would like to argue for in this study (1977: 40–2).

Mansour dismisses the notion that a single African language serving as the official language is problematic. He believes, much like Bokamba and Tlou, that a plural language policy can exist while one indigenous language serves as the official language. Further, " . . . there is no contradiction between the promotion of a single African language to official status and an otherwise pluralist language policy. When Tanzania adopted Swahili as its official language it was not at the expense of the local languages but at the expense of English (Mansour 1993: 126)."

THE MYTH OF "ANGLOPHONE" AND "FRANCOPHONE" AFRICA

Like other myths that swirl around Africa, the notion of a "French-speaking," and an "English-speaking" Africa is among the most popular. African countries are multilingual indeed. But European languages are by no means dominant in the homes of most Africans. The language of the elite or the language of government is not the language of the people. In West Africa, for example, among the so-called "English-speaking" nations, the number of English speakers falls between 10–20% (Bokamba 1991: 497). Bokamba accurately asserts that English is learned almost exclusively through formal education. It is reasonable to assume, he contends, that the actual number of speakers in these countries does not exceed that of elementary and post-secondary school enrollees and graduates. For instance, Ghana uses English as her official language, an inheritance from Britain, yet most Ghanains do not speak English as their first language (Andoh-Kumi 1997: 41). Adegbija further clarifies the language situation when he reveals:

> [Terms] such as "English-speaking Africa;" "French-speaking Africa" and Portuguese-speaking Africa" are commonly heard and used even by well-informed scholars . . . such terms are very deceptive because less than 30% of Africans speak such ex-colonial languages (in fact, in many parts of East Africa, English is spoken by probably less than 10% of the population). In spite of this, however, and to high-light the dominance of European languages, one could point out that in virtually all Sub-Saharan African countries, indigenous languages are not used as the medium of higher education, except, sometimes, in the teaching of the languages themselves (1994: 17–18).

The same is true for so-called "Francophone Africa." It is estimated that only 18% of the people in former French colonies actually speak French (Sanders 1993: 217).

CONCLUSION

Under colonial administrations, and in large part today in post-colonial Africa, few Africans have access to education. If access, for whatever reason, is not gained to these institutions, then French, English or any other colonial language is not acquired. And as we have been discussing, the colonial language affords the colonized and the newly independent access to government positions and other "well-paying" jobs.

Given its linguistic situation, why do we continue to identify countries in Africa with terms that do not reflect the reality of the people of Africa? Part of the answer lays in the fact that European domination, colonial and post-colonial, dictates that we view all reality from the vantage point of the colonizer. The reality of the colonized is irrelevant in this scheme.

The legacy of colonialism in Africa has had a profound impact on the languages and cultures of the continent. So much so, that the way many view their language and culture is beneath the languages and cultures of their former colonial masters. The colonial language policies of Britain and France (and certainly others) are still being reflected in today's language policies in the post-colonial era. Although the British introduced the use of indigenous languages as a means of cultural, political and linguistic domination and the French used French at all levels attempting to create "African French-men," both were intended to suppress African people and exploit the continent's resources.

REFERENCES

An African Survey Revised 1956: A Study of Problems Arising in Africa South of the Sahara. Oxford University Press. 1957.

Adegbija, Efurosibina. *Language Attitudes in Sub-Saharan Africa: A Sociolinguistic Overview.* Mulitlingual Matters, Ltd. 1994.

Akinnaso, F. Niyi. *Language Policy and Symbolic Domination in Nigeria.* Unpublished. 1998.

Alexandre, Pierre. *Languages and Language in Black Africa.* Northwestern University Press. 1972.

Andoh-Kumi, Kingsley. *Language Education Policies in Ghana.* Crigle Press. 1997.

Asante, Molefi K. Ed. *International Journal of Black Studies.* Vol. 25, No. 1.

Bamgbose, Ayo. Ed. *Mother Tongue Education: The West African Experience.* Awoniyi, Timothy. "Mother Tongue Education in West Africa: A Historical Background." Hodder and Stoughton LTD. 1976.

Bamgbose, Ayo. Ed. *Mother Tongue Education: The West African Experience.* Bamgbose, Ayo. "Introduction: The Changing Role of Mother Tongue Education." Hodder and Stoughton LTD. 1976.

Bokamba, Eyamba. *English Around the World.* 1991

Coulmas, Florian. *Language and Economy.* Black Well Press. 1992.

Diop, Cheikh Anta. *Black Africa: The Economic and Cultural Basis for a Federated State.* Africa World Press & Lawrence Hill Books. 1987.

Eastman, Carol. *Language planning.* Chandler & Sharp Publishers, Inc. 1983.

Fishman, Joshua A. Ed. *The Earliest Stages of Language Planning.* Ka, Omar. "Seneglese Languages in Education: The First Congress of Wolof." Mouton De Gruyter. 1993.

Fishman, Joshua A. Ed. *Advances in Language Planning.* Spencer, John W. "Colonial Language Policies and their Legacies in Africa." Mouton & Co. N.V., Publishers. 1974.

Fishman, Joshua A., Ferguson, Charles A., & Das Gupta, Jyotirindra. Eds. *Language Problems of Developing Nations.* Zima, Petr"Hausa in West Africa: Remarks on Contemporary Role and Functions." John Wiley and Sons, Inc. 1968.

Hargraves, John D. Ed. *France and West Africa: An Anthology of Historical Documents.* MacMillan St. Martins Press. 1969.

Kennedy, Chris. Ed. *Language Planning and Language Education.* Harries, L. "The Nationalization of Swahili in Kenya." George Allen & Unwin Publishers, Ltd. 1983.

Komarek, Kurt. *Mother Tongue Education in Sub-Saharan Countries: Conceptual and Strategic Considerations.* Deutsche Gesellschaf fur. 1997.

Kotey, Paul F.A. & Der-Houssikman, Haig. *Language and Linguistic Problems in Africa: Perceptions of the VII Conference on African Linguistics.* Bokamba, Eyamba & Tlou, Josiah S. "The Consequences of the language Policies of African States Vis-à-vis Education." Pgs. 35–53. Hornbean Press, Inc. 1977.

Laitin, David D. *Language Repertoires and State Reconstruction in Africa.* Cambridge University Press. 1992.

Mansour, Gerba. *Multilingualism and Nation Building.* Clevedon Press. 1993.

Mazama, Ama "An Afrocentric Approach to Language Planning." Journal of Black Studies. 1994.

McEwan, P.J.M. *Twentieth Century Africa.* Oxford University Press. 1968.

Wa Thiongo, Ngugi. *Decolonizing the Mind: the Language of African Literature.* Hieneman Press. 1986.

Owomoyela, Oyekan. *A History of Twentieth-Century African Literatures. Owomoyela, Oyekan.* "The Question of Language in African Literature." University of Nebraska Press. 1993.

Richmond, Edmun B. *New Directions in Language Teaching in Sub-Saharan Africa: A Seven-Country Study of Current Policies and Programs for Teaching Official and National Languages and Adult Functional Literacy.* University Press of America, Inc. 1983.

Sachs, Wolfgang. Ed. *The Development Dictionary.* Escobar, Arturo. "Planning." Zed Books, Ltd. 1992.

Sanders, C. Ed. *French Today: Language in a Social Context.* Bokamba, Eyamba G. "French Colonial Language Policies in Africa and Their Legacies." Cambridge University Press. 1993.

Sanders, C. Ed. *French Today: Language in a Social Context.* Lafage, Suzanne. "French in Africa. Pgs. 215–36. Cambridge University Press. 1993.

Some, Malidoma. *Of Water and Spirit: Ritual, Magic and Initiation in the life of an African Shamon.* Tarcher/Putnam. 1994.

Tollefson, James W. *Planning Language, Planning Inequality: Language Policy in the Community.* Longman Press. 1991.

Chapter Seven

Thinking and Responding to Difference: Pedagogical Challenges for African Education

George Sefa Dei[1], University of Toronto

INTRODUCTION

I enter this discussion on social difference and schooling as a racial minority, Ghanaian-born scholar who is privileged to teach in an institution of higher learning in North America. My sojourn in this educational setting has often presented me with opportunities to critically reflect on the challenges of schooling and teaching students from diverse backgrounds. Like many others, I long for a school system that effectively responds to the needs and concerns of a diverse student population. This paper pinpoints some of the challenges and possibilities in this endeavor.

As educators, we have a responsibility to utilize our place and location in school, college and university spaces to launch (along with students and other allies) a critique of conventional schooling. It is equally important to engage in struggles of resistance to contest and subvert the work of the academy. Among the many vital pedagogic challenges of resisting conventional schooling, I continually navigate around difference while understanding the institutional and systemic conditions that structure both the process of schooling and the lives of diverse bodies within schools as a collective. There are perils and desires in working with difference within communities. In working with critical and alternative ideas for example, how do we as scholars from minority groups think through our concepts and avoid an easy, seductive slippage into the form, logic and implicit assumptions of that which we are contesting.

In this paper, I discuss the pedagogical challenges of confronting difference in African schooling. The empirical work done in Ghana examined how ethnic, cultural, religious, and linguistic minorities, as well as women and students from low socio-economic/class background engage in the school system. The study sought to answer the following key questions: How do schools consider diversity and difference in their local student population? How do schools respond to the relational aspects of difference (class, gender, ethnicity, religion, language and culture) in educational practices? How do schools take into account students' home, off-school culture, and [local] cultural resource knowledge in their educational practices? And finally, how do schools seek out and integrate Africa-centered resources in classroom instructional, curricular, pedagogical and communicative practices? (Dei, 1994; Dei, 1996; see also Banks, 1993; Ghosh, 1996; Asante, 1991, Hilliard, 1992).

As argued elsewhere (see Dei 1999, 2000, 2003a), many Ghanaian educators espouse the view that students go to school as disembodied youth. The racial, ethnic, cultural, linguistic, religious, sexual and gender identities of our students are consequential for how these bodies engage schooling. Moreover, prevailing discourses on nationhood and citizenship work to deny rather than affirm the strengths of difference and diversity (Banks, 1997). This situation is not unique to Africa. In fact, current educational innovations in European-American schools, including Canada, seek to enhance the teaching, learning and administration of education for a diverse body of students. In articulating concerns about minority youth's schooling and education in European-American contexts, some critical educational researchers and practitioners view schools as "contested public spheres" (Fine, 1993: 682), and as political sites for the reproduction of power and social inequality (see also Apple and Weis, 1983; Giroux, 1983; Apple, 1986; McCarthy, 1990; Willis, 1977, 1983). These authors also see structural poverty, racism, sexism and social and cultural differences as consequential to schooling outcomes, particularly of minority youth. This is a significant departure from conventional views that focused on family-school relations, conceptualizing homes and families as sites and sources of student educational problems and pathologies. It also marks a shift away from the conventional false separation between homes and schools in accounting for educational successes and failures.

This paper utilizes on-going debates of "inclusive schooling" in European-American contexts as a base from which to interrogate African education. In North America, the debate on school inclusivity may be conceptualized in two broad categories (see Banks and Banks, 1993; Goldstein, 1994; and Bracy, 1995): "diversity as a variety perspective" and "diversity as a critical perspective." The first approach to inclusion is exemplified as viewing diversity in terms of teaching and sharing knowledge about the contributions of diverse cultures to enrich pluralistic communities. The second approach views schooling as a racially, culturally and politically mediated experience. The focus is on dealing directly with marginalization and exclusion in school contexts by centering all human experiences in the student's learning process, as well as placing a calculated focus on the twin notions of power and domination in order to understand and interpret social relations and structures (see Goldstein, 1994; Bracy, 1995: 3, Anderson and Collins, 1995).

While the issues of North American schooling may be conceptualized differently from the African context, some broad parallels can be identified. For example, North American education is struggling to deal with state cuts in funding and a reneging of fiscal responsibilities to schools. Schools have to contend with ways to promote inclusive learning environments that have broad representation of staff, curriculum and instruction in a climate of lack of resources and an absence of political support. There is a contestation of how we (as educators) ensure that education is made relevant to wider society. In this contest the imperatives of market forces are "winning." The dominant, conventional discourse of "return to basics," "standards matter the most," "quality education" alongside with the disturbing shift towards the "marketization of education" has only helped to sideline equity considerations. Market considerations determine how we come to understand social justice and equity education in schools. Equity cuts have also become a central feature of schooling reform around the globe (see Dei and Karumanchery, 1999; Hatcher, 1998). In places where equity has not been examined critically for its implications for schooling, the promise of educational reform to produce change has been short-lived (Hatcher, 1998; Craig, 1990; Samoff, 1996; Federici, Caffenttzis & Alidou, 2000).

Africa is affected in profound ways by the "marketization of education." The cost of schooling has become unbearable for large segments of local populations. Class divisions have intensified in these societies where education is seen as a major tool for social mobility. Africa has not benefited from the encroachment of corporate capital in supplying computers and other information technologies into schools. Faced with scarce resources, government policies on educational funding have exacerbated social inequities. As the state sheds its responsibilities from publicly funded schooling and actively seeks the unfettered involvement of the private sector in education, existing social inequities have become clear (Biddle,

2001). Furthermore, by allowing education to serve the needs of increasingly global corporate capital, different priorities have been established for financial budgeting. Within such a climate, addressing the immediate concerns of social equity and justice has not always registered with governments and educational policy makers.

Education in Africa today is often said to be in a "crisis" (Ragwanja, 1997). The current "crisis" is in part a colonial legacy of misguided educational policies and practices (curriculum, texts, pedagogies) that fail to 'speak' adequately to the variety of human experiences, diverse history of events and ideas that have shaped and continue to shape human growth and African development. But the problem of African education is more than colonialism. Current educational policies and practices of most sub-Saharan governments are not appropriately contextualized in the local human condition and African realities (see Banya, 1991; 1993, Banya and Elu, 1997; Bloch, Bekou-Betts, and Tabachnick, 1999). Fortunately, in some communities, local scholars have been pioneering new analytical systems based on indigenous concepts and their interrelationships for promoting education (see Lawuyi, 1991; Dei, 1994). There are signs of cultural renewal and a revitalization of an African cultural resource base to address current social problems (Brock-Utne, 1996; Tedla, 1994). To promote genuine educational alternatives in Africa, it is argued that we must begin to "know from within" and highlight local responses to the issues of internal differentiation and the social politics of schooling and difference (Dei, Asgharzadeh, Eblaighie-Bahador, and Shahjahan, 2004). The question is: what can be learned from these convergences and divergences between North American and African educational systems?

HISTORY AND CONTEXT

As noted elsewhere (Dei, 1999), the educational reforms implemented in Ghana in the 1980s and 1990s come under the general rubric of economic adjustment reforms pushed on a number of Southern countries by Northern capital interests. Initially introduced under "structural and sectoral adjustment programs," these reforms became the cornerstone of the international financial community's approach to "improved" educational systems in Ghana (like much of Africa), meaning improved systems directed toward human capacity building and social development (Altbach, 1989; Kwapong and Lesser, 1989; Moock and Harbison, 1988; World Bank, 1988, 1989).

General educational reforms are normally instituted to respond to perceived problems in the school system. Admittedly, chronic problems have afflicted Ghanaian education. These problems include stagnating school enrolments, lack of textbooks and instructional materials, inadequacy of teacher training, diminishing educational finances, and inefficiency in educational administration and management practices. More and more Ghanaian children do not have access to basic education. In some regions school enrolment rates in Ghana are low. Nsiah-Peprah (1998) reported that in 1990 only 66.8% (2.33 million) of children in the school going population (ages 6 to 15) of 3.49 million were enrolled in schools. The situation is worse in certain parts of the country. For example, in the Upper East region "registrations were 28.47% while in Central region it was 84.17%" (p. 8). Moreover, those fortunate enough to graduate from school barely gain employment. The few available jobs are often incongruent or incompatible with the skills of recent graduates and the demand of the job market. While many of these problems have been long-standing, others can be attributed to the dismal failure of the post-colonial, patriarchal state in altering the existing system to reflect changing times, circumstances and social realities.

Over the years, these issues have driven policy makers and educators to clamor for genuine educational reforms. These changes are usually directed at schooling structures rather than the content of curricula and school texts. For example, the educational reforms of the 1980 and early 1990s called for the introduction of a 6–3–3–4 educational structure; that is, a structure comprising of six years of primary education and three years of junior secondary education (JSS). This nine-year basic education was followed by three years of senior secondary or technical/vocational education (SSS). Graduates of the SSS can then apply for admission to the tertiary cycle, either in university, polytechnic or teacher-training programs. As Nyalemegbe (1997) points out, "[w] ithin an expanded concept of second cycle education, technical institutes and vocational schools are now considered as second cycle institutions. This second cycle of education leads to tertiary education which constitutes four years of university education or studies in diploma awarding institutions" (p. 7).

The overall economic and political objective of the reforms was to increase cost-effectiveness and cost recovery through the strategic use of allocations and the involvement of parents, communities and private business groups in funding education (e.g. provision of school infrastructure such as buildings, furniture, tools and equipment for workshops). User fees for school services, equipment and laboratories (e.g. health service fees, sports and recreational fees, textbook and stationery fees), parent-teacher association fees, and room and board charges for institutions of higher learning have been introduced. The state has reduced recurrent expenditures on staff, staff training, and textbooks (Apusigah, 2002; Konadu-Agyemang, 2001).

Later reforms encouraged the idea of 'community-based' schools. They have large day student populations and have made second-cycle education accessible to more students than in the past when a significant proportion of the secondary schools were boarding institutions. To some educational practitioners, the idea of community-based schooling is also an attempt to deal with the problem of regional, sectoral and socio-economic disparities (north-south, rural-urban and poor-rich) in education. Other significant changes under the 'improved reform' package are the inclusion of religious/moral education emphasizing religious and cultural values at both the basic and senior secondary levels and the teaching of additional Ghanaian languages, life skills and culture.

With all these changes, educational reforms have neglected questions of difference as a way to work powerfully with the implications of social difference for schooling. Beyond the material inequities that characterise schooling (regionally, locally and nationally) there are questions about the way gender, religion, socio-economic class, language and ethnicity play out as sites of difference and power in schooling.

METHODOLOGY

Data for this paper were gathered through a qualitative study of how educators understand and deal with questions of difference, diversity, equity and power sharing in schools. In-depth interviews provided study participants (educators, school administrators and students) with the opportunity to center their lived experiences in the local educational process. The study is part of a longitudinal study in Ghana that has extended from 2000 into 2003. This study concentrates on the work undertaken in 2000. During a summer of fieldwork in Ghana, I conducted thirty-two (32) individual interviews with Ghanaian educationists at the Ministry of Education and Ghana Education Service, teachers at two senior secondary schools (SSS), as well as prominent Ghanaian educators. I analyzed policy documents at the Ministry of Education and the Ghana Education Service in Accra and conducted ethnographic observations of classroom teachers holding summer classes at selected schools.

Throughout the longitudinal study, the data gathering approach was framed to maximize the voice to local subjects. This qualitative approach captured the in depth understandings of students' schooling experiences. For the 2000 study, the study sample was randomly selected. Senior administrators referred teachers at the colleges/secondary school level based on the criteria of teachers we developed for the study (e.g., diverse ethnic, religious, linguistic, cultural, gender and socio-economic backgrounds). Ministry of

Education and the Ghanaian Education Service officials were accessed through personal contacts. The interviews (both individuals and focus group) were carried out at schools by Canadian and Ghanaian research assistants. Open-ended questions were asked in a semi-structured interview style. Participants were asked to speak from their experience, were given time to reflect on their responses and to present other issues of interest or concern.

In the individual interviews, participants were asked about their understandings of difference and diversity, the notion of inclusion in schools, who and what constituted a minority/majority status in the school system, what they like about school systems and what they disliked and why, how they saw schools responding to ethnicity, language, religion, culture, social class and gender backgrounds. They were also asked to comment on the significance of subject identity for schooling and knowledge production and how questions of marginality and dominance, subordination and power played in daily interactions in schools and who these could be accounted for. The group discussions allowed for researchers to tease out contentions in subject voices as participants responded to issues that emerged from the individual interviews.

The focus of the data analysis was to identify specific educational initiatives (instruction, pedagogy curriculum and policy) targeting inequity; to explore educators' use of diverse histories, experiences and viewpoints in teaching and learning practices and the means by which schools account for students' concerns and interests around ethnicity, culture, language and difference; and to investigate school support activities aimed at the inclusion of all students. Moreover the data was qualitatively analyzed for general trends in innovative inclusive practices. Through triangulation, I have been able to compare individual narratives between and among teachers, administrators and officials working at the primary, college and university levels and locate general patterns.

The study used participants' words to highlight the tensions, struggles, contradictions and ambiguities in subject (ive) accounts of dealing with difference in diversity. As noted elsewhere (Dei, 2004), the importance of "voice" allows readers to bring their own interpretations to the data. Participant voice moves the analysis beyond an abstract, theoretical discussion of inclusive schooling to reveal a nuanced interpretation of the meaning of inclusive education. For the critical researcher, voice provides insight into the historical and present contexts that contribute to participants' standpoint knowledge. For this study, we highlight voices that reflect a diverse, sophisticated understanding of the complexities and relations of difference.

Moreover, as the researcher, I am implicated in this study by minority status in Canada and as a scholar studying difference and inclusion in schooling in Ghana. My knowledge of the minoritized experience within schooling systems has shaped my critical interrogation of Ghanaian schooling. My experience provides greater insight into the subject voice, given my own experience with marginality and exclusions in the dominant relations of schooling. This situates me in the study rather than outside of it as the usual privileged, objective, 'detached' researcher. While my voice has been integrated to the interpretation of subjects' accounts I do not profess this research as a "mirror to the real."

THE THEORETICAL/DISCURSIVE LENS

The "discursive framework" approach used here to make sense of particular schooling practices is an approach to knowledge production that allows educational researchers to present events, occurrences and actions as dictated by the subject. I use the term "discursive framework" to refer to a theoretical lens "through which things are sorted out, related and omitted from thought, [rather than] a set of propositions to test" knowledge or human action/behavior (Popkewitz, 1998: 15). This epistemological distinction supports interpreting the empirical world in which actual human practice and events involve the interplay of thought and social action.

Theoretically, I adopt a critical anti-colonial discursive framework[2] to understand the issues of culture, social difference, identity, and representation in schooling and the implications for genuine educational options in an African context. "Colonial" is conceptualized not simply as "foreign" or "alien," but rather as "imposed and dominating." The anti-colonial framework is a theorization of issues emerging from colonial relations. It deals with the implications of imperial/colonial structures for knowledge production and [in] validation, the understanding of local indigenousness and the recourse to agency and resistance. In other words, the anti-colonial perspective is an interrogation of the configurations of power embedded in ideas, cultures and histories of knowledge production and use (Fanon, 1963; Memmi, 1969; & Foucault, 1980). The anti-colonial approach recognizes the importance of locally produced knowledge emanating from cultural history and daily human experiences and social interactions. The creation of knowledge begins with where people are situated. This means understanding knowledge from multiple sites and sources—formal, informal and non-formal learning cultures. Knowledge is socially, culturally and politically relevant if it maintains a fit with people's aspirations, lived experiences and practices.

The anti-colonial discursive framework allows for research to highlight issues and questions about knowledge production, identity and representation in schooling and education in diverse contexts. It draws out insights of local knowledge, individual agency and resistance for rethinking schooling and education in African and North American contexts.

The issues of minority schooling play out differently in different contexts. In Canada, for example, difference is affirmed, though educators have not necessarily responded to difference. The acknowledgement of difference has not led to educators and schools instituting measures that concretely address the implications of difference. One may hear educators boasting about their schools diversity. Yet, classroom-teaching practices to ensuring students are presented with a diversity of ideas and events that shaped and continue to shape human growth is often not attended to. Responding to difference also requires that educators address the power-saturated issues of schooling, since difference itself provides the context for power and domination. Similarly, African education, since historical times, is fundamentally based in national development. In emphasizing the goal of national integration, post-independence, "post-colonial" education in Africa has denied heterogeneity in local populations, as if difference itself was a problem. With this orientation, education has undoubtedly helped create and maintain the glaring disparities and inequities, structured along lines of ethnicity, culture, language, religion, gender and class, which persist and grow. However, this pattern can be disrupted through the voices that speak about such inequities and challenge complacency (see Dei, 2003a).

SUBJECTS' VOICES

These narratives focus on Ghanaian educators (secondary school/college teachers) and officials working at the Ministry of Education and in the Ghana Education Service. Most have several years of working experience in the educational system to draw on when addressing questions about dealing with difference in schools.

NEGOTIATING DIFFERENCE

Yafo[3] has been teaching for thirty years specializing in Geography. He notes carefully that the diversity of Ghanaian society requires that educators minimize difference and promote the commonalities shared by Ghanaians. He sees this as strategically enhancing social cohesion and nation building.

See, Ghana is a multi-ethnic nation. So, if we do not try to minimize
our differences, and if we emphasize the differences, then, nationhood
in the true sense will be very difficult to attain. [07/20/00]

According to Yafo, the difficulty in achieving a collective sense of a nation
is rooted in teachers' attempts to accentuate what divides rather than unites
Ghanaians. Ada, a Vice-Principal of the Teacher Education Division of the
Ghana Ministry of Education disagrees and sees the challenge of nation
building as thwarted by schools that negate differences. In fact, he sees such
reasoning as nothing but a denial of difference. Ada states poignantly:

We keep saying that we are not considering these differences, that we
are not affected by the differences among ourselves. However, when
we look at the negative side of some of these things, we see that they
are really affecting us. It is just like a scenario of children watching
television. Some people think that when you're exposing the children
to television, you are spoiling the children. So, they only talk about the
negative side of television; nobody bothers to talk about the positive
side of it. [07/21/00]

Ada expects educators to emphasize the positive aspects of difference
because school aged youth are not oblivious to such differences. Educators,
like students, must grapple with issues of difference rather than sweeping
such matters under the carpet. Bali, has been an educator for twenty-five
years. She is currently head of the Technical Vocation section in the Curriculum Development Division of the Ghana Ministry of Education. She is
also a mother with children in the school system. She concurs with Ada and
thinks that relevant is what educators see as their pedagogy of difference:

I think we should be able to approach the differences in such a way
that, while we maintain our differences, for example our religious differences, at the same time we remain united and together. You know you
are different, I am different; but that shouldn't separate us [08/01/00].

Here she refers to notions of unity in sameness and difference. Our differences connect rather than divide groups and community of learners.

GENDER ISSUES

Ideological representations of gender in schooling are also crucial in exer-
cising and maintaining ethnic, patriarchal, class, and sexual domination in

society (see Collins, 1990). Gender identities, like other forms of difference, implicate how we come to understand ourselves and the valued goods and services of society. Discussing gender, therefore, is essential to challenging definitions and practices that build subordination and domination into social categories.

In the Ghanaian educational practice, gender education is receiving increasing attention both for students and teachers. The establishment of a Girl-Child education unit with the Ministry and the Ghana Education Service has helped, at least rhetorically, in this shift. Today, one could say that gender differences are being acknowledged as relevant for understanding schooling. But it should be said that not all students, educators and school administrators explicitly point to the importance and relevance of gender for the experience of schooling (e.g. curriculum, pedagogy, and distribution of power). The old gender-neutral approach continues.

In pluralist education, we (whether as educators, students, school administrators) must address gender to understand both the gendered relations of schooling, as well as learning with multiple forms of difference (see Diller, 1996). Research should not simply document the extent to which schooling is patriarchal, sexist and heterosexist, but more fundamentally must tease out how the social organization of knowledge implicates gender and gendered categories (see also Ayim and Houston, 1996). Patriarchal structures and relations of schooling accord male privileges, which can be refracted in the everyday practices of male and female interactions in schools. A critical knowledge of gender and schooling should move beyond 'gender sensitivity' (Martin, 1981 cited in Houston, 1985, p. 360) to the examination of how the current structures of educational delivery (structures for teaching, learning and administration of education) work to sustain subordination and domination along lines of gender and other forms of social difference.

Gender differences are power hierarchies, which work systematically to sustain material, ideological, symbolic and institutional advantages for different segments of society. Thus, our ability to theorize gender and its implications for schooling has a bearing on how we can create genuine educational equity. When Ghanaian female students ask for, or see female teachers as role models, we must also articulate the relations between gender and knowledge production and what such relations imply for transforming the entire school curricula (e.g., the link between identity, representation and education).

When educators, school administrators and policy makers acknowledge gender stereotypes and address gender differences in schools, they transform learning. Adosa has been an educator for twenty-seven years. He has taught Commerce, Economics, and Accounting in a number of schools over the years and notes that:

Female students are different. There are things that they [students] can learn from female teachers. I had a friend who was teaching in a school where there was no female teacher, and he, as a male teacher, was made to act as a housemistress! He found it very difficult to do that job. [07/20/00]

Adosa recognizes the importance of female teachers as role models for all students, but particularly female students. The theme of role models and gender identification is also articulated by Jete, an Assistant Headmaster teaching Economics. He has also been working for twenty-five years. He recognizes the importance of having female representation on staff:

In a school that there are female students, it's very, very important and necessary to have female teachers. There are certain problems about which girls are shy and uncomfortable to come to male teachers. [07/26/00]

Female students can be more reluctant to approach male educators with certain issues. Female staff can foster a discussion of personal issues between students and teachers. Female students also strive harder when they see female teachers on staff. For males, it challenges their notions of the capabilities of women and men. This point is not lost on Rena who has taught for twenty-seven years and has held her current position as Senior Housemistress for the past ten years. She speaks broadly of the culture of schooling and how this characterizes and informs students' expectations, performance and goals:

It helps the students especially the female students, to see that if a female teacher has been up to this point, then they can also learn to reach that height. In the last term there was an example here. A female math teacher came to the school, and these ladies here, they weren't doing so good. So this teacher rounded them up and started giving them tutorials and at the end of the year we got to know that [in] this year's exams [the school] had a higher grade [mark] on the math examination. So she had inspired them a lot. [07/28/00]

Both female and male teachers have a role of motivating female students to do well in school especially in subjects like science and mathematics.

SOCIAL ECONOMIC STATUS AND EDUCATION

Students' social class and family socio-economic background continues to be a major concern in African schooling (social economic status defined both in terms of Marxist analysis of social class—wealth and prestige- and in Weberian sense of power). The severe economic constrictions and the resultant rising costs of education exacerbate this situation. The severe national and global economic contraction in recent years has led governments to cut budgets for basic social services, including education and health. In Ghana, the structural adjustment economic policies intended to address the sectoral imbalances in global, regional, national economies resulted in the government reducing expenditures on services. As a result communities and families shoulder a great deal of the responsibility for education (see Konadu-Agyemang, 2001; Hutchful, 1996).

Increasing material poverty further exacerbates these class distinctions. The introduction of educational reforms in the 1980s intensified the hardships of local parents as they accessed education for their children. In fact, parents are paying for public education at the primary/basic level despite the fact that such education is "free." The rise in private schooling (both at the elementary and secondary/technical school levels) with exorbitant fees further aggravates Ghanaian socio-economic divisions. Even within the public school system free tuition at the basic level has been accompanied by a steep rise in incidental fees. The situation is more severe at the additionally costly secondary and tertiary levels.

Table 1 below gives a breakdown of information on school fees that I collected for primary/JSS, SSS and University levels for the 2000–2001 and 2002–2003 school years. Between 2001 and 2003, the percentage increase in incidental fees for day students in their first year, SSS1 (senior secondary students in Year 1 who lived at home and attended secondary schools) was about 22%. The corresponding percentage increase for SSS3 (senior secondary students in Year 3 of study) from 2001 to 2003 was 115%. The cost of boarding school at SSS1 (for those fortunate enough to live on campus) rose by about 43.8% between 2001 and 2003. Corresponding percentage increase for SSS3 was 68%.

Table 1. School Fees (Incidental Fees)—SSS

	DAY	BOARDING		
LEVELS	2001	2003	2001	2003
SSS 1	C889, 000	C1, 085, 000	C1, 600,000	C2, 300,000
SSS 3	C317,000	C684,000	C892,000	C1,500,000

Note: Forex Bureau exchange rate (2001), C5, 000 = $ US 1; and in 2003, C8, 500 = $US 1

Table 2. Registration Fee—JSS/SSS

LEVELS	2001	2003
JSS	C 68,000	C 84,000
SSS	C 295,000	C 350,000

Moreover, registration fee for JSS increased by 23.5% between 2001 and 2003, while those of SSS increased by 18.8% (see Table 2 below). School fees for the JSS ranged from C53, 000 per child in 2001 to about C73, 000 in 2003.

In theory, tuition at the university level is free. But there are huge expenses involved in receiving university education. Table 3 shows that at university levels, Residential Facilities' fee at the university increased by about 30.5% between 2001 and 2003. At the same time, the Academic Facilities' fee decreased slightly by 0.7% (see Table 3). An average university student spends a minimum of about C10, 000 to C12, 000 per day on feeing cost alone. The minimum daily wage in Ghana in 2001 was C5, 500 and C9, 200 in 2003, and unemployed Ghanaians do not receive any social security benefits/ payments. Emma, a college level novice teacher of Social Studies makes a similar point:

> Money is keeping a lot of people out of the school. In our schools, we can deal with ethnicity, we can deal with gender; but when you don't have money . . . that is a whole different thing. [07/20/00]

Wealthy and some less privileged families struggling to pay fees are now opting to send their children to private schools or overseas. Tempo, now an Assistant Headmaster who has been teaching since 1974, notes that a two-tier class system has been created in schools for "the haves and the have-nots":

> Yes, because more and more of the rich are sending their kids to private schools that they think are better schools. And some of them even are sending their kids abroad. So we have this kind of haves and have-nots. [07/28/00]

Table 3. University Fee for the Period 2000 to 2003

FEE TYPE	2000-2001	2002-2003
Residential fee	C 168,500	C 220,000
Academic fee	C 688,000	683,000

Whether in public or private schools, one could easily see how family economic background affects schooling outcomes for youth. Foku, a Geography teacher for thirty years notes:

> For students who come from a poor family background, a payment of the school fees is a major problem. . . . And the embarrassment of being asked. . . . especially in front of their classmates. . . . To go for fees is quite annoying. It affects their studies. [07/20/00]

Moreover, while school administrators and teachers try to understand their students' financial circumstances, usually if they cannot pay the fees, they may not be allowed to attend school and sit for exams. As Koku explains:

> You see, currently we are ending the year, but there are some children who have not paid their fees. We had to print up questions according to the number of students, and yet we have students who haven't paid their fees. What do you do then? Well, we allow some time for these students, so their parents come and make arrangements to pay their dues [fees], little by little over time, until things are settled. [07/26/00]

ETHNICITY, LANGUAGE AND RELIGION/RELIGIOUS DIFFERENCES

In this paper, ethnicity is defined as a social relational category determined by socially selected cultural characteristics. These characteristics may include a conflation of language, culture, history and religion. While this definition does not subsume these characteristics under ethnicity, it is noted that in the narratives of some local subjects, culture and ethnicity for example can be conflated. Rather, I argue that language, ethnicity, religion; culture should be treated separately as parallel notions of difference that build on each other. For example, one may belong to an identified ethnic minority, practice the dominant religion, and speak the language of the dominant fluently. Cultural minority status is not dependent on numerical statistics. Instead, minority status results from cultural status rather than the numbers of bodies in the school. In Ghana, the Ewes or Northerners, for example, make up a larger proportion of the school population, yet are perceived as culturally inferior.

The designation of a religious, ethnic, linguistic minority status must be understood in terms of the tensions of cultural, religious, linguistic or ethnic domination and not in the representation of physical bodies. By addressing the separate and distinct aspects of one's identity, we are able to tease out the complexities and relational difference unique to identity.

The challenge for educators is that histories, experience and cultures while unique may be contingent and intertwined.

Ethnicity

Elsewhere (see Dei, 2003a), I have addressed the question of ethnicity and education as it relates to schooling in Ghana. Ethnicity is read differently by diverse educators. Some insist that accentuating students' ethnicities ferment divisions, while others maintain that identity is important and must be linked with schooling and knowledge production.

> Ethnicity is a relative rather than bounded categorization. We need to understand ways in which "groups identities necessarily form through interaction with other groups through complicated experiences of conflict and co-operation and in the structural contexts of power" (Espiritu, 1999: 512). In a sense, forms of difference reveal ethnic groupings as equally heterogeneous; their cultures varied and unfixed their boundaries unstable and changing within political contexts and situations.

Bubi, an agricultural science teacher with twenty-seven years experience, says he is aware of the ethnic differences among the student population. Yet, he is uncomfortable speaking of differences for fear of subverting the project of developing a common Ghanaian identity:

> Well, in fact, formerly we did not look at groups as dominant and so forth because we look at each other as Ghanaians. But personally, even now, when I go to classes and a student tries to say 'I am this and that,' normally I don't like that; because it brings about a lot of problems. So personally, in my class when someone says that 'I am Fanti' and such, I emphasize that we are all Ghanaians. I don't want to bring that at all into the classroom. [07/20/00]

This thinking and pedagogical practice are only marginally useful. As an ethnic minority from the northern part of the Ghana, Bubi brings a particular historical knowledge to regional stereotyping. He sees his presence in the school system significant to challenging commonly held stereotypes. As a role model for students of his ethnicity, he has a better understanding of their experiences and is therefore more easily approachable. Jete, an Assistant Headmaster who has taught Economics for twenty-five years supports Bubi's view:

> There is nothing wrong with having teachers from different backgrounds. Then the students from the same background would also

relate to them very well. Let's say here we have students from different religious backgrounds such as Protestants and so on; they also have their own associations related to their grouping. So if there is any religious conflict, we just call the teachers in charge to straighten things out. So, this is very necessary. We are saying that if one particular tribe [ethnic group] feels aggrieved in a way, they will easily confide in the teacher from the same tribe [ethnic group] than in other teachers. So it really helps. [07/26/00]

Teachers, then, are not only role models but also role players. They can help students develop self-esteem, self worth and pride essential in cultivating mutual and respectful interactions with other peers. Having a teacher of their own group attests to what they can accomplish, may help students overcome stereotypes, develop positive identities and relate to other groups with confidence.

Teachers from different ethnic groups also constitute an important source of cultural knowledge. Bajo, a Social Studies teacher since 2001 and a member of a dominant ethnic group (Akan) sees the pedagogic and instructional relevance of having teachers who represent different ethnicities:

I believe if there are teachers from different ethnic groups, it will help a lot. Not only they will serve as role models for others, but also we could share their experiences. Let me take myself as an example. There are certain topics related to ethnic groups that I teach in my social studies class. I just read and teach the theoretical aspect of it, without knowing what it really means in practice. So, if I had colleagues, say from Ewes, from this and that, I could go to them and share their knowledge. [07/21/00].

Language as a Site of Difference

Language and linguistic differences present challenges for African schooling (see Dei; Asgharzadeh, 2003). And, instituting a national language policy in schools has not made teaching easier for educators. The pull for a common language of instruction alongside the politics of identifying local languages to promote national culture continues to create tensions. Dowu, a Ministry of Education official, had this comment about the language policy in schools:

Ghana has a language policy for education, and the policy says that when children enter school, the first three years, the medium of instruction should be a Ghanaian language. And when they move up the third year we use English as the medium of instruction. . . . Unfortunately, we are having so many problems with this policy, because here in this country we have about 60 different languages. . . . So, in most cases English is used as the medium of instruction from the first year. Unfortunately, our colonial past is not doing us any good. People tend to believe that if you speak English well, then you are a better.

Language can be a trope for domination in school settings. It connects powerfully with the ethnicity and identification of dominant ethnic groups. When asked about language policy and practice in the school system, Jete, the Assistant Headmaster and Economics teacher, describes how language and power are linked:

> We force them to speak English. When they come to the House [school dormitory], they are to speak English. [07/26/00]

Mana, a Ghanaian educationist renowned for her children's stories, noted this about the secondary school where she currently teaches:

> In fact, language differences are not so salient here, because the insistence is on speaking English. And in fact, a student might be punished if he or she is found speaking a local language in the classroom! [07/24/00].

Ironically, African literary critic Ngugi wa Thiong'o (1986) said the same about British colonial education in Kenya; students found speaking the local Kikuyu language suffered humiliation and punishment under the hands of British colonial educators.

RELIGION/RELIGIOUS DIFFERENCES

Religion is an important site of difference among Ghanaian students. Historically, religion and colonial missionary education have also been a source of tension in schools. Today, tension arises out of public education's incorporation or omission of students' and educators' religious belief. Dabo, a college-level mathematics teacher asserts that his school has been tolerant of all religious faiths.

> In this school we all move together and worship together. We invite pastors from various churches, not necessarily from one particular church. Somebody can come from Presbyterian, somebody from

Methodist, some Evangelist, all over. Even Muslims, too, are allowed to worship . . . but they have to obey the school regulations as well. [07/20/00]

While students are free to practice their faith, schools' codes of conduct must be followed regardless of the students' religion. Problems emerge when students perceive this code of conduct to conflict with their faith. Fesu, a History and Religion teacher, notes that some Muslim students feel that schools are largely informed by the dominant Christian faith (though he believes he can persuade them that this is not really the case).

Muslims should not think we are trying to Christianize them. We are only seeing the same God through different perspective. So if you go to the university, for example, we are going to teach all religions there. We teach Christianity, we teach Islam, we teach Hinduism, we teach Buddhism, we teach philosophy of religion, psychology, and sociology. So, I tell them these things and immediately the student accepts. So, the students see that we are not there to take anything from them. So such an approach I think always makes the students comfortable. [07/26/00]

Rena, a school administrator, is emphatic when discussing the merits of religion and abhors any attempts to force religious beliefs on others. She discusses this in relation to students who attend missionary school:

I feel religion should not be forced on individuals. You have to use your own free will. So if it happens that you attend the mission [school], that doesn't mean any religion should be imposed on you. Although, one may say, 'after all, you have your own churches, and they have this training there, why didn't you go there?' But it is not like everybody is able to get admission. I personally do not side with the way the students are forced to worship at the missionary schools. [07/28/00]

Dade, a male Chemistry teacher, sees the need for teachers in multi-faith schools to reflect the different religions represented in the school and/or community:

Muslims too, need to cater [to] their religious needs. So, for [ethnic] . . . and . . . . ethical balance in the school and also in society, I think we need to have Muslim teachers. [07/20/00]

Koku, of the Ministry with thirty years' of college teaching experience, explains that religious diversity within teaching staff is important because of differences in knowledge relevant to the curriculum:

> I would argue that, if there are certain things that only a Muslim teacher is equipped to address, then we could say that we really need this Muslim teacher here at the school. For example if there are parts of the syllabus that non-Muslim teachers cannot handle very well, then we could ask for a Muslim teacher. [07/26/00]

DISCUSSION

As noted elsewhere (Dei, 2003a), the colonial and post-colonial politics of schooling in Ghana emphasized nation building, the creation of common citizenship and citizenry, and the promotion of social integration/cohesion. Quite evidently the narratives of Ghanaian subjects trouble these politics. The above local voices add to our critical understanding of the role of language, religion, culture, ethnicity, class, and gender in schooling in the African contexts. Difference is one aspect of the discourse on schooling that has been neglected in discussions of African schooling and education. This paper points to the challenge of responding to difference in schooling. A key question is how to understand difference as both a site of important knowledge and a source of discriminatory practice in schools.

The question of difference has been examined in many pluralistic contexts (see Ghosh, 1996). There are also points of convergence between the Ghanaian case study and the way difference is taken up in some North American contexts. For example, some North American and Ghanaian educators see accentuating difference as problematic. Speaking of difference creates discomfort for North American educators who would rather speak about commonalities. Difference is deemed negative. For example, authors such as Neil Bissondath (1994); Diane Ravitch (1990) and Dinesh D'Souza (1995) deny racial differences as significant and see individuals and groups as raceless.

On the other hand, authors such as Christine Sleeter (1993), Michele Fine (1991) Keren Brathwaite and Carl James (1996); Dei, James–Wilson, Karumanchery, and Zine (2000); Dei, Mazzuca, Mc Isaac and Zine, (1997) affirm the consequences of race. Sleeter (1993) and Dei, Mazzuca, McIsaac and Zine, (1997) show how race positions bodies differently in the North American school system. Acknowledging [racial] difference is not inherently problematic; rather it is interpretations and understandings of difference that may be challenging. Difference is understood as negative. Difference can also be totalizing such that students are seen as their ethnicity, gender, class, language, religion or simply culture. This failure to see the student as a complex subject negates some aspects of a student's identity.

Although concepts such as race, ethnicity, gender, culture, religion and language are social constructions, they have real material and political effects. These identities are constructed differently over time, as are their real effects. Ethnic differences are significant in that they carry powerful political and material effects for people who can be advantaged or disadvantaged on the basis of their ethnic affiliations. Similarly, our bodies are marked by gender, class, linguistic and religious differences each of which carry currency in the social setting. To misrecognize one's identity and fail to show the complexities of the subject denies a part of the self. The non-recognition of an aspect of one's identity is equally oppressive (See Taylor, 1994:25).

How are these issues of difference articulated and acted upon in Ghanaian and Canadian/ North American contexts? What comparative lens can be brought to the subject of how educators engage difference in school settings? Concepts like "North American schools" and "African schools" are indeed complex and the challenges facing schools whether in the US, Canada, Ghana and other parts of Africa are monolithic, but let us engage the broader philosophical and theoretical discussions that cut across the specificity of schooling in these diverse contexts. The intellectual engagement with North American schooling emerges from my prior research work with Canadian schools and the much-acquired knowledge on how the possibilities of inclusive schooling can help inform ongoing challenges of promoting inclusive schooling in Ghanaian contexts.

The negation of the ethnicity of Ghanaian students is shared in the denial of race in North America. Race is a taboo subject (Tatum, 1992), an unsettling issue for many Canadians as is ethnicity in Ghana. That "ethnicity" is a troubling issue for most Ghanaians becomes evident in the different voices that speak to "ethnicity" in the interviews. This is understandable given the politics of colonization and the history of colonial education (Bassey, 1999: Brock-Utne, 2000). In this case study, ethnicity is differently read when juxtaposed with other forms of difference such as gender, class, religious, linguistic and cultural forms. It is in this juxtaposing where ethnicity is rendered "difficult knowledge." Ethnicity evokes a colonial history of distinctions, which fosters unhealthy tensions and competition among groups and communities with interrelated histories. This "divide and rule" tactic formed part of the pre-colonial administration. Unfortunately, the post-colonial era has not succeeded in addressing this issue, and in some cases, the problem has been intensified.

In Ghanaian schooling we note that difference is also evoked to either affirm or deny the complexity and contentions of integrating different bodies in schooling. While some school administrators, teachers and students do not critically engage the asymmetrical power relations that structure the lives of learners, difference is clearly relevant to the understanding everyday practices of schooling. In Ghana, while multicultural education may not be directly practiced, still the assumptions underlying multicultural education (e.g. importance of culture, students' identities and the links to knowledge) are revealed discussions about global and citizenship education. Educators' strategies to achieve global/international and citizenship education varies from an approach that avoids difference to a recognition of specific contributions of diverse groups, and their acknowledgement as members of a community. But, like Canadian and North American contexts, for schooling in Ghana to promote the strengths of difference, we need an integrative analysis that recognizes the power of difference and how questions of identity (ethnicity, gender, class, religion, language and culture) implicate knowledge production.

As in other pluralistic contexts, schooling is a process and a practice mediated by the powerful intersections of ethnicity, class, gender, language, religion and culture. An inclusive schooling system in Ghana (as elsewhere) is one capable of responding to ethnic, cultural, linguistic, religious differences among the community of learners. Inclusive schooling is about a demonstrated commitment to address the diverse needs of all students. It requires an acknowledgement of the historical and institutional structures and contexts that sustain educational inequities in schools. Narratives of some Ghanaian subjects about the marginalization of difference in the school system suggest new theoretical and practical conceptions of difference for effective social and political practice and educational change.

There are important points of divergence when examining Ghanaian and Canadian/North American schooling. In addition, there are diverse and different ways majority or dominant students minimize the issue of 'minority' status. While "minority" in Canadian contexts is basically a question of power, the narratives of Ghanaian subjects reveal a myriad of conceptions and understandings of "minority." For example, "minority" is viewed both in terms of power and in terms of quantity of people. The history of colonial education and the concentration of schools in the South have ensured that Ghanaians from the southern parts of the country occupy most influential positions in the government and business. Because historically there have been large [disproportionate] concentration of schools, colleges and universities in the South, students from the North in these educational sites often constitute the minority. Those interviewed were quick to establish that, today; students from the South attending schools in the northern parts of the country are the minority in these regions. This does not translate, however, into these students being the minority in society broadly. When students speak of "dominant/majority" status in Ghana, often they are referring to the large linguistic groups such as the Akans, and in some occasions ethnic groups holding power. This complex reading of minority-majority status points to how geography, history, politics and ethnicity combine to conflate understandings of "minority" in Ghanaian schooling contexts.

The foregoing discussion informs the pursuit of a practice of inclusion in both Canadian/North American and Ghanaian schooling. Ghanaian educators have an understanding of 'inclusive schooling' as schools that are not just 'inclusive' in terms of students sense of belonging but, as schools that address local needs and fit the local context and situation. The notion of 'inclusive schooling' is understood as place-based schooling/education. The local community is identified with the school to the extent that educators make learning and teaching relevant to community needs and rely on local experiences in classroom pedagogy and instruction. Local narratives of "inclusivity" reveal a connection between schools and the local community. There is a call for systemic integration, such as moving 'schooling' into the local community and teaching through culture. This is another form of critical teaching that helps students to be culturally and socially responsible (see Dei, 2003b).

In order to appreciate the social and political conditions that shape students' experiences of schooling, educators must acknowledge in their teaching students' diverse realities. To affirm difference therefore requires working with contextualized teaching and learning. There are philosophical and practical implications for intersecting language, religion and culture with ethnicity, class and gender differences. A particular strength emerges when students and educators question difference. Dominant discursive manipulations in schools and particularly classroom instructional practices reveal that educators assume power by disempowering bodies in schools. By refusing to critically engage difference, part of a student's identity is denied. This denial can have political, social and emotional consequences as students engage and disengage with the school system.

In another work (Dei, 2003b), I noted that some Ghanaian students want role models they can identify with in schools. Students identify strongly with these bodies and by extension, schooling. In schools students produce knowledge and make sense of their education through their individual and collective histories, identities and experiences. We can begin to appreciate the difference when we "think in circles" rather than "in hierarchies." When thinking in circles, I borrow from Aboriginal peoples' philosophies and epistemologies (Castellano, 2000, Couture, 2000) which connects every participant to the circle, even if and because each participant has a unique contribution. Learners are joined in a circle in recognition that excellence (whether defined socially or academically and including multiple arenas of activity) is equitably distributed within the circle population.

The tensions between educating for nation building and recognizing difference is not endemic to Ghanaian society, but rather, are located in the relations of schooling. The creation of a shared "Ghanaian" identity has been viewed in conflict with support for various ethnicity and their cultures. The Ghanaian community is a community of differences. These difference need to be affirmed (rather than denied) to strengthen community building. For educators to work with ethnicity and difference in positive (i.e. solution-oriented) ways, we must uphold the virtues of difference and deal with the asymmetrical power relations in the classroom.

Young's (1990) essay is informative here in examining the tensions between education for nation building and recognizing differences. Education can foster a shared sense of identity and collective belonging. In her important essay, "The Ideal of Community and the Politics of Difference," Young (1990) argues for a "concept of social relations that embody openness to unassimilated otherness with justice and appreciation. . . . [along with]. . . . a discourse and institutions for bringing differently identified groups together without suppressing or subsuming the differences" (p.320). At both the philosophical and practical levels, she criticizes dominant articulations of the ideal "community" which obfuscate difference. The privileging of unity can be seen in progressive politics that suppress difference [in] directly, explicitly or implicitly to exclude persons with whom one does not identify. While Young makes direct reference to the politics of community in Diasporic/North American contexts, (where racism, homophobia, sexism may necessitate that the marginalized and oppressed group celebrate a common culture) her work is relevant to interrogating anti-colonial politics of nation building that subsumed difference under a shared national project. The struggles against European colonialism may have justified such politics but in today's postcolonial realities we must be wary of extending such into the "fear of difference."

Schooling and education in postcolonial societies has the enviable task of establishing speaking about community and nation as marked both by sameness and by difference. To achieve this educational goal, "desire for unity or wholeness in discourse [cannot] generate borders, dichotomies and exclusions" (Young, 1990: 309). Educators must not deny difference within and between learners. While learners may be encouraged to define community with respect to a shared heritage, social identity, culture and values, this defining becomes problematic if it used as an "oppositional differentiation from other groups who are feared or at best devalued" (Young 1990:311). Rather than deny or suppress differences, schools must uncover differences among learners and educators and harness this wealth of knowledge to further educational goals. The just, un-oppressive community of learners embodies difference, as education must embrace differences through an openness to the differences of culture, religion, language, ability, sexuality, ethnicity, gender and social class.

In this essay, I also interrogate how and why some Ghanaian educators collapse their classroom discursive practice of the "universalist/generalist" student. While educators that say "all our students are 'Ghanaians'" may be furthering the politics of nation building and a sense of "national" community, we must remember that community is never homogenous. Ghanaian educators can negotiate the multiple identities of their students in order to affirm the common bonds (similarities) and the ties (differences that connect the group). Tensions arise when students perceive themselves as simply or only having different ethnicities, cultures, and linguistic and cultural affiliations. Tensions produced by such processes of identification are not necessarily productive. Because identities (whether structured along the lines of gender, ethnicity, class, religion and culture) are themselves constructed to have powerful social and political meanings, these identities ought to be engaged in schools and within schooling processes.

A universalistic approach to identity may, at times, sit uncomfortably with difference. Difference notes particularities and connections, and the fact that our histories, while disparate and unique, are also interconnected or intertwined. So, the universalistic conception of humanity needs unsettling through a greater emphasis on the particular, specific and the contextual. This particularity of experience for students and educators offers a way for the latter to understand and appreciate the unique contributions the diverse bodies bring to their classrooms while we work to build a community through our shared ties and histories.

To recognize differences structured along the lines of culture, language, religion, ethnicity, gender and class is to acknowledge one's own power, privilege and history. This recognition is about self-affirmation and collective worth. Knowledge of the self is made possible through the affirmation of difference (Hall, 1987: 5). Difference is often rendered invisible through processes of normalization. Ghanaian students and educators are challenging and resisting this normalization when they problematize the lack of attention to difference. As in other pluralistic contexts when Ghanaian youth from minority ethnic, religious, socio-economic and linguistic backgrounds insist on acknowledging and responding to difference (despite the understanding that 'we are all Ghanaians'), they are in fact resisting their marginality in dominant schooling practice.

CONCLUSION

This paper has focussed on educators' views and perspectives on how schools deal with social difference. Educators can be best placed to appreciate the importance of accounting for identities through the learning process. In order to enhance learning outcomes for Ghanaian youth, educators must acknowledge and respond to difference. How teachers ensure that difference is appropriately engaged and not dismissed in their classrooms/schools remains a great challenge. Classroom teachers open the door to academic and school success by welcoming all students into the class and ensuring that each has the right and the responsibility to an equal voice. Learning happens when we develop humility for others' knowledge and appreciate students' and teachers' diverse backgrounds, histories and contributions.

As educators, our thinking must be critical if our teaching is to be truly transformative. Difference cannot separate the collective. Learners want a pedagogic and instructional approach to difference that affirms our connections with each other. Difference need not be an "either/or" value of division or connection. Difference should be about our uniqueness as well as our connections to each other. It is through difference that we begin to appreciate each other and to value our collective sense of worth.

While there is a general recognition among educators in Ghana of the important role that difference plays in the school system, a more critical reading of difference (e.g. ethnicity, gender, class, religion, language) that allows for questioning of the school curriculum, classroom pedagogy and official texts is lacking. We need a critical understanding of how schools reproduce and sustain social inequities and differentiation. This requires teasing out issues around gender, ethnic and class power, the discretionary use of authority and the evocation of privilege and how they work in tandem in schools systems to establish unequal outcomes for students.

NOTES

1. Acknowledgments: Many individuals have assisted my research in Ghana. I would like to acknowledge the assistance of Dr. Margarida Aguiar for helping with the work on tape transcriptions and data analysis, and also Alireza Asgharzadeh, Lems Crooks, Bijoy Barua, and Gulnara Medebeukova all of

OISE/UT who at various times worked as graduate researchers with me in Ghana. I thank Bathseba Opini and Tania Principe of OISE/UT for going over the paper, and, particularly, Bathseba for helping to address reviewers' comments. I am indebted to Mr. Paul Akom, Dean of Students at the University College of Education at Winneba for his invaluable assistance on my research project. Many thanks to Messrs Dickson K. Darko, Martin Doudo, Esther Danso, Paul Banahene Adjei, and Mrs. Ntow of Ghana; all who served as my local research assistants. My sincere gratitude goes to the many Ghanaian educators, students and parents who gave their time for the interviews during my fieldwork. I would also particularly like to mention Ms. Evelyn Oduro of the Ghana Ministry of Education, Accra. Kayleen Oka of the Department of Sociology and Equity Studies at the Ontario Institute for Studies in Education of the University of Toronto (OISE/UT) read and commented on a working copy of the paper. Cheryl Williams of OISE/UT provided editorial assistance on the manuscript. The Social Sciences and Humanities Research Council of Canada (SSHRC) provided funding for this study.

2. The anti-colonial framework has roots in the decolonizing movements of colonial states that fought for independence from Europeans at the end of the Second World War. In the specific case of Africa the ideas of Frantz Fanon, Albert Memmi, Aimé Césaire, Cabral and Kwame Nkrumah, to name a few, were instrumental in shaping the nature of the anti-colonial struggles. In particular, Fanon's (1967) and Cabral's (1970) writings on the violence of colonialism and the necessity for open resistance and Memmi's (1969) discursive on the relations between the colonized and the colonizer helped instill in the minds of colonized peoples the importance of engaging in acts of resistance against the violence of colonialism. After independence a new body of 'anti-colonial thought' emerged. This discourse appropriately labeled within the 'post-colonial' (see Ashcroft, Griffiths and Tiffin, 1995, Gandhi, 1998) have largely focused on the interconnections between imperial and colonized cultural practices and the discursive possibilities of hybridity and alterity (see also Bhabha, 1990; Spivak, 1988). In understanding these interconnections post-colonial theorists employ the pointed notion of difference and the embedded power relations of claiming race, class, gender, ethnic, linguistic and religious identities (see also Shohat, 1992). Current anti-colonial theorizing has stressed local knowings of colonized and the recourse to power and subjective agency for resistance.

3. Names of research participants used in the text are all pseudonyms.

REFERENCES

Altbach, P. (ed.). 1989. "Symposium: World Bank Report on Education in Sub-Saharan Africa." [Summary of World Bank Report]. *Comparative Education Review* 33(1): 93–133.

Anderson, M. L. and Collins, P. H. 1995. Toward Inclusive Thinking through the Study of Race, Class, and Gender. In M.L. Anderson and P.H. Collins (eds.) *Race, Class and Gender* (2nd ed.) Belmont, CA.: Wadsworth Publishing.

Apple, M. 1986. *Teachers and Texts: A Political Economy of Class and Gender Relations in Education*. New York: Routledge & Kegan Paul.

Apple, M. & L. Weiss. 1983. "Ideology and Practice in Schooling: A Political and Conceptual Introduction." In. *Ideology and Practice in Schooling*. Philadelphia: Temple University Press.

Apusigah, A. (2002). *Reconsidering Women, Dvelopment and Education in Ghana : A Critical Transformation*. Unpublished Ph.D. dissertation, Faculty of Education, Queen's University, Ontario, Canada.

Asante, Molefi K. 1991. "The Afrocentric Idea in Education." *Journal of Negro Education* 60(2): 170–180.

Ashcroft, B. Griffiths, G. and H. Tiffin. (eds.). 1995. *The Post-colonial Reader*. New York: Routledge.

Ayim, A and B. Houston 1996. "A Conceptual Analysis of Sexism and Sexist Education." In. A. Diller, B. Houston, and K. P. Morgan. (eds). *The Gender Question in Education: Theory, Pedagogy and Practice*. Boulder, Co.: Westview Press, pp. 9–30.

Banks, J.A. (1997). *Educating Citizens in a Multicultural Society*. New York: Teachers College Press.

Banks, J. 1993. "The Canon Debate, Knowledge Construction and Multicultural Education." *Educational Researcher* 22(5): 4–14.

Banks, J.A. and C. A Banks 1993. (eds.). *Multicultural Education: Issues and Perspectives*, Boston, Mass.: Allyn and Bacon.

Banya, K. 1993. "Illiteracy, Colonial Legacy and Education: The Case of Modern Sierra Leone." *Comparative Education*. 29(2): 159–70.

———. 1991. "Economic Decline and the Education System: The Case of Sierra Leone." *Compare*, 21(2) 127–142.

———. and J. Elu. 1997. "Implementing Basic Education: An African Experience." *International Review of Education* 43(5/6): 481–496.

Bassey, M.O. 1999. Western Education and Political Domination in Africa: A Study in Critical and Dialogical Pedagogy. Westport, CT : Bergin & Garvey.

Bhabha, H. K. 1994. *The Location of Culture*. London: Routledge.

Biddle, B.J. (ed.). 2001. Social class, poverty, and education: Policy and Practice. New York: Falmer Press.

Bissondath, N. 1994. *Selling Illusions: The Cult of Multiculturalism in Canada*. Toronto: Penguin Books.

Bloch, M., J. A.Beoku-Betts, and R. Tabachnick. 1998 (eds.). *Women and Education in Sub-Saharan Africa: Power, Opportunities and Constraints*. Boulder, Co.: Lynne Rienner.

Bracy, W. 1995. "Developing the Inclusive Curriculum: A Model for the Incorporation of Diversity in the Social Work Curriculum." Paper presented at the 41st Annual Program meeting of the Council on Social Work Education." San Diego, California, March 2–5, 1995.

Brathwaite, K. and C. James 1996. (eds.). Educating African-Canadians. Toronto: James Lorimer Publishers.

Brock-Utne, B. 2000. Whose Education for All? The Recolonization of the African mind. New York: Falmer Press.

Brock-Utne, B. 1996. "Reliability and Validity in Qualitative Research within Education in Africa." *International Review of Education* 42(6): 605–621.

Cabral, A. 1970. "National Liberation and Culture." The 1970 Eduardo Mondlane Lecture, Program of Eastern African Studies of the Maxwell School of Citizenship and Public Affairs, Syracuse University, February 20.

Castellano, M. 2000. "Updating Aboriginal Traditions of Knowledge." In G. Dei, B. Hall and D. Goldin Rosenberg (eds.). *Indigenous Knowledges in Global Contexts: Multiple Readings of Our World*. Toronto: University of Toronto Press.

Claussen, B. (ed). 1994. *Aspects of Globalization and Internalization of Political Education*. Hamburg: Kramer.

Collins, P. H. 1990. *Black Feminist Thought: Knowledge, Consciousness and the Politics of Empowerment*. New York: Routledge.

Couture, J. 2000. "Native Studies and the Academy." In G. Dei, B. Hall and D. Goldin Rosenberg (eds.). *Indigenous Knowledges in Global Contexts: Multiple Readings of Our World*. Toronto: University of Toronto Press.

Craig, J. 1990. *Comparative African Experiences in Implementing Educational Policies*. Washington: The World Bank.

Dei, G. S .1994. "Afrocentricity: A Cornerstone of Pedagogy." *Anthropology and Education Quarterly* 25(1): 3–28.

Dei, G. S. 1996. *Anti-Racism Education: Theory and Practice*. Halifax: Fernwood Publishing.

Dei, G. S. 1999. "Education Reform Efforts in Ghana." *International Journal of Educational Reform*. 8(3): 244–259.

Dei, G. S. 2000. "Local Knowledges and Education Reforms in Ghana." *Canadian and International Education*. 29(1): 37–72.

Dei, G. S. 2003a. "Dealing with Difference: Ethnicity and Gender in the Context of Schooling in Ghana." *International Journal of Educational Development*. [Forthcoming].

Dei, G. S. 2003b."Critical Teaching in an African Context: Indigenous Knowledge and Educational Reforms." In. W. Tettey, K. Puplampu, and B. Berman (eds.). *Politics and Socio-Economic Development in Ghana*. The Netherlands: Brill Publishers, pp.365–388 .

Dei, G. S. 2004. *Schooling and Education in Africa: The Case of Ghana*. African World Press, Trenton, New Jersey.

Dei, G. S. and L. Karumanchery. 1999. "School Reforms in Ontario: The 'Marketization of Education" and the Resulting Silence on Equity." *Alberta Journal of educational research* XLV (2): 111–131.

Dei, G. S, J. Mazzuca, E. McIsaac and J. Zine. (1997). *Reconstructing "Dropout": A Critical Ethnography of the Dynamics of Black Students' Disengagement from School*. Toronto: University of Toronto Press.

Dei, G. S, I. James, S. James-Wilson, L. Karumanchery, and J. Zine. (2000). *Removing the Margins: The Challenges and Possibilities of Inclusive Schooling*. Toronto: Canadian Scholar's Press.

Dei, G. S, S. James-Wilson and J. Zine. (2002). *Inclusive Schooling: A Teacher's Companion to Removing the Margins'* Toronto: Canadian Scholar's Press.

Dei, G. S. and A. Asgharzadeh. 2003 "Language, Education and Development: Case Studies from the Southern Contexts." *Language and Education* [in press].

Dei, G. S, A. Asgharzadeh, R. Shahjahan, and S. Eblaghie-Bahador, 2004. *Power, Knowledge and Social Difference in African Schooling.* [forthcoming]

Diller, A. 1996. "An Ethics of Care Takes on Pluralism." In. A. Diller, B. Houston, and K. P. Morgan. (Eds). *The Gender Question in Education: Theory, Pedagogy and Practice.* Boulder, Co.: Westview Press, pp. 161–169.

D'Souza, D. 1995. *The End of Racism: Principles for a Multiracial Society.* New York: Free Press.

Easterly, W.R. 2001. *The Effect of IMY and World Bank Programmes on Poverty.* Helsinki: United Nations University, World Institute for Development and Economic Research.

Espiritu, L. 1999. Disciplines Unbound: Notes on Sociology and Ethnic Studies. *Contemporary Sociology* 28(5): 510–515.

Fanon, F. 1963. *The Wretched of the Earth.* New York: Grove Weidenfeld.

Fanon, F. 1952 (translated 1967). *Black Skin, White Masks.* Grove Press, N.Y.

Fine, M. 1991. *Framing Dropouts: Notes on the Politics of an Urban Public High School.* New York: SUNY Press.

Fine, M. 1993. "[Ap] parent Involvement: Reflections on Parents, Power and Urban Schools]" in *Teachers College Record* 94(4): 682–710.

Federici, S., Caffenttzis, G. & Alidou, O. 2000. A Thousand Flowers: Social Struggles against Structural Adjustment in African Universities. Trenton, NJ: Africa World Press.

Foucault, M. 1980. *Power/Knowledge: Selected Interviews, 1972–77.* C. Gordon, (ed.). Brighton: Harvester Press.

Gandhi, L. 1998. *Postcolonial Theory: A Critical Introduction.* Columbia University Press: New York and Chichester, West Sussex.

Giroux, H. 1983. *A Theory of Resistance in Education: Pedagogy for the Opposition.* South Hadley, Massachusetts: Bergin and Harvey.

Ghosh, R. 1996. *Redefining Multicultural Education.* Toronto: Harcourt Brace.

Goldstein, L. 1994. "Achieving a Multicultural Curriculum: Conceptual, Pedagogical, and Structural Issues." *Journal of General Education* 43(2): 102–16.

Hall, S. 1987. "Minimal Selves." In *Identity: The Real Me.* London: The Institute of Contemporary Arts. pp. 44–6.

Hilliard, A. 1992. "Why Pluralize the Curriculum" *Educational Leadership.* 49(4): 12–15.

Hatcher, R. 1998. "Social Justice and the Politics of School Effectiveness and Improvement." *Race, Ethnicity and Education* 1(2): 267–289.

Heneveld, Ward and Helen Craig. 1996. *Schools Count: World Bank Project Designs and the Quality of Primary Education in Sub-Saharan Africa.* Washington, D.C.: World Bank.

Houston, B. 1985. "Gender Freedom and the Subtleties of Sexist Education." *Educational Theory* 35(4): 359–369.

Hutchful, E. 1996. "Ghana: 1983–1994" In P. Engberg-Pedersen, P. Gibbon, P. Raikes & L. Udsholt (eds.). *Limits of Adjustment in Africa.* London: Villiers Publications.

Jones, P. W. 1992 *World Bank Financing of Education: Lending, Learning, and Development.* London and New York: Routledge.

Konadu-Agyemang, K (ed.). *IMF and World Bank Programs in Africa: A critical appraisal of Ghana's program, 1983–1999.* Aldershot, Hampshire, and U.K.: Ashgate International.

Kwapong, A. and B. Lesser (eds.). 1989. *Capacity Building and Human Resource Development in Africa.* Halifax: Lester Pearson Institute for International Development.

Lawuyi, T. 1991. Personal communication on: "Maintaining the Infrastructure of Development for Africa." Received at the annual meeting of the Canadian Association of African Studies, York University, Toronto, Canada.

Martin, J. R. 1982. "Excluding Women from the Educational Realm." *Harvard Educational Review* 52: 133–148.

Martin, J. R. 1981. "Sophie and Emile: A Case Study of Sex Bias in the History of Educational Thought." *Harvard Educational Review* 51(3): 357–372.

May, S. 1999. "Critical Multiculturalism and Cultural difference: Avoiding Essentialism." In S. May (ed.). *Critical Multiculturalism: Rethinking Multicultural and Antiracist Education.* Farmer: London., pp. 11–41.

McCarthy, C. 1990. *Race and Curriculum: Social Inequality and the Theory and Politics of Difference in Contemporary Research on Schooling.* Basingstoke: Falmer Press.

Memmi, A. 1969. *The Colonizer and the Colonized.* Boston: Beacon Press.

Ministry of Education, Ghana. 1990. "Keynote Address by Mrs. Vida Yeboah, Deputy Secretary for Education at National Seminars on the Education Reform Programme." January 1990. Accra.

Moock, P. and W. Harbison. 1988. *Education in Sub-Saharan Africa: Policies for Adjustment, Revitalization, and Expansion.* Washington, D.C.: The World Bank.

Morgan, K. A. 1996. "Freeing the Children: The Abolition of Gender: Two Instructive Anecdotes." In. A. Diller, B. Houston, and K. P. Morgan. (Eds). *The Gender Question in Education: Theory, Pedagogy and Practice.* Boulder, Co.: Westview Press, pp. 41- 49.

Nelson, J.M. 1999. Reforming health and education: the World Bank, the IDB, and complex institutional change. Washington, DC: Overseas Development Council; Baltimore, MD: The Johns Hopkins University Press.

Nsiah-Peprah, Y. 1998. "Ghana's Educational Reform." *Ghana Review International* 052, June. pp. 8–9.

Nyalemegbe, K. 1997. "The Educational Reforms So far." *Daily Graphic* [Ghanaian national daily] (February 28), 7.

Orenstein, P. 1994. *School Girls: Young Women, Self Esteem and the Confidence Gap.* New York: Doubleday.

Popkewitz, T. S. 1998. "Restructuring of Social and Political Theory in Education: Foucault and a Social Epistemology of School Practices." In T. Popkewitz and M. Brennan (eds.). *Foucault's Challenge: Discourse, Knowledge and Power in Education.* New York: Teacher's College Press., pp. 3–55.

Ragwanja, P.M. 1997. "Post-Industrialism and Knowledge Production: African Intellectuals in the New International Division Labour." *CODESRIA Bulletin* 3:5–11.

Ravitch, D. 2000. *The American Reader: Words That Moved a Nation.* New York: HarperCollins.

Rich, A. 1979. "Claiming an Education." In. *On Lies, Secrets and Silence.* New York: W.W. Norton & Co.

Samoff, J. 1996. "African Education and Development: Crises, Triumphalism, Research, Loss of Vision." *Alberta Journal of Educational Research* 42: 121–147.

Shohat, E. 1992 . "Notes on the 'Post-Colonial.'" *Social Text* 31/32: 99–113.

Sleeter, C.E. (1993). How White Teachers Construct Race. In C. McCarthy & W. Crichlow (Eds.), *Race, Identity and Representation in Education* New York: Routledge, pp. 157–171.

Spivak, G.C. 1988. "Can the Subaltern Speak?." In C. Nelson and L. Grossberg (eds.), *Marxism and the Interpretation of Culture,* Macmillan Education: Basingstoke.

Tatum, B. 1992. "Talking about Race, Learning about Racism: An Application of Racial Identity Development Theory in the Classroom." *Harvard Educational Review,* 62, (1), 1–24.

Taylor, C. 1994. "The Politics of Recognition." In A. Guttman (ed.). *Multiculturalism: Examining the Politics of Recognition.* Princeton: Princeton University Press. pp. 25–74.

Tedla, E. 1995. *Sankofa: African Thought and Education.* New York: Peter Lang.

wa Thiong'o, N. 1986. *Decolonizing the Mind.* London: James Carrey.

Willis, P. 1977. *Learning to Labour.* Farnborough: Saxon House.

Willis, P. 1983. "Cultural Production and Theories of Reproduction." In L. Barton & S. Walker (eds.), *Race, Class and Education.* London: Croom Helm.

Wit, Hans de. (2002). *Internationalization of Higher Education in the United States of America and Europe: A Historical, Comparative, and Conceptual Analysis.* Westport, CT: Greenwood Press.

World Bank. 1988. *Education in Sub-Saharan Africa.* Washington, D.C.: The World Bank.

———. 1989. *Sub-Saharan Africa: From Crisis to Sustainable Development.* Washington, D.C.: The World Bank.

Yang, R. 2002. *Third delight: The Internationalization of Higher Education in China.* New York: London: Routledge.

Section III

African Women, Children, and Families

Chapter Eight
African Women: Re-centering the Issues for the 21st Century

Filomina Steady, Wellesley College

INTRODUCTION

The study of women and gender in Africa in the 21st century cannot escape the realities of post-colonial hegemonic domination of Africa by Europe and North America. This is expressed through the reproduction of colonial-like policies that are supported by international financial institutions and international corporate laws. The patriarchal and racialized ideologies of this new market imperialism are being sustained and reinforced by corporate globalization.

It is no surprise then that despite significant epistemological challenges to this new imperialism by post-modern scholarship, Eurocentric concepts, methodologies and paradigms continue to be applied to the study of women and gender in Africa. They remain the compelling and pervasive force responsible for presenting one-dimensional, frozen and simplified writings about women and men in Africa.

This paper examines the impact of external concepts, methodologies and paradigms in the study of gender in Africa as evidence of the influence of academic structures in enabling the exploitation of Africa. It also proposes African-centered approaches based on an understanding of African socio-cultural realities, philosophical proclivities and feminist traditions.

The aim is to develop gender-focused frameworks of analysis that can bring out the multiple and varied social locations of African women, while maintaining their specific identities and priorities and developing linkages with other women. Hopefully, this will allow for new approaches in gender research that will promote greater understanding of gender issues, gender equality, social transformation and women's empowerment.

In this regard, the paper uses historical, cultural and post-modernist analyses to argue for an emphasis on culture. It also makes a case for the relevance of oppositional discourses in the study of systematic domination. These approaches can best address and challenge both the continuities of patriarchal myths and 'tradition' and the impact of colonial patriarchy and racism as they continue to be expressed in global economic domination.

THE PERSISTENCE OF EUROCENTRIC PARADIGMS: NEW WINES IN OLD BOTTLES

Academic interests in Africa historically stemmed from the need to maintain systems of colonization and exploitation through value-maintaining ideologies that included scientific racism. Today, corporate globalization, a new and more insidious form of domination has replaced the colonial project accompanied by corresponding neo-liberal paradigms.

Concepts of the African woman continue to be central to the development of these paradigms since gender is an organizing principle in the accumulation and operation of colonial and transnational capital and in the allocation of resources and privilege. What is interesting is the way in which these paradigms continue to reproduce themselves.

The discipline of anthropology, the most influential in African Studies, had three main approaches that reinforced colonial domination and racism; Social Darwinism, structural/functionalism and "acculturation" theories. Anthropology was often linked to colonialism and anthropologists helped to develop the image of the "savage" which according to Macquet, helped to justify colonial expansion and domination (Maquet, 1964).

Many of the earlier theoretical distortions were criticized as biased, myopic and based on faulty methodologies and unreliable data. Nonetheless they became reinforced through modernization theory which promoted the notion of 'stages' of growth. Modernization theory is now rearing its ugly head through the prism of neo-liberalism, the pillar of corporate globalization. Neo-evolutionalists echo modernization theorists through their proclivity for dichotomies.

Conceptual frameworks applied to Africa are often presented in Eurocentric-oriented dichotomies of rural/urban, formal/informal, traditional/modern, developed/underdeveloped and so forth. Whatever the division, Africa always ended up on the lower rung of the social evolutionary ladder and in methodological schemes of classification.

The equilibrium model of the British school of structuralism-function-alism also had a colonial *raison d'etre*. It provided analyses of "tribal" law and order so that the "natives" could be effectively governed through the policy of "indirect rule." This policy was in effect quite misleading since the British established a number of "warrant chiefs" and "district commission-ers" that served as puppets of the British colonial government.

The equilibrium model mystified reality and regarded colonialism as a given (Owosu, 1975). It also ignored the destructive consequences of three centuries of the trans-Atlantic slave trade involving more than 20 million Africans (Galt and Smith, 1976). Structuralism/functionalism continues to be relevant through the essentializing tendencies of globalization, a new form of colonization. The colonial economy has been replaced by a "new and improved" international colonial system whose structure and function depends on domination by a single functioning market controlled by the North. Today, neo-liberal paradigms justify globalization in much the same way as their antecedents, namely social Darwinism, modernization theory and structural/functionalism justified colonialism. Liberal-oriented inter-national relations studies privilege Western political institutions within a global political system dominated by Western capital and patriarchal ide-ologies (Pettman, 1996).

The "acculturation" model found mostly in studies of social change in Africa is not much different. It assumes the inevitability of assimilation to Western norms, values and lifestyles as a result of contact with the West. Seldom is the reverse shown to illustrate the impact of Africa on the West through music, religion, intellectual traditions and so forth. Acculturation studies have for the most part been concerned with what Magubane refers to as "symbols of Europeanization" and "Westernization." Such symbols are measured by European attire, occupations, education and income and have resulted in the inferiorization of African culture, values and esthet-ics. Because colonialism was ignored, these studies also ignored the lack of free choice and decision-making and the role of coercion in the pro-cess of acculturation. In effect, colonialism not only blocked indigenous processes of decision-making, it also destroyed indigenous processes of knowledge generation. The result is a form of scientific colonialism sus-tained by scientific racism. Historical studies were no less Eurocentric and racist. Africa was presented as having no history, no civilization and no culture. Studies of the classical period have consistently denied the con-tributions of Africans to Egyptian civilization and to the civilizations of ancient Greece.[1]

Most of the themes of social science research fashioned by colonial con-quest, imperialistic designs or neo-liberal motivations have also influenced gender studies and the feminist discourse. With the exception of Boserup, whose analysis was a critique of the gender bias in economic development (Boserup, 1970) modernization theory tends to see African women at a lower stage of development (read evolution) compared to women of the West; structuralism-functionalism imposes a functional explanation in the study of gender relations that is essentialist in nature. Acculturation studies have been replaced by "women in development" or "gender in development" studies which seek to "integrate African women in development" by making them more like Western women.

COUNTER-HEGEMONIC DISCOURSES

Post-colonial and post- modern discourses are providing a revisionist examination of epistemologies and paradigms that justify Euro-centric hegemonic control. They are challenging and reframing many of the philosophical and theoretical underpinnings that are derived from a strongly positivistic, universalizing and evolutionary tradition of Western scholarship. They are concerned with the historical and modern imperatives of the destructive global political economy controlled by the Global North. It is within this trajectory that gender research in Africa can yield the best results.

Eurocentric paradigms can lead to a justification of hegemonic policies. It can also provide and justify an abstract mapping of systems of stratification, rather than a more profound interrogation of the very institutions that determine such lines and parameters of social inquiry. The widespread poverty among women in Africa requires an understanding of the construction of social inequality at the global level which privileges some countries and its men and women,(primarily among groups in the North) at the expense of others, notably in the South.

Revisionist historiography and the work of Diop, Bernal, Asante, UNESCO, Black Studies programs and Afro-centric paradigms are challenging the tenacity of scientific racism posing as scholarship. Revisionist historians, economists and other social scientists focusing on the impact of the international political economy on Africa have made significant contributions in challenging the scientific colonialism and racism inherent in Eurocentric scholarship.

Rodney's *How Europe Underdeveloped Africa* was a major milestone in this development and has been reinforced by dependency theorists. Their counter-hegemonic discourses provide a basis for understanding how and why the underdevelopment of Africa has continued and how it has become intensified through corporate globalization (Rodney, 1981;

Amin, 1974; 1997; Bernal, 1987; Asante, 1990; Amadiume, 1997; Fall, 1999; Pheko, 2002). Corporate globalization, supported by neo-liberal paradigms, is the process that directs the market with the aim of ensuring the unfettered flow of transnational capital. In this process, nation states are rendered powerless through laws that protect multinational coopera- tion and that are regulated by the World Trade Organization. Interna- tional financial institutions such as the World Bank and the IMF impose conditionalities of Structural Adjustment Programs designed to promote macro-economic stability through loans that stifle the economic growth of countries of the South. The result is a reverse resource flow thought debt servicing of at least 14 billion U.S. dollars a year from Africa to the affluent nations in the North. This is greater than the amount received in *real* international aid. Corporate globalization is increasing marginaliza- tion of African countries in the global economy, a process that transcends gender but that has gender implications. Globalization has a compounded effect on women because of certain structural disadvantages in the global and national division of labor and inequalities in the distribution of assets and power.

FEMINISTS OF AFRICA AND THE SOUTH CHALLENGE EUROCENTRIC PARADIGMS

The Association of African Women for Research and Development (AAWORD) was among the earliest women's organizations of the South to adopt a critical approach to research and to challenge Eurocentric para- digms from a feminist and post-colonial perspective. As early as the mid 70s, it called for the de-colonization of research and established a critical gender research agenda. It also has a major research agenda on globaliza- tion (Fall, 1999). In the mid 80s, following the lead of AAWORD, The Development Alternatives for Women in a New Era (DAWN), a research organization of women of the South also challenged the destructive neo-lib- eral model of development and its impact on women of the South.

Throughout the 80s and 90s feminist scholars of color in the South and North led an intellectual movement that challenged essentialist notions of womanhood and insisted on recognizing and interrogating difference. Crucial to this task was the need to understand how the social location of women is determined by race, ethnicity, class, status and access to privilege. Those at the lower end of the scale face powerlessness, exclusion, despair and vulnerabilities. Such constructions of social inequality confer power on some at the expense of others (Steady, 1981; Sen and Grown, 1986; Essed, 1990; Mohanty, 1991; Imam, 1997).

Methodological challenges in investigating gender

There are some fundamental assumptions in investigation of gender that do not fit the African reality, even when controlling for African diversity. One is the belief in the universal subordination of women. Another is the separation of the public and private spheres into gendered spheres that gave men an advantage by participating in the public sphere. From this analysis followed studies seeking to explain asymmetrical relations between men and women.

If one is to believe the universal subordination argument, then one has to ignore the ways in which social location based on race, ethnicity, class, color and so forth confers power and privilege. Furthermore, one has to question the sensitivity of the research tools used to investigate "subordination" and also the methodological approaches used to apply it cross-culturally. The "universal subordination of women" argument forces us to settle for the highly contested notion that "biology is destiny" and to ask the following questions: Whose biology? Whose destiny? Are all female biologies socially constructed the same way? What if they come in different colors? What if they are stunted by poverty and malnutrition? What if they are subject to trafficking like a commodity? What if they cannot carry a fetus to full term because of poor health?

Similarly, if one accepts that gender is a metaphor for relations of power, how do we define power? Do all men have power? Do some women have power? How are the people with the most power socially constructed? In many African societies, power is not only vested in political organizations. Women can derive power from their position in religious systems, in female secret societies such as the Sande of Sierra Leone and Liberia as well as through their roles as mothers, especially when the society is matrilineal and has matrifocal ideologies.

The post-modernist challenges of the 80s by feminist scholars of the South included serious critiques of methodologies, which questioned the right of Western feminists to assume dominance on feminist discourses. They also questioned their essentializing proclivities without regard to race, nationality and so forth. Mohanty, following others, also questioned the production of "Third World Women" as a homogeneous category in Western feminist texts and as subaltern subjects (Mohanty, 1985). A major critique along this line also centered on the essentialist proclivity of lumping all women in one basket without clarifying who is being spoken about and who is speaking for whom, or who has greater credibility in framing the issue (Nnaemeka, 1998).

Problems of framing are also problematic when filtered through the racist and sexist biases. For example, Narayan, writing on women of India challenges the tendency to use so called "cultural" explanations of practices like sati and dowry murders in India while ignoring murders due to domestic violence in the United States. This has led to the visibility of dowry murder in India and to the comparative invisibility of domestic violence murders in the United States (Narayan, 1997, 95).

While not condoning harmful traditional practices with patriarchal origins, nevertheless genital surgical interventions in Africa have been over-sensationalized. African women are presented as savages or damaged victims worthy of nothing better than scorn. At the same time, harmful plastic surgery to reconstruct healthy vaginas, breasts and other body parts in the West are ignored. Also ignored, is the fact that they are also responding to cultural dictates that define the ideology of womanhood. Western plastic surgery, as Foucault would put it, is an example of "docile bodies" succumbing to the coercive pressures of Western patriarchal culture. (Foucault, 1992).

AFRICAN WOMEN AND THE "GENDER" PROBLEMATIQUE

The term "gender" is a highly contested concept when applied to Africa. "Gender" has become the main focus of Western feminist discourse during the second wave of feminism. Like other systems of thought it has been exported to the South as a concept, an analytical tool and as a policy initiative. The domination of Western concepts and terminologies has thus become apparent in the term "gender." It is well established in development circles of the United Nations which in turn influences the agenda and budget of national governments and even academic research.

In 1981, I pointed out in the introduction to the book *The Black Woman Cross-Culturally* that within a racist political/economic hegemony, white women can become primary oppressors. It is now widely accepted that women are a non-essentialist category and represent diverse groups with different social locations. "Gender" can therefore mean different things to different people since it carries the ideologies of the socio-cultural context in which it is constructed.

Without doubt, the term "gender" carries a Western bias. It tends to be myopic, inventive, and can obscure other differences. Because it is Western, it reveals white Western middle class biases and obscures other differences based on race, class, ethnicity, religion, sexuality and so forth. In this regard, it fails to recognize the role of women themselves in other structures of oppression.

"Gender" is analogous to difference but contains within it notions of inequality and is often viewed as a metaphor representing relations of power. However, analysis of power is often restricted to male/female power relations only, ignoring power relations based on race, class, ethnicity, age, nationality and so forth. Thus the various ways in which gender has been used, namely, as a basis organizing principle of society; as a heuristic tool, as a crucial site for the application of dichotomous models and as an indicator of progress in the development process have to be questioned.

Furthermore, the term "gender" tends to represent a proclivity towards dichotomous models that do not often fully represent the African reality, although exceptions can be found. For example, a study of cultural boundaries and social interactions in Africa has argued that trans-social and transactional cultural flows are inherently gendered and that gender is a crucial site of intersection between "inside" and "outside" (Grosz-Ngate and Kobole, eds. 1999, p.8).

TWO MAJOR EXAMPLES CHALLENGING THE CONCEPT OF "GENDER" IN AFRICA

African societies are complex and recognize exceptions to general normative rules. They use other concepts that convey a cyclical ordering of social life in addition to oppositional and hierarchical ones or on ones based on biological classification. For an example, changes in the lifecycle can alter women's status so that post-menopausal women can assume political functions and serve as elders and advisers on the same basis as men.

Similarly, female ancestors can share equal status with male ancestors. Moreover, "third genders," "agendered and trans-gendered entities," and "alternative genders" have been discovered in many parts of the non-Western world. In Africa, institutions such as 'woman marriage' and the ambiguity of the gender of some deities have challenged the dichotomous model of the West.

Major challenges of the term 'gender' have come from African women, the most celebrated of whom are Amadiume and Oyewummi. Amadiume's book, *Male Daughters, Female Husbands* was ground breaking in deconstructing the word "gender" in the Igbo context. In her analysis of sex-gender distinctions, she exposes what she described as the racism and ethnocentrism of earlier studies of Igbo society by Western scholars. She convincingly demonstrates how misleading biological categories can be in studying sex and gender since either sex can assume socially viable roles as male or female.

Oyewumi in *The Invention of Women: Making An African Sense of Western Gender Discourse* further challenges the heavy reliance of Western scholarship on what is seen: "world view" rather than what is perceived through other senses: "world sense." She argues that although "gender" is deemed to be socially constructed, biology itself is socially constructed and therefore inseparable from the social. Hence the separation between "sex" and "gender" is superficial since "sex" itself has elements of construction. She insists that this "biologization" inherent in the Western articulation of social difference is by no means universal. Through imperialism it has been imposed on other cultures resulting in the imposition of the term "gender" which, being socially constructed, may not have existed at all in some societies.

She argues that "Gender" has become important in Yoruba studies not as an artifact of Yoruba life, but because Yoruba life, past and present, has been translated into English to fit the Western pattern of body-reasoning. This pattern is one in which gender is omnipresent, the male the norm, and the female the exception; it is a pattern in which power is believed to inhere in maleness in and of itself. It is a pattern that is not grounded in evidence (Oyewumi, p. 30).

Oyewumi agues that in the written discourse of the Yoruba, gender is privileged over seniority only because of Western dominance in the conceptualization of research problems and in social theory. In Yoruba society, seniority takes precedence over gender and many Yoruba such as *oba* or *alafin* nouns are gender-free. The creation of "woman" as a category was one of the very first accomplishments of the colonial state since in pre-colonial societies, male and female had multiple identities that were not based on anatomy. "For females, colonization was a two-fold process of racial inferiorization and gender subordination" (Oyewumi, p. 124).

THE NEED FOR ALTERNATIVE AFRICAN-FOCUSED METHODOLOGIES

There is a need to critique and challenge the Eurocentric models in the study of women in Africa. Since most models are linked to political conquest through colonialism and corporate conquest through globalization, oppositional discourses inherent in various forms of Marxism, post-structuralism, post-colonialism and post-modernism are still relevant to African gender research.

Such approaches will of necessity have to include one or more of the following: a historical perspective, a holistic perspective, multidimensionality, multiple time frames, multiple levels of analysis, multiple identities and realities, relational and dynamic contexts, comparative methods, oral history, life history and so forth.

The need to link theory and praxis is essential. Given the empirical reality of poverty, economic exploitation and marginality, theory for the majority of Africans is a luxury. The thrust towards praxis will expose and centralize invisibility, voicelessness and autogenic social processes need to act and change retrograde developments. It will also help to reconcile universal and post-modernist tensions.

AFRICAN-FOCUSED AND GENDER-SENSITIVE APPROACHES

One of the major constraints to gender research in Africa is the weak data base and the lack of a critical mass of gender researchers due to the low priority given to social science research and to the brain drain. The challenge is greater than the resources and available capacity. For example, African research on gender has to develop methodologies for criticisms and revisionist endeavors as well as methodologies for alternative research. The same standards for data gathering procedures that will satisfy the basic scientific requirements of validity, reliability and replicability have to be applied. Added to this will be new methods related to language and to indigenous systems of thought so that the framing of gender will be determined within the context of the relationship of language to culture.

Crucial to the redefining of an alternative approach to research from an African perspective will be the following:

- Policy-orientation
- Viewpoint and value orientations
- Time orientation
- Geographical orientation
- Levels of analysis
- An emphasis on culture.

All of these factors will be conditioned by the type problem to be investigated, the kinds of data available, research instruments to be employed and the need to prioritize the research problems to be investigated. (Steady, 1977).

Given the diversity of Africa, theoretical applications have to be developed through dynamic, multi-dimensional and heterogeneous methodological approaches and adjusted for contextual validity. However, it is quite legitimate to speak of an African perspective or an African reality even if only one or two African countries are indicated. This type of typological projection can become a valid heuristic tool. When one speaks of Eurocentric models, one does not have to indicate which particular European country or people is being referred to.

POLICY ORIENTATION

Western scholarship places a high value on theorizing and theory-building at the expense of pragmatism and relevance. Hence higher prestige is given to theoreticians. For Africa, there are many economic and social problems, not least of which is its dependency on the West and its marginalization through globalization, which theory cannot solve. Lack of interest in practical problems has been shown to lead to an insensitivity to the people studied and to an emphasis on professional advancement by the researcher. Over 40 years ago, a European scholar Galtung in referring to what he called "scientific colonialism" compared the researcher who extracts data for professional profit to the colonialist who exports the resources out of Africa. In the following analogy, he demonstrates a parallel between the two systems of extraction and processing:

> . . . to export data about the country to one's own country for processing into manufactured goods, such as books and articles. . . . is essentially similar to what happens when raw materials are exported at a low price and reimported as manufactured goods at a very high cost. The most important, most rewarding and most difficult phase of the process takes place abroad (Galtung, 1967; p. 296).

Critique of Donor-Driven Research

Given the ideological nature of development policies in Africa that are often driven by the neo-liberal agenda and the dictates of globalization the research agenda on gender tends to be determined by external priorities and policy orientations that reinforce the re-colonization of African social science. Donor-driven research can also undermine academic programs if the faculty is motivated by the pursuit of funds for research especially in light of the economic difficulties of the continent and the low salaries of faculty. African researchers have to be critical of donor-driven and donor-sponsored research.

Particular attention must be paid to various projects sponsored by international donor agencies and to certain types of externally-designed research. Some research on health care, nutrition, agricultural production, migration and education may be designed to promote neo-liberal policies related to making African markets and labor more accessible to exploitation.

External gender research priorities can also center on concerns about fertility regulation, female circumcision, rather than to the global economic forces and liberalization policies that result in increasing malnutrition and poverty. Nor is enough attention being given to the dumping of guns, other lethal weapons, drugs, pornographic material and dirty technologies in Africa. Little interest is also shown in the illegal trafficking of young girls from Africa to Europe to be used as prostitutes and domestic servants under slavery-like conditions. The destructive impact of debt, structural adjustment policies, unemployment, export-oriented industries, sex tourism and so forth are often also overlooked.

Social Impact and Basic Research

Social impact research is critical. A number of studies can be conducted as intensive micro-level studies for purposes of evaluating the impact of "development projects in small communities." Although a number of international projects have an evaluation component built in, such an evaluation need not have local input and may reflect the vested interest of certain interest groups abroad. It is important that evaluative research be given a high priority by African social scientists.

Micro-level research can also be conducted as basic research that can have policy implications. Intensive research, using both qualitative and quantitative methods can be most useful and yield relevant information from which valid conclusions can be drawn. Intensive social surveys can provide useful information about food distribution, income distribution and demographic changes and can provide a good profile of the health status of a community. For example, it can lead to a clearer evaluation of the fertility rates in a given country by taking cognizance of factors such as infertility, infant mortality and mortality from the HIV/AIDS epidemic as well as fertility. Governments will then be presented with realistic projections on which to base a population policy.

Viewpoint and Value Orientation

The researcher is not a neutral observer. He or she brings existentialist limitations to the scholarly endeavor. The values and biases of the researcher are inevitably injected into the research. A researcher has a certain obligation to become involved in the realities and problems of the 'subjects' under study. Research in Africa has to be geared towards a certain degree of involvement and inter-subjectivity.

Indeed the aim should be to contribute to improving the life of the people studied rather than to exploit them for professional advancement. Very often there is an in-difference and a patronizing attitude to the "subjects" of research, especially when the researcher is a foreigner with vested professional interests outside of Africa. Very few researchers bring back to the community the results of their study or give anything back. The subject/object or insider/outsider dichotomy is increasingly being challenged by both Western and scholars from the South. Most scholars of the South now insist on the study of culture from the inside by an insider.

The overriding problem facing Africa today is that of the destruction of African societies by forces of corporate globalization resulting in poverty, illiteracy and disease. The major mission of a scholarly endeavor in the social sciences should be the elimination of the conditions that produce massive poverty and human misery among the masses of African people. The new researcher has to be involved in improving the well being of African people.

Involvement would necessitate abandoning the subject/object dichotomy of social science to one of "intersubjectivity" more akin to an indigenous model with elements of advocacy, protest and social engineering. Such approaches will also of necessity be multidisciplinary, policy-oriented as well as participatory both on the side of the researcher and of the people being studied. The aim would be to demystify the research process itself since data gathering procedures will be linked to problem solving and can be participatory.

Quantitative and mathematical research instruments designed for use in more technologically complex societies may have limited relevance when applied to Africa. They may also be more prone to bias due to the variability of the research capacity and data base. Research instruments, data-collecting and data-analyzing procedures have to be sensitively designed and made uncomplicated to encourage participation and involvement and to have practical relevance. Research methodology from an African perspective has to be partisan- i.e. dedicated to the progress and advancement of the African people. An appropriate value orientation would lead to research formulations and projects that aim to be action and policy oriented, problem solving and focused on the improvement of the African condition.

Time Orientation

Emphasis should be given to an analysis of social processes on a continuum that will involve the past, the present and the future. A historical perspective will be essential in understanding the role of conquest and colonization in shaping the themes and trajectory of research in Africa as well as in developing new forms of colonization such as corporate globalization. Urbanization and social change will be seen, not as inevitable processes of modernization but as a distortion of African indigenous development through economic domination.

The African worldview encompasses dimensions of the past, present and future. Stated simply, the dead, the living and those yet to be born are essential for maintaining cosmological balance. This balance has been destabilized and has important gender implications leading to a loss of social status for women not only in the political and economic spheres but also in the realm of ritual and religion.

Geographical Orientation: Incorporating the African Diaspora

Africa is no longer confined to its geographical entity. The Transatlantic slave trade led to the dispersal of Africans on a massive scale. Today, Africans move as migrants, refugees and international civil servants to all parts of the world. The study of Africa must now include "Global Africa" in all its historical, socio-cultural, political and economic dimensions. In a book I edited recently, this concept was central to an analysis of Black Women of Africa and the African Diaspora within the current international political economy. I advanced the notion of African Feminism as a theory and praxis for the liberation of African women from gender-based discrimination compounded by racism, the legacy of colonialism, and the injustices of the international political economy.[2]

Levels of Analysis

A useful orientation in terms of level of analysis is one that combines both macro-and micro-levels of analysis within a given national or international boundary. This orientation can be used to demonstrate the larger systems of interaction that exist between the rural area and the urban area. Thus, rural and urban areas can be seen as systems in a larger framework rather than as fossilized units presented in monographs. This perspective of rural/urban interaction is missing in most studies of Africa. The interconnectedness of phenomena across broad spatial domains has also been absent from most studies of African urbanization.

Orientations that show dynamic interactions rather than atomized unitary systems are essential to understanding the fluidity of the African social situation requiring linkages among the political, economic and cultural systems as well as geographical linkages between rural and urban areas and even between countries and sub-regions. This orientation will also facilitate pan–African research and the strengthening of African research networks designed to build capacity for indigenous research in which similar problems can be examined in a number of countries in Africa.

A continuum must also be maintained between the macro-and micro level and the holistic and particular. In our attempt to understand the position of African societies within the international economic system and the historical conditions that have shaped the relationship of inequality between the rich and the poor nations, a macro-level perspective of global dimensions is a useful one.

Here we will need to re-examine neo-Marxist methodology in the context of Africa. Its theoretical and political significance as it affects social science research ought to be given greater attention. This will lead to an understating of how forms of imperialist domination affect a country in terms of means of production, property ownership and the relationship between class, gender and the family.

We need to study the relationship of imported ideologies, religions, educational systems and other aspects of the superstructure to the oppression of the African masses. The South has produced eminent scholars who have articulated this view. The research efforts of African scholars must continue to study the theoretical and political implication of oppositional discourses and methodologies in the context of Africa.

An Emphasis on Culture

Culture is a collective pattern of living that conveys the norms and values of society that is handed down from generation to generation. It is both dynamic and resilient and has positive, negative and neutral attributes. The study of African cultures have to include an inquiry into the continuities of gender discrimination and to determine where the cultural, historical, gendered and racial markers uphold, distort and undermine the "real" and the "authentic."

Because culture represents routine behavior that carries norms and values of a society, they are often not easily changed. Okeke has argued against the tendency to regard gender discrimination inherent in cultural practices as being acceptable because it is the "tradition." She shows how patriarchal continuities, even when they contain contradictions can support claims of the rightness of tradition.

For example, the contradictions between statutory and customary law and the weaknesses in statutory law can lead to the strengthening of traditional justifications that still privilege men in relation to property rights, inheritance laws, etc. This can result in "relations of power which keep in place an inequitable social structure that privileges the dominant gender" (Okeke, 2000, p. 6)

Essed in her study of gendered racism in Europe has shown how everyday racism is the interweaving of racism in the routine of day to day life, in a way that makes racial injustices seem normal and a part of what can be expected. She notes that the focus on everyday manifestation of systemic inequality extends outside the field of race relations as well. This contributed to granting "the everyday generic meaning, everyday inequalities, everyday sexism" (Essed, 2002, p. 210).

An examination of the role of gender in the socio-cultural construction of hierarchies and hierarchy sustaining structures has to continue as an important research agenda for African social science. For example, the gender implications of the legacies of colonialism, apartheid and racism have only been systematically studied within the last 20 years. We still do not have comprehensive studies of the role of gender as a central aspect of armed conflict, civil wars and the erosion of the African state.

Gender-based analyses are also important in our understanding of the patriarchal myth which is being sustained by forces of globalization that privilege men in cases of privatization of land, liberalization of markets, etc. and can lead to alliances among men that ordinarily would be enemies on the basis of East/West, North/South and White/Non-White divisions.

The idea of culture has valuable and positive assets that provide effective models for gender research that can lead to the empowerment and advancement of African women. African feminism as defined in 1981 outlined the value of African women in the ideological, institutional and customary realms. Women's power bases are partly derived from cultural values that stress the potency of a female principle governing life and reproduction though motherhood and the centrality of children. Women can also control political and ritual spaces.

Women's indigenous groups can provide important leveraging mechanisms for women and are instrumental in promoting sustainable development projects. So rather than dismiss African cultures as archaic, we need to conduct more studies using culture as the paradigmatic framework that has the potential of producing action-oriented research capable of transforming society and empowering women.

THE CONTINUING RELEVANCE OF OPPOSITIONAL DISCOURSES: THE POLITICAL ECONOMY PARADIGM

The major problem confronting most women in Africa today is poverty. This compounds their lack of access to strategic resources, facilities, basic literacy and economic and political decision-making. In addition, they are faced with health and nutritional problems, including the HIV/AIDS epidemic and deteriorating environments that can no longer sustain them. In order to fully comprehend and address the deepening poverty in Africa, a comprehensive study is needed of the causes and consequences of poverty and its chronic and protracted nature in the African context. Analysis of the conditions and processes involved in the production, reproduction of poverty and its structural nature must be conducted in its spatial and temporal context as well as from a cross-cultural perspective within Africa.

Globalization facilitates the movement of capital across national boundaries and is characterized by a deepening of markets across borders aided by communication technologies, international laws and the monitoring role of the World Trade Organization. It affects countries differently and uses traditional institutions, the informal labor market and women's labor to facilitate the process of forging a 'single market' dominated by the North.

While some countries are experiencing growth and market integration, others, including many in the South, especially Africa are being marginalized. The term "a market apartheid" has been applied to this process. Inequality has increased between and within countries. Even the World Bank, one of the sponsors of globalization paints a dismal picture.

"One sixth of the world's population produce 78% of the world's goods and services and get 78% of the world's income, an average of $70 per day. Three-fifths of the world's people in the six poorest countries receive 6% of the world's income; less than $2 a day. However, this poverty goes beyond income. While 7 out of 1,000 children die before age 5 in high-income countries, more than 90 out of 1,000 die in low-income countries."[3]

The Human Development Report of 1999 showed an increase in inequality between countries. Within the past decade, the number of individuals in Eastern Europe and Central Asia living on less than U.S. $1 rose to 13 million. The corresponding number of 35 million in South Asia and in sub-Saharan Africa, the number actually tripled to 39 million.[4] One can only imagine the gender implications when compounded with gender-based discrimination. Macro economic policies often makes gender disaggregated impacts difficult to assess because of the way in which they are conceptualized and the focus on official policy rather than the realities on the ground.

The World Bank figures are even higher and show that between 1987 and 2000, the number of people living on $1 or less (65 cents) a day increased by more than 80 million in sub-Saharan Africa. According to Dembele, "One of the most dramatic impacts of trade and investment liberalization in Africa has been the weakening, even the collapse of many African states. Among the factors that contributed to this collapse are the huge revenue losses, resulting from sweeping trade and investment liberalization" (Dembele, 2002, p. 78). African countries experience huge losses in revenues from import taxes from which they derive 90% of their fiscal revenues. The losses have meant greater dependence of up to 80% of their budget on external sources.

In spite of these grim realities, the policy preference for the international community controlled by the North and the IMF and World Bank, the major international financial institutions is to develop strategies for poverty reduction within the context of the market and the instruments of liberalization and privatization. The mantra is "trade not aid."

Free trade is now well recognized as being anything but free, and trade liberalization is viewed as a major contributor to poverty in Africa with serious gender implications. According to Dembele, sub-Saharan Africa is the only region in the world where poverty has steadily increased during the last two decades and all development indicators reveal a continuing deterioration. Trade liberalization is a major contributor to this human crisis.

The political economy approach offers one of the best explanatory models for full understanding of the political economy of African countries that is shaping gender relations. According to Pheko, multilateral financial institutions are forcing insidious policies of liberalization and globalization, market ascendancy and the diminished roles of the state, that have been unsuccessful in industrialized countries. She urges African women to be aware of the dangers of trade liberalization and resist it.

The role of gender research and gender researchers as activists in this process is crucial since privatization and the private sector are notoriously gender biased. The public sector has been the most advantageous for women's formal sector employment but Structural Adjustment Policies mandate retrenchment in the public sector and cut backs in the social sector, such as health and education, that are of extreme importance to women.

"As women, we need to continue applying a gender analysis to all trade agreements and globalization processes. The human rights analysis should also be applied while strong South/South dialogue among women should be promoted, especially regarding the impact of international trade and macroeconomic policies, in particular, their formulation and implementation. African women should also call into question, the liberalization and globalization agenda by building civil society's understanding of the issues and by bringing about mass mobilization in a global, regional and coordinated fashion" (Pheko, 2002, p. 105).

CONCLUSION

African feminist inquiries have articulated the strong link between Western neo-liberalism and European domination that are implicated in colonial oppression and corporate globalization and bolstered by racist ideologies and institutions. There is a need for a revisionist analysis of external concepts, canonical theories, methodologies and paradigms that have distorted gender studies in Africa. There is also a need to critically examine gendered readings of mainstream research of the West in the fields of science, history, the social sciences and the academy from an African perspective. There is also a need for an African feminism that will reflect the paradigmatic complexity of gender research in Africa.

African feminism, as I define a brand of it, operates within a global political economy in which sexism cannot be isolated from the larger political economy and economic processes responsible for the exploitation and oppression of both men and women. The result is a kind of feminism that is transformative in human and social rather than in personal, individualistic and sexist terms (Steady, 1981). Given this orientation, the following are among important research questions to be asked.

- How does an academic context shaped by the injustices of the Transatlantic Slavery, colonialism and imperialism and justified by racist and sexist stereotypes and myths about Africa and Africans, affect gender research in Africa?
- How relevant is the Eurocentric search for universal women's oppression when other forms of oppression based on race, nationalism, ethnicity, class and so forth and the global economy threaten the very existence of most Africans?
- How do the pressures of globalization and the market economy impact on social institutions such as marriage, the family, male/female relations and positive and negative cultural practices?
- How has the donor community influenced the research agenda of Africa and distorted African realities based on preconceived assumptions and biases?
- How do we deepen our understanding of the importance of matrifocal traditions of Africa of which Diop wrote and the dynamic interplay between these traditions and patriarchal systems, especially the modernization of patriarchal domination through globalization?
- How is the link between women's roles in production and reproduction significant in understanding the continuities between the public and the private spheres in the context of a rapidly changing political economy and a socio-cultural crisis of major proportions?
- How are gender relations in the domestic sphere supporting or impeding women's decision-making and control over their lives?
- To what extent are African women's bodies becoming commercialized, and a potential target for trafficking and violence, in the age of globalization?
- How is the HIV/AIDS epidemic affecting notions of sexuality, fertility, gender relations, well-being and collective survival in Africa?

NOTES

1. See Diop, 1974 and Bernal, 1987, and Asante, 2000, for challenges to these positions.
2. See Steady, 1981, 1987; 2000; 2001; 2002).

3. World Bank, 2000, *World Development Indicators*, 2000, New York, OUP.
4. UNDP, 1999, *Human Development Report*, New York. UNDP.

REFERENCES

Amadiume, I. 1987, *Male Daughters, Female Husbands: Gender and Sex in an African Society*, London, Zed Books.

Amadiume, I. 1997, *Reinventing Africa: Matriarchy, Religion and Culture*, London, Zed Books.

Amin, S. 1974, *Accumulation on a World Scale: A Critique of the Theory of Underdevelopment*, New York, Monthly Review Press.

Amin, S. 1997, *Capitalism in the Age of Globalization: The Management of Contemporary Society*, London, Zed Press.

Asante, M. 1990, *Kemet: Afrocentricity and Knowledge*, Trenton: Africa World Press.

Asante, M. 2000. *The Painful Demise of Eurocentrism*. Trenton: Africa World Press.

Bernal, M. 1987, *Black Athena: The Afroasiatic Roots of Classical Civilization*, New Brunswick, Rutgers University Press.

Boserup, E. 1970 *Women's Role in Economic Development*, London, George Allen and Urwin.

Dembele, M. 2002, 'Trade Liberalization and Poverty in sub-Saharan Africa' in F.C. Steady, ed. *Black, Women, Globalization and Economic Justice: Studies from Africa and the African Diaspora*, Rochester, Schenkman Books.

Diop, C. 1974, *The African Origin of Civilization: Myth and Reality*. Translated from French by Mercer Cook, New York, L. Hill.

Essed, Ph. 1990. *Understanding Everyday Racism: An Interdisciplinary Theory*, Newbury Park, CA. Sage.

Essed, P. 2002, 'Gendered Racism in Diasporic Locations: Opposition and the Use of Eyewitness Testimonies in Global Struggles' in F. C. Steady, ed. *Black Women, Globalization and Economic Justice: Studies from Africa and the African Diaspora*, Rochester, Schenkman Books.

Etienne, M and Leacock, E. eds. 1980, *Women and Colonization: Anthropological Perspectives*, New York, Praeger.

Fall, Y. ed. 1999, *Africa: Gender, Globalization and Resistance*, Dakar, AAWORD.

Foucault, M. 1992, *The Archeology of Knowledge and the Discourse on Language*, New York, Pantheon.

Galt, A and Smith, L. 1976, *Models and the Study of Social Change*, London, John Wiley and Sons.

Galtung, J. 1967, 'After Camelot' in I. Horowitz, ed. *The Rise and Fall of Project Camelot*, Cambridge, M.I.T. Press.

Grosz-Nagate, M and Kobole, O. eds. 1997, *Gendered Encounters: Challenging Cultural Boundaries and Social Hierarchies in Africa*, New York, Routledge.

Imam, A, Mama, A, Sow, F. eds. 1997, *Engendering African Social Sciences*, Dakar, CODESRIA

Macquet, J. 1964, 'Objectivity in Anthropology' Current Anthropology, vol. 5: 47–55.

Mohanty, C. 'Under Western Eyes' in C.Mohanty, A. Russo, L. Torres, eds. *Third World Women and the Politics of Feminism*, Bloomington and Indianapolis, Indiana University Press.

Narayan, U., 1997, 'Cross-Cultural Connections, Border-Crossings,' and 'Death by Culture: Thinking About Dowry-Murders in India and Domestic-Violence Murders in the United States' in Narayan, U. 1997, *Dislocating Cultures: Identities, Tradition and Third World Feminism*, New York, Routledge.

Nnaemeka, O. ed. 1998, *Sisterhood, Feminisms and Power: From Africa to the Diaspora*, Trenton, Africa World Press, Inc.

Okeke, P. 2000, 'Reconfiguring traditional women's rights and social status in contemporary Nigeria' in *Africa Today*, Bloomington, Winter, 2000.

Oyewumi, O. 1997, *The Invention of Women: Making an African Sense of Western Gender Discourse*. Minneapolis, University of Minnesota Press.

Owusu, M, ed. *Colonialism and Change*, Essays presented to Lucy Mair, The Hague, Mouton, 1975.

Pettman, J. 1996, *Worlding Women: A Feminist International Politics*, London, Routledge.

Pheko, M. 2002, 'Privatization, Trade Liberalization and Women's Socio-Economic Rights: Exploring Policy Alternatives' in F.C. Steady, ed. *Black Women, Globalization and Economic Justice: Studies from Africa and the African Diaspora*, Rochester, Schenkman Books.

Rodney, W. 1981, *How Europe Underdeveloped Africa*, Washington, D.C. Howard University Press.

Sen, G. and Grown, C. 1986, *Development, Crises and Alternative Visions: Third World Women's Perspectives*, New York, Monthly Review Press.

Steady, F.C. 1977, 'Research Methodology from an African Perspectives' in *Echo*, Dakar, AAWORD.

Steady, F. C. ed. 1981, *The Black Women Cross-Culturally*, Cambridge, Schenkman Publishing Company.

Steady, F.C. 1987. 'African Feminism: A Global Perspective' in R. Terborg-Penn and A. Rushing eds. *Women of the African Diaspora: An Interdisciplinary Perspective*, Washington, D.C. Howard University Press.

Steady, F.C. 2001, *Women and the Amistad Connection: Sierra Leone Krio Society*, Rochester, Schenkman Books.

Steady, F.C. ed. 2002, *Black Women, Globalization and Economic Justice: Studies from Africa and the African Diaspora*, Rochester, Schenkman Books.

U.N.D.P. 1999, *Human Development Report*, New York, U.N.D.P.

World Bank, 2000, *World Development Indicators*, 2000, New York, Oxford University Press.

Chapter Nine
African Mothers: A Case Study of Northern Ghanaian Women

Nah Dove, University of Ghana

Like their ancestors before them and the generations to come, African Mothers including Diasporan sisters, wherever their location, will either help to betray or redeem Africa knowingly or unknowingly. The ability of Mothers to make any conscious decision in this regard is tempered by the impact of European and Arab cultural imperialism, materially, mentally and spiritually. Two significant groups of Mothers who hold allegiance to their ancestors are identified. One group includes sisters of the diaspora, living outside Africa, some of whose ancestors have not lived in Africa for centuries. Their consciousness has grown from the cultural remnants of their historical legacy as descendents who arrived in Europe and the Americas at different times for different reasons ranging from enslavement and refugeeism to finding work. The other group of Mothers are indigenous to Africa practicing Traditional values and beliefs that have been handed down for millennia under continuous unbroken assault.

What happens to these Mothers in the 21st Century will have a significant effect on the integrity of cultural redemption in the African world.

To elucidate, this chapter uses some original studies and focuses on an important study of 835 rural Traditional Mothers in Ghana and some of the difficulties they encounter raising their children under western models of governance and development. A study on the struggles of disaporan Mothers shows some of the similarities in raising children in UK and US contexts that debase African humanity. Both groups of Mothers are integrally bound spiritually through their ancestral links and the desire for their children to have knowledge of their ancestors.

AN AFROCENTRIC CONCEPTUAL FRAMEWORK

The European and Arab worlds have become powerful and rich based on their historical and cultural relationship to Africa. They exploited indigenous knowledge in the interests of advancing their own societies from the time of Kemet (Ancient Egypt) until now. They took ideas of theology, literacy, urban development, architectural skills, agricultural specialization, astrological and astronomical wisdom, medical expertise, democratic governance and formalized education and so on. They forced African people to build their societies to their specifications either on the continent or off.

Prior to the conquest of Africa Motherhood and Mother centered values[1] in contrast to their low status in the west were so valuable to society that social development was centered on them. Mothers participated in the top echelon of religious, legal, medicinal, political and educative institutions. Female and male reciprocity the core of Traditional religion instituted social justice and equality the basis of their great societies. As a result of European and Arab invasion Traditional religion eroded, corrupted and went underground. Male supremacy overrode the necessary social disciplines that inspired harmony, equality and justice imposing instead anarchic social hierarchies founded on spurious arguments about the inferiority of some humans based primarily on their color, sex and social class[2]. In this work the fall of Africa is perceived as the fall of Traditional religion.

Deculturalization[3] describes the characteristics of cultural imperialism affecting African people both on and off the continent. It is historical, ancient and purposeful in assisting the transition of knowledge, resources, energy, wealth and lands to non-indigenous control. Most importantly, it facilitates the manipulation of cultural identity by demonizing indigenous Traditional religion so that ancestral respect is lost; thus resulting in confusion and chaos. Arabs conquering the north of Africa centuries ago enslaved indigenous people using religion as a tool of domination so that non-acceptance meant certain death. European enslavement led, in some cases, to stronger Nations conspiring to do their bidding in order to save themselves from annihilation. Such Nations were insured favoritism in the ensuing colonial power structures. Many of these old unjust hierarchies remain within westernized Nation states and colonial boundaries have concretized them creating the potential for and reality of interminable conflict. These Africa-wide tensions, considered past animosities harbored by "tribal" people, are instigated whenever it is politically expedient. Over the centuries indigenous people, forbidden to speak of past atrocities have borne generations of children who practice non-indigenous religion as their own accepting sometimes their subservience to other members even within their Nations.

In this regard, the role of African Mothers as central to family stability and as culture bearers is so vital to social change that if during the continuing process of deculturalization links to the ancestors are severed this can lead to self loathing and contempt for African people. The chapter brings to light the pro-activism of some indigenous Mothers who counteract this pervasiveness by maintaining their Traditional religion and some diasporan sisters who send their children to schools that affirm their African forebears in spite of the negation of Africa.

AFRICAN MOTHERS IN THE UK AND US

African Mothers (1998) honors the role of Mothering in opposition to the west's devaluation of women, in particular Mothers. The study brought to light Mothers who were aware of the children's miseducation and abuse in state schooling particularly regarding their treatment and the misrepresentation of Africa and her people in the UK and US. They voluntarily worked to challenge the system by initiating and supporting the creation of schools that revered their African ancestors. This accomplishment was regarded as a feature of "cultural unity" a concept asserting that a cultural unity exists among people of African descent traceable spiritually, materially and mentally both on and off the continent in spite of deculturalization.

In the UK Mothers who sent their children to culturally affirming schools were involved with the Supplementary school movement that began by challenging the underachievement of African descended children attending racist state schools, the root of which was traceable to the Caribbean. Mothers in the US using culturally affirming schools were linked to the Independent Black school movement whose origin was traced to the African effort to institute mass schooling in the US. These Mothers were considered part of an historical global human rights movement, challenging attempts to maintain a caste system, relegating their girls and boys to the bottom of the UK/US social order.

TRADITIONAL AFRICAN MOTHERS

This research continued the thrust of the earlier work broadening its parameters to include a study on African indigenous mothers more closely aligned to their Traditional values. They represent those indigenous people who retained the fabric of their Traditional religion refusing to submit to centuries of brutal conquest by Arabs and Europeans alike. Like their ancestors they remain devoted to their beliefs. Today there is little evidence of their past glory and there are no temples.

From as far back as the 1950s until around 1990s, anthropologists and others took an interest in studying the child upbringing practices of Traditional breastfeeding Mothers. Data revealed that Traditional infants were more advanced in their psycho-social, behavioral and physical development than European middle-class infants. Ainsworth's (1954) research in Uganda led this trend. She suggested that the advanced sensorimotor results were based on the Mothers' high standards of sensitive care in their breastfeeding practices, availability and awareness of their infants' development. The implications of these results had far reaching effects. They pointed to inadequacies in the childrearing practices of western mothers e.g., not breastfeeding, not breastfeeding on demand, ceasing breastfeeding too early, not carrying infants at all times, isolating infants during sleeping times, not attending to their needs etc., thus challenging the logic of European superiority. How could neglectful parenting produce advanced people and culture?

Studies rose to challenge these findings surmising that although Traditional infants showed advancement in their early stages of development they later regressed compared to white middleclass infants in the US and more significantly to westernizing non-Traditional African infants. Traditional Mothers were therefore seen to be cosseting their infants to produce obedient, placid dependent children for primitive life and westernized and European descended Mothers were raising less well behaved infants in preparation for technically advanced life.

No references were made to cultural and historical relations of white Mothers to African Traditional Mothers. In keeping with racist evolutionist theory aspersions were cast upon the potentiality of African children. Instead of viewing Traditional models of upbringing practices as entirely appropriate for raising children (noting urbanity and the great achievements accomplished in the past) they viewed caring Mothering skills as outcomes of primitivism. In this vein instead of viewing western models as appropriate for raising affluent white infants to dominate less affluent white people in their cultural milieu as well as members of other cultural groups globally, they viewed child neglect and bad behavior as outcomes of advanced societies.

The current view of Traditional Mothers and their upbringing practices has taken a new turn. No longer considered caring wonderful Mothers they are viewed as neglectful and ignorant. Western Mothering is now considered the epitome of parenting. This change in perspective has resulted from the west's unending manipulation through IMF, World Bank, Loans and Aid legitimizing western style Nation States in the interests of furthering western investments and profits by any means necessary. New leadership cultivated from these conditions now looks at Africa with the western eye of falsehood allowing and inviting the architects of sustained indigenous conflict over land and resources in the guise of peacemakers like NGOs, aid donors and religious bodies, to help settle the problems of the fallout.

Western models of governance and development have become synonymous with the accumulation of wealth for powerful urban, political, religious, business and professional families and the possibility (not guarantee) of having some basic needs met for some rural Traditional people. Like the white researchers of the 50s and onward western NGO personnel, aid donors and religious entities are trained to not know the history of the role of Africa in advancing the western world. Instead westerners and westernizing African men and women citing ignorance and abject poverty as resulting from the promulgation of Traditional values, beliefs and practices have produced countless studies and reports. Thus creating a perceived need for western development ranging from childcare, schools, health, dietary knowledge, hygiene, to women's rights, of which Europeans are considered the experts.

Consequently, so-called development requires the relinquishment of Traditional religion, the foundation of Indigenous Knowledge and the basis of family and Nation organization, stability and cultural unity. Set apart from other studies this research challenges the notion that western (or Arab) imperialist democracy is a panacea for global human development. The Mothers from the UK/US study bore testimony to this as they struggled to raise their girls and boys in conditions that despised their humanity, where African descended men and women were vastly overrepresented in prisons and war, underemployed, impoverished, underachievers in schools, underrepresented in universities and professional work, had lower life expectations and overrepresented in criminalized activities creating untold wealth for the weapons and drugs industry, the two greatest profit producing industries in the western world.

Development strategies presently used in Africa are considered part of a larger program of continuing destabilization, undermining indigenous religious knowledge so that allegiance is severed or weakened in preparation for full-blown New World Order control. Those who fail to abandon their beliefs will find themselves more and more isolated without access to basic needs and in this way genocide can be viewed as a natural occurrence resulting from primitiveness. Mothers are the prime targets for the success of this devil-opment program.

POVERTY

The rural Traditional Mothers in this study lived in insecure vulnerable circumstances mainly in northern Ghana. Overall, the Mothers were non-literate and lacked basic needs i.e., clean and or running water, sufficient food, paved roads, electricity, telecommunications, appropriate schools, proper healthcare, religious freedom etc. They are the poorest regions and becoming increasingly poorer partially through the desertification of lands. Afram Plains set in the Eastern Region, although a more fertile place, none-theless suffered impoverishment. Interest in survival and sustainability does not rest entirely on monetary concerns but rather on the people's spiritual ancestral relationship to the land and the ability of their lands to produce an abundance of food, medicine and water. In the present circumstance in order to survive their lands must produce enough to:

- Sustain the lives of the members of the family
- Help others
- Be sold/exchanged for extra necessities

In the main the majority of these families could barely survive. Rela-tionships to Traditional lands have been compromised as a result of the complexities of historical exigencies stemming from movements of Nation people escaping from war, refugee-ism, enslavement and colonial confines. Western style governments often exacerbate rather than ameliorate land issues Africa-wide in concert with their interests in land usage and the nec-essary deconstruction of Traditional power to this end.

Background of the Mothers

For the study, Mothers were used as the main source of information regard-ing their children's development. While they were not regarded as experts in these fields their perceptions were corroborated across districts and Nations. Thus, the magnitude of their insight was recognized. This unique study provided a foundation for a more holistic understanding of child upbringing practices and children's development.

The Mothers came from rural farming communities. Seven hundred and seventeen came from Northern Ghana and the rest from the Eastern region. They represented 27 Nations and practiced 3 main religions, Tra-ditional, Moslem and Christian. A perfect example of cultural unity in this study was that over 80% of the Mothers admitted practicing Traditional religion whether Moslem or Christian. More would have attested to being so but there was pressure to downplay Traditional practices since a major source of income to some teachers (interviewers) in some areas was predicated on their allegiance to the Church or Mosques and their ability to create converts and deny Traditional practices. This attempt was in contradiction to the study, which sought to discover Traditional ways of raising children.

The median age for the Mothers interviewed was 36 years and the median number of children was 3. The number of children they hoped to have was between 4–6 and all children were breastfed. The median age for Mothers to have their first child was 20 years and the spacing between children was 2–3 years. Except for 2 Mothers who were single and one widowed, 832 were married at the time of the study. Many Mothers lived in compound housing where walls between the houses of women and men enclose the family. Other Mothers lived in separate housing in their family groups.

Marriage

Five hundred and forty three Mothers were in polygynous marriages living in the same families as other wives some of whom also had children. There were some Christian wives in polygynous marriages as well as some Traditional and Moslem wives in monogamous marriages.

Monogamously married partners lived in compounds and communities with other relatives, married and/or unmarried and in this way shared the responsibilities of childrearing. Some marriages appearing monogamous could change for these reasons:

- A young wife may later become the first wife of a number of wives.
- A young wife may become the only wife if the senior wife passes away (died).
- An older wife may bring her own relatives, e.g., a younger sister to marry her husband and help with the children.

Some monogamous marriages are for life whether Traditional, Moslem or Christian. Monogamous and polygynous marriages did not differ greatly in terms of childcare and Mothers' support. They rather constituted particularized family structures that could adequately care for the infants while at the same time provided support for family members to carry out their responsibilities. In the current circumstances polygynous families allowed Mothers to farm, manufacture, trade, cook and raise children thus enhancing the chances of survival for people under threat of extinction.

Some Marriage Experiences

The status of marriage is the basis on which families are created particularly among Traditional families less affected by western values. Raising children is a family and community commitment that requires the input of all members for the successful transmission of practices, skills, values and beliefs. Choosing husbands is complex requiring some knowledge of the background of prospective families. Marriages form the union of families and parents want their daughters to marry reputable men who have enough resources to support her and raise her children. Parents generally know or seek to know the ancestral background of the families this is what gives the potential union credibility. The expectation is that they will be life partners. Most Mothers had been married for years to the same husband.

The study showed that marriage was a central focus in the Mothers' lives. Their happiness and unhappiness was mainly dictated by the success of the relationships formed with the men who became their husbands. The role of parents, particularly Mothers, in choosing or influencing the choice of husbands is still powerful even amongst more urbanized and westernized families.

A few stories have been selected as examples of some of the marriages Mothers' experienced.

> Ayariselie from Builsa aged 40 has six children. She was the last born of her Mother's four children from a polygynous family. She is happily married and the only wife. She met her husband when she was sixteen in the rice fields of Gbedembilisa her village. Courting commenced. This led to the performance of "Akayali" the customary rite performed by the prospective husband to indicate that "your daughter is staying with me, do not therefore look for her." In other words she is married and safe with me. Next according to Ayariselie came the following real marriage of "Nansuik Ligka," which means the closing of the gate, meaning this is the finalization of the marriage. She has been with her husband for 24 years.

Sometimes a Mother was betrothed to her potential husband before birth or when she was a tiny girl. The belief that these marriages work is very powerful because so many Mothers found the husbands their parents chose, suitable. They often respected their husbands for their kindness and support. Some marriages did not work out so the women left their husbands and married again. These examples show the concerns the Mothers had regarding their ability to become Mothers.

> Adzadouklie, is 30 years old. She is the daughter of a farmer and began to look after cattle at the age of 7 years old. She was later sent to Kumasi. While there she met her husband who was from the same district. She married him at the age of 17 and they decided to return home. Time passed and life became unbearable for Adzadouklie she decided to escape from the marriage and returned to her family home. From there she remarried to her present husband at the age of 20. She has given birth to three children and wishes to have five.

> Donno was married at the age of 29 years to a husband she did not like. Her marriage was under duress from her father. She accepted the marriage to please him. "As time passed I did not give birth and decided to run away." Before she could leave, her husband took her to a priest to be given some herbs to help her conceive. She informed her father about her continued failure to get pregnant. While the father sympathized he urged her to stay with the husband because of the dowry. Her father advised her to return to the priest. Instead she told her mother secretly and decided to run away with her blessing. She stayed away for sometime and one day on a visit to the market she met an old boyfriend. An arrangement was made and she married him. At first the father did not want to accept but he was obliged to. Six months after the marriage she became pregnant. She had three children altogether. Owing to her failing health she was unable to have more.

In discussions on meeting their potential husbands, many Mothers thought of them as friends and spoke often of love between them. Some Mothers went against their parent's wishes in order to marry their friends. A Bassare Mother found her own husband when an arranged one fell through.

> I went to stay with a man who married me. Because my father and brother were not in favor my brother took me illegally from the man and sent me to learn a trade. After completion the man came back and pleaded with my father to be allowed to marry me. It was finally agreed and the present husband was made to pay the expenses I incurred in learning the trade.

Some Mothers were the first wives of a polygynous marriage and they accepted their "rivals" as women who would serve and help them with their responsibilities in raising children. By the time of the interviews many of these Mothers were still married to their husbands after many years and sometimes many wives later.

> Sana is the first wife of three. She has been married for fifteen years and is 34 years old. She has five children. "I was born at Tusani where I lived with my parents and served them. When I grew up I made a choice of my future husband and when I was 18 years I married. Within one year I had my first born who was a girl. My business is farming and she-abutter extraction with the other women (wives) I support my husband to feed the children. I will have as many children as God gives me."

Pinyann, a Konkomba Mother agreed to marry the man her parents chose for her. She is one of three wives and has nine children. Pinyann learned her trade of pito brewing when she was a girl earning enough money from her brewing and cutting firewood to help her mother and family buy cooking utensils for her marriage. At the age of 25 years she married and her first child was born a year later. "My husband loves me and I also love him as he is helping me and our children and the family. Our children and our family work together to make the family lasts longer."

Aunties played a major role in the lives of many of the Mothers. As young girls some Mothers were sent away from their communities stay with more affluent Aunties when they were very young and "served" them. They learned about womanhood. In the main the Mothers remained very close to their Aunties in later life although there were instances where these Aunties mistreated the girls. There were examples of this custom in the data in the UK/US study in families living in the Caribbean and in the U.K. Usually the Auntie is better able to provide more for the child than sometimes the family can. Auntie caring is also viewed as a way of extending the family.

> When Fuseina, now 34, was 7 years old her Auntie adopted her as a household help. She was the firstborn of her parents. While staying with her Aunt she performed her work perfectly to the admiration of those around her. She was able to gain skills and when she grew into womanhood she was a well-behaved girl. At the age of 17 years her mother returned her to her parents' home. A year after she returned to her father's home she married. At her matrimonial home she gave birth to two girls. Sadly her daughters died and then three years later her husband also died. After two years she remarried and had three children with her current husband. She wishes to have three more children.

Azara, from Yendi, was a child she was given to her Aunt to raise. "My Auntie was very nice to me. She gave me good morals and taught me good behaviour." When it was time for marriage Azara was given the freedom of choice. She chose a husband who was a poor farmer but his love for her knew no bounds. He worked so hard to maintain her. He never gave up the struggle to survive. "He would move mountains for me." Their marriage was blessed with children. Shortly after her third child he became ill. The sickness was mental insanity. "I wept all night when I heard the news." It was the beginning of a life of misery she could not believe. Azara's Auntie took her and the children away from this situation. She married again believing the fate of her children rests with faith. Although their father is still insane she still hopes for his recovery.

It was evident from the overall data that the commitment to and the status of marriage are highly regarded, as is the status of motherhood. This belief is so critical for the stability of the family and the environment that the infant will be born into. The concept of family, marriage and motherhood is culturally constructed and cannot be separated from Traditional religious values and principles. Having children out of wedlock is frowned upon since there is less guarantee that the child, a spiritual member of two families and their ancestors, will receive the appropriate blessings, safeguards, inheritance and commitment to her development that a child born into wedlock must receive.

Living in deprived situations is a major handicap for Traditional people who have historically been living in a state of war for centuries so that their practices are un-free to expand and develop. There is little control over their lives except to survive and preserve what little they have and the threat of death from ill health, contaminated water, malnutrition, war etc., is imminent. The protection of women and children is paramount and strict marriage rules assure their survival and the transmission of traditional beliefs.

COMPARISONS OF FAMILY AND MARRIAGE

In concert with western values, and in antithesis to the African extended family model the nuclear family model in the UK and US is based on the supremacy of the father. It is considered the ideal family setting for the accumulation of wealth in that financially it holds allegiance only to its household family members. Generally, the wife is expected to stay at home to raise the girls and boys, while the husband is away at work and rarely sees the children. There are varying types of this family model based mainly on income. Mothers from wealthier families may hire the help of full-time strangers to raise their children. In poorer families Mothers may receive government remuneration to put their infants in nurseries and play-centers, again with strangers, so they can earn incomes to support their families. In such cases Mothers may have to return to work early forfeiting breastfeeding or adequate breastfeeding.

While the monogamous marriage is the ideal marriage for the nuclear family, unlike the monogamous extended family in Africa it mostly excludes family help in raising children. Because of its isolated nature the nuclear family can cultivate unsavory family relationships where the maltreatment of family members, often women and girls and boys can take place unobstructed cloaked in secrecy and often undetected. There were examples in the UK/US study of Mothers receiving abusive treatment at the hands of parents or caregivers. For example one Mother had a child to her abusive father when she was 14 years and another managed to run away just before her father could rape her. The high rates of child molestation, pornography, torture, incest and murder that occur in the UK and the US are less likely to happen in the openness of extended family relationships in Traditional African families where behaviors are strongly monitored.

Amongst the Traditional Mothers only 3 out of the 835 interviewed were single, yet 10 out of the 21 Mothers who told their histories in the UK and US were single and overall 53% of the 116 parents interviewed as the background to the study, were single. Data revealed many cases of intergenerational single parenting experiences within most of the Mothers' families by grandmothers, great grandmothers, grandfathers, fathers and aunties.

In the present era high rates of single parenting among the poor in the UK and US are encouraged by policies that penalize Mothers through lower benefit payments or housing opportunities if their children's fathers or prospective husbands live with them. This condition is perceived as part of the ongoing attack on families of African descent to increase and maintain insecure lives preventing unity by undermining male and female power relations. African women have become more easily employable since their energy can be hired for less than European women and men as well as African men. The rise in the employability of African women is in concert with the un-employability of African men and can be seen as a worldwide phenomenon. This is also linked with the engagement of men in "illegalized" money making activities.

Despite these circumstances the high rate of single parents in the UK/US data is significant in that these Mothers were some of the most serious advocates for the development of culturally affirming schools. Their interest was attributed to their desire not only to educate their children but also to liaise with likeminded Mothers and parents interested in creating appropriate environments for educating their children for the purpose of extending their family networks. The Mothers' tenacity in this regard is related to a cultural similitude noted in the Traditional Mothers' study where the interdependency of women is cultivated in the family structures. Mothers participate in women's institutions, run their own businesses, farm, raise children and live in their own houses. This interdependency is nowhere more highly demonstrated than in breastfeeding sharing practices where Mothers will breastfeed other Mothers' babies when Mothers die, have no milk, need to work and want to do something for themselves.

EDUCATION

Non-literacy is used as an important justification for the implementation of development. Literacy supposedly gauges the level of advancement of people from so-called primitiveness. Arguments abound propounding erroneous beliefs that Africa never had indigenous literacy rather it arrived in Africa through Arabs and Europeans. The current lack of literacy rather denotes outcomes of centuries of ravishment, destabilization, refugee-ism and genocide etc.

This study strove to show that literacy could not be used to determine the level of intelligence and development among Traditional people in their present circumstances. It was hoped that the attainment of certain skills from pre-birth to walking, childcare, animal husbandry, weaving etc could act as indicators of the spiritual, physical, mental and psychological attributes necessary for their accomplishment. In this way, it would be possible to analyze their achievements, in order to show that levels of attainment could be compared to what infants and children accomplish in other societies.

Attempts to categorize the children's skills using Werner's cognitive, perceptual, gross motor and social and emotional definitions as well as Piaget's cognitive development stages proved futile. Some levels the children in the study exhibited in developmental processes were arrived at sometimes years before they were expected to. In concert with earlier research that looked at child precocity in relation to breastfeeding, data showed that Traditional children were being developed to attain important skills and were still advanced to western children.

In support of the findings, Hilliard's (1995) argument was that new western insights on infant development show their cognitive baseline is further advanced than ever realized. He noted that contrary to the findings of Developmental psychologists, like Jean Piaget, babies as young as 3 months old understand some physical and spatial properties of hidden objects. Furthermore, research shows how more sophisticated tasks for infants demonstrate more complex cognitive development previously not recognized or quantified. In reality, mainstream authoritative information on the psychological development of infants and children is still undergoing its own developmental process. New ways of thinking about how a child grows are still embryonic as the study shows.

Kagitcibasi, (1996) following mainstream thought on cognitive development and white superiority, pointed out that children from Africa and Traditional societies who gain the type of skills identified in the study have learned them through a process of "nonverbal observational learning and noninductive obedience oriented child socialization." She goes on to explain that while this process is culturally relevant to Traditional societies, this type of learning style does not accommodate the "cognitive/linguistic complexity" necessary for the demands of western societies.

Hilliard warned that serious problems arise for children if stylistic differences among them are viewed as evidence of capacity rather than the preferred method of learning. This bears great relevance to the types of schools being imposed to bring literacy to Traditional children that will be touched upon later. The assumption of the study was that Traditional rural people had an education structure in place for the development of their children. This study moved away from mainstream ideas that these children were uneducated and therefore unintelligent. In the west being educated usually refers to the attainment of literacy and having attended Arab and western-oriented institutions.

INTELLIGENCE

Serpell's (1992) research on the meaning of intelligence is interpreted in Chi-Chewa by children the majority of who had never attended school in a cluster of Traditional villages in rural Zambia. Highly complex definitions were elicited from their vocabulary. Serpell argued that indigenous perspectives for conceptualizing children's intellectual development are rarely explicitly articulated or affirmed in public discourse in Zambia or other modern African states. He further argued that the aspect of social responsibility delegated to intelligence is omitted in mainstream psychology. For the Chewa and other indigenous African Nations, a person who acts in a manner that is unconscionable (unprincipled or unscrupulous) cannot be intelligent.

This concept ties into ancient ancestral beliefs on intelligence propounded in Kemetic (Ancient Egypt). Intelligence was regarded as one of the 7 dimensions of the soul and considered rational, spiritual and ethical. During the judgment of the deceased before God, one's intelligence was measured by whether one had used it to cultivate harmony in her/his ethical or moral being. Intelligence is rather seen as critical for transforming a corrupt society into a purified one and not feeding passion but elevating and transcending it enlighten the heart.

In Kemet, students who underwent training to become priests competent in their fields of study, like the modern university, comprised three grades.

- The Mortals, probationary students who were being instructed, but who had not yet experienced inner vision.
- The Intelligences, those who had attained the inner vision.
- The Creators, those who had become united with true spiritual consciousness

These students were expected to understand Grammar, Rhetoric and Logic as moral disciplines. The comprehension of Geometry and Arithmetic sciences was the key to problems of one's being. Astronomy dealt with knowledge of the destiny of individuals, races and nations. Music was perceived as the living practice of philosophy, the route to harmony with God, and the cure of disease. The individual was expected to cultivate the Arts and Sciences along with virtue and through this understanding seek to become godlike while on earth.

These principles are completely synchronistic with current Traditional religious principles. The children are raised to be intelligent in order to live morally good lives so they may be qualified to fulfill their social responsibilities and eventually become ancestors.

SKILLS DEVELOPMENT

A compilation of children's accomplishments from the ages of 0–9 years was developed from the data. While no tests were taken to study psychomotor and psychosocial development the results from the data show that children could be considered precocious by mainstream standards in terms of the development of their skills and familial and social responsibilities by the time they were 9 years old. These findings complement results from earlier studies on Traditional infants all over Africa.

Wilson's (1978) list of the results of the early Psychomotor Development of African infants, based on western instruments of deduction, helps provide an idea of the infants' capabilities.

1. Nine (9) hours old, being drawn up in a sitting position, able to prevent her/his head from falling backward.
2. Two (2) days old, with head held firmly, looking in the face of the examiner.
3. Seven (7) weeks old, supporting herself in a sitting position and watching her reflection in the mirror.
4. Five (5) months old, holding herself upright.
5. Five (5) months old, taking the round block out of its hole in the form board. Five (5) months old, standing against the mirror.
6. Seven (7) months old, walking to the Gesell Box to look inside.
7. Eleven (11) months old, climbing the steps alone.

The findings from the study corroborated Wilson's test findings. Girls and boys were found to achieve the same skills levels at the same ages, regardless of district, Nation and religion. By the time the children are between the ages of 8 and 9 they were competent enough to carry out adult female and male responsibilities.

The parents had a heightened awareness of:

*   Infants' capabilities
*   Infants' consciousness of the world they interact with.

Unlike most child development studies this study is underpinned by the knowledge that Mothers were spiritually connected to their children and that it played a critical role in communication and the children's development. Unborn babies were able to communicate likes and dislikes to Mothers spiritually and physically. In many cases when probed for information, Mothers revealed they were aware of whether they carried daughters or sons prior to birth. Some of the more westernized interviewers did not think it possible that the Mothers knew their children's sex prior to birth so did not pursue that line of investigation.

Children were introduced into experimentation and learning stimulated through play. Mothers expected their children to be destructive in the early stages of social skills development, but these experiences were considered amusing. According to the Mothers, infants were stimulated to laugh and see the fun in life. This light-hearted approach to teaching was fortified through breastfeeding, considered God given, a joy and comfort to infants, that is continuous until between the ages of two and three years and in some cases after the age of three years. In this way learning was strengthened by optimistic loving, caring relationships. In contradiction to reports purporting child neglect and underdevelopment among Traditional families, these findings confirmed earlier positive studies written over the last 50 years.

Pre Birth

Analysis

Mothers were acutely aware of the importance of protecting the life of the unborn infant, the child was perceived in some cases to be a returning ancestor. The Mothers' awareness of and sensitivity to their unborn infants' needs, was supported by modern research carried out by the Pre and Peri-Natal Psychology Association of North America (PPPANA) that showed that universally, unborn infants respond to light, pain and music stimulation. Infants are also known to suck their thumbs in the womb. Their reaction to music stimulation demonstrates the first known awareness of the significance of music prior to birth. Musical expression is the philosophical and spiritual milieu of the African child known for over millennia to be integrally connected to health and wellbeing.

In line with the PPPANA findings the data showed that prior to birth, infants had sensibilities and made demands. As self-interested entities they were able to direct messages to the mother to make appropriate changes to their conditions in the womb. For example, they influenced choices the mothers made regarding food intake, positioning and physical exertion. When the Mother was behaving inappropriately (overworking and not eating), regarding her/his physical needs and/or care the infant was able to signal, usually through movement, "turning" as the Mothers put it, her/his discontent. A Mother could feel nausea after ingesting something her child was not happy with, or before she took inappropriate food. She also found that she craved certain food believing this to be the result of her children's wants. Mothers also observed that even after birth their children would continue to eat food they had favored whilst in the womb.

0–3 months

In compound or village life the mother is the primary carer but the infant has access to many caretakers from siblings, to rivals, grandmothers, sisters, aunties, fathers, grandfathers, uncles and brothers. The early psychosocial and physical development of the infant is contextualized by the expectations of the family and community. The tabula rasa concept is unknown to Traditional people this is why the name of the child is reflective and a reminder of the child's potential.

During the first 7 days a libation using water is performed to thank God for her/his safe arrival, to welcome the infant to the physical world, and to protect her/him. The infant is centered in learning to understand her/himself particularly as a physical being. Physical skills attainments like trying to sit and stand, rolling and kicking legs are encouraged with joy. S/he knows when her/his name is called and alerts the Mother of her needs. S/he produces sounds and gestures recognizable to her carers who use their psychic and spiritual skills to understand. Lullabies and songs are sung throughout the children's lives. They transmit messages that provide culturally relevant information to infants even before birth to reaffirm their spiritual connection particularly in tragic cases perhaps if the infant experiences negative situations like war or starvation or if the Mother died during childbirth and also when there is cause to celebrate or just express love etc. Babies rarely have reason to cry since they are closely monitored, everything is explained and all their needs are taken care of.

3–6 months

Analysis

Trying to stand and crawl involves the development of the infant's physical/spatial understanding of the distance to and from her/his Mother/carer by moving and being carried. When carried on the back of the Mother s/he views the world from a position of safety, able to observe peacefully interaction among people and animals that s/he would otherwise miss in a pram or pushchair. From this vantage s/he is constantly learning interactive social skills. The infant's level of contentment is always heightened by the fact that s/he remains on the back of the Mother or carer throughout the day, breastfed on demand and traveling to the farm or market and calmed by the Mother's heart-beat, spiritual protection and presence.

At this age infants discriminate against strangers. They are extremely perceptive about the deeper thoughts and feelings of others. This unspoken and deep psychic/spiritual awareness babies have is often overlooked in the west because they are not considered spiritual entities. They are able show their personal preferences for people in their gestures, words, crying and/or trying to move away and/or pushing away the stranger.

By now the infants' ability to understand and obey instructions are growing. They are listening very carefully to directives from carers and constantly supervised so their own needs are recognized. In this way, personal development is heavily influenced by family values and infants quickly learn family expectations especially since they are often raised and guided by examples of behavioral practices from older children.

6–9 months

Analysis

The infant is better able to follow instruction and obey commands in part because of her/his physical ability. S/he becomes increasingly articulate, signals and gestures become clearer and dexterity is more specialized. The dexterity gap between infants and adults is vast compared to the physical differences between infants and children with whom they are surrounded for much of the time. Thus, the desire and ability to achieve skills is more easily attainable.

Crawling, trying to walk and walking calls for specialized dexterity and balancing skills. Fetching small items entails the ability to follow instruction, obedience and logic. The infant wishes to please her/his parents and/or other carers because she understands the joy and satisfaction brought to them that is then transferred back. During this period the baby continues to be carried in the lapa providing security and the capacity to concentrate, observe, learn and be patient. Viewing the world from a higher vantage helps in developing spatial awareness and social integration. A child can be far more confident and aware of what is happening when s/he is trying to crawl, walk, explore and discover.

Laughing is always encouraged particularly with the achievement of a simple deed. The infant's preference for any item or object is influenced by the value it is given by the carers. During religious events infants understand the spiritual and moral values surrounding singing and dancing because of community involvement. These events instill and reinforce the musical connections made prior to birth.

The infant's close attachment to her/his mother, leads her/him to miss her when she is away and is characteristic of the acknowledgement of spiritual connection not just the attachment to her for breast milk. Other Mothers, sisters, grandmothers or older siblings are given responsibility for the infant so s/he is easily satisfied.

9–12 months

Analysis

This is a very busy age, she is walking and becoming more involved with family activities and making demands to carry out tasks. This is often amusing to the older siblings. S/he can now articulate wants and follow instruction.

The child is able to articulate her illnesses and places of pain on the body. S/he also observes the scientific and spiritual connection in ritual that leads to her healing. In some cases Traditional families used both Traditional and western medicines in the treatment of their children. In some districts in the north of Ghana, only Traditional healing was used. If given the choice the majority of Mothers wanted to have access to both forms of medicine in the event that one type of medicine did not work.

The art of speaking intelligibly and singing presents infants with new possibilities for communicating and learning. Older children teach their Traditional songs in the way the western children learn nursery rhymes. Infants accompany older children to special places where the children play. They also accompany older children carrying out chores so they learn first from observation and then from experimentation. Infants are carried by older siblings, whenever necessary. Older children whether from the direct family or not will always attend to any infants in distress.

Independent play is encouraged. Learning housework in this early phase is viewed as playful so that the child is able to learn dexterity at an early age yet realize its significance to daily survival. Children of all ages are taught they have responsibilities as teachers and role models for younger siblings. The social skills the children were learning to practice at this age ranged from sweeping, bodily hygiene, bathing, feeding fowl to fetching calabashes and important items for the Mother.

1–2 years

Analysis

The child's engagement with community affirms the emotional and social skills particularly around behavior, instruction and obedience that are being learned inside the family base. Members of the community have the same expectations of all children as they do of their own. In this way expectations are clear and children learn quickly how they must behave and what they should do.

Purchasing items is very important in rural life and marketing, for the child it requires mathematical knowledge development and this begins at this early age although observing trading whilst being transported by the Mother from birth will have introduced the sounds and behaviors associated with these business transactions. Mathematical skills are developed through knowledge of the members of households and animals owned by families. The child is becoming involved at the most basic stages of animal husbandry in learning how to feed the fowl and shoo the goats. They learn the personalities of the animals, developing their own relations with them. They are also taught the boundaries of their movement around humans. These skills are very complex bringing the child into the knowledge of ecosystems and religion through the role of animals in the spiritual and physical survivability of the family and community.

By this age, Mothers believed their children understood the protective role of amulets, bracelets and waist beads against negative spirit forces. Their emotional, spiritual and psychic skills have been enhanced since they were in the womb. Unlike western children they are taught to understand there is no dichotomy between the spiritual and material world. This helps the children develop a holistic and scientific understanding of their world.

The majority of children according to the data were able to take solid food independently using their own bowls. The ability to eat at the same plate as older siblings is a skill not usually acquired by the majority of children until they are 2–3 years old. There is a certain ritual practiced among children who eat from the same plate that must be followed and younger children have to be adept before they can learn it. It is also around this time that the infants are coming off the breast.

Play is critical for developing social skills. The children play in the earth with natural objects like broken calabashes, stones, sticks, leaves, empty containers and fashion them into cooking utensils imitating cooking and other social skills. At the same time the earth keeps the connection to farming and learning about insects and creatures that frequent their natural habitat.

Fetching a stool for visitors marks the accomplishment of a social grace. To carry out this act without instruction is evidence of understanding respect for elders and visitors etc., and is viewed with great respect.

The child bathes and relieves her/himself in the right location and cleans her/himself appropriately. Children are interested in their sexuality and often inquire about differences between girls and boys. Mothers answered such questions simply and to the point. In concert with and a compliment to the acknowledgement of differences, the data shows that female/male roles-orientation takes place at the next stage around the age of 2–3 years.

2–3 years

The boy's relationship to the father becomes more serious. Until now, both the boy and girl have been following their mother because of breast-feeding. Thus, the mother has directed most of their earlier learning. The boy's role as a man is now being defined through his relationship with his father.

Boys serve their father's table and can eat and work with him. Age differentiation is critical for maintaining social orders. As mentioned earlier younger children are the apprentices of the older children. This relationship instills older children who are teachers with responsibility for educating the younger ones. Girls begin to follow their mothers for the specific intention of becoming women.

In Chiok Wiaga (Builsa) the son begins his apprenticeship for Blacksmithing training. He follows his father, uncles and senior brothers to sit with them and observe this ancient work. Like Blacksmithing, cooking is an ancient science that requires training in the form of apprenticeship so girls will gain an holistic understanding by going with their Mothers to farm and produce the vegetables and cereals that will be pounded and used in cooking and manufacturing and trading. They learn the cycle of food production from seed to planting to caring to reaping and food preparation. Boys, will also be expected to cook for their fathers on some occasions.

Caring for the babies helps the children develop Mothering skills and become good parents, community and Nation members. Both girls and boys are able to identify with the needs of babies because they are so emotionally close to them. They have the intensity of compassion and sensitivity to understand them. Their sensitivity is highly developed in terms of forming symbiotic and empathetic relationships while at the same time understanding the temperaments and intentions of the babies in their charge. These competencies require a holistic, spiritual and emotional awareness of infant needs. The children love to care for their younger siblings they love to be cared for by them in return. Children are given the trust and responsibility to care for the babies under supervision, unlike their peers in the west.

Children are given the important responsibility for delivering messages or objects. They are safe in their communities and able to travel freely in the knowledge that their safety is paramount to all the children and adults they are likely to meet. It is not unusual to witness tiny children traveling safely independently and with confidence.

Girls and boys are perfect dancers, they have been dancing before they could stand. Singing and dancing are expressions of social morality, involving the meaning of events that range from the celebration of birth, harvesting to the transition from the material to the spiritual world (death) in the lives of these children. All events are connected to astronomy, the seasons and the destiny of people.

The children follow their Mothers and older siblings to the water every day. To begin with, younger children carry small containers on their heads to help develop the strength, balance and dexterity necessary for this work. Observing their Mothers carrying water when carried helps the children to gain knowledge of spatial and physical realities as well as the critical social need for water to survive and the great life/death responsibility it holds for the carriers to bring it home to the families. This domain belongs essentially to the women and the girls, although boys carry water if a family has mostly boys. In this case boys must do the work that girls would normally do, and girls would have to carry out boys' tasks if the majority of children are girls, for example minding cattle. Boys do not feel ashamed to carry water nor girls to mind cattle it rather shows the status of the family regarding the acquisition of girls and boys.

Learning about herbs and their medicinal characteristics begins at 2–3 years old, developing throughout all the age categories. Most rural children will gain some basic information about herbs and their healing properties. Parents are observing their children's interests in herbs.

3–4 years

Analysis

At this age the majority of children are no longer breastfeeding and there is a looser attachment to the mother. Their knowledge of community expectations is now sophisticated and they have the foresight and self-assurance to realize them.

Girls and boys sing the songs they have learned to help sooth crying babies. Memories coupled with the deeper understanding of songs help children retell them to the babies in their own words.

The scientific logic required for connecting the spiritual and natural world with healing is understood at this early age so that girls and boys can receive instruction about the healing attributes of specific plants. The children's predilection for understanding plants and healing is monitored. Some children are born to be healers and parents know before their birth, others show signs of interest during their development and others are descended from women and men who are Traditional doctors.

Throughout their childhood, the children meet to play and take time to communicate with each other outside the earshot of their parents and other adults. This happens both at home and in the community. Mostly, they congregate under a shady tree. During these times they pass information to each other and share ideas. Communication among children provides the greatest form of educational transmission particularly regarding social mores. Younger siblings listen and learn from the older ones. They do not speak out of order. Even amongst each other they are learning when it is appropriate to speak. As Yankah (1998) argues, speaking in Traditional societies is a discipline and language is used carefully because speech as sound is a powerful purveyor of good or evil.

4–5 years

Analysis

Children of this age are quite accomplished with regard to personal hygiene, the articulation of their health standards and their ability to accomplish tasks more efficiently.

Mathematical logic is now substantial because family survival depends on it. Girls work closely with her mother learning cooking from preparing fresh ingredients to cleaning up afterwards and purchasing goods, in preparation for petty trading later on. Weaving baskets is an ancient skill that is both artistic and practical the product of which is considered a symbolic expression like literacy that uses mathematical logic.

The laying out of the father's mat is a great privilege for boys, although symbolic of respect for the father and becoming men not all Nations practice this. Boys have been serving their fathers since 2 years old, keeping the father's home clean, fetching water to drink and serving food etc. The boys go with their elders to graze the cattle learning how to care for them and sometimes traveling with them for miles to find adequate grazing. They are able to find food for the chickens, like certain grubs and feed them and put them in their coops. In the Eastern Region young boys begin fishing and diving from the boats into deep waters developing their physical skills. They are also using their artistry to mend their nets.

5–6 years

The girls and boys at this age are competent to work on their parents' farms. Boys farm independently and have their own gardens. Girls have reached a stage where they have a need for privacy and a desire to dress like their mothers. This signals a stage of maturity in their thoughts about personal identity as women. The construction of feminine identity falls within the expectations and values of the community and family. These developing womanly desires are natural to children of the same ages in western-oriented societies and are linked to the biological and psychological changes taking place.

Manufacturing Pito brewing is a complex science carried out by women and learned by the girls. Pito is made from millet and includes several stages of fermentation. During the first stage of brewing the millet is boiled and in this form can be taken as an herbal remedy even by babies, it is rich in iron. During fermentation it has stages of maturation. Alcoholic strength differs at every stage until it is fully matured. It may be used as a social drink and as a Shrine offering.

The boys are dexterous and agile. They have developed some knowledge of the habits of wild birds that by now they are able to hunt with a catapult.

6–7 years

Boys and girls have learned some of the complexity of their role in the family home and community. Both girls and boys care about their personal hygiene and girls are focusing on their femininity.

7–8 years

Girls were able to petty trade and spin, evidence of their artistic and mathematical acumen. At the same time, boys were also using these skills for learning Blacksmithing, carving, making musical instruments and dyeing materials. All artistic accomplishments have a spiritual function. Artifacts are made with God in mind. Aesthetic quality fits into the requirements dictated by the spiritual world.

The boys were more involved than girls in the religious arena learning ritual and shrine work regarding sacrifice. Boys accompanied their fathers to festivals and funerals. Although some girls become priestesses more boys become priests and Traditional doctors. Owing to the necessary protection of women in these vulnerable conditions there were fewer women involved in these vocations than would otherwise be if conditions were more conducive to life, abundance and societal development.

8–9 years

By the time the girls reached this age they were able to run a home, care for children, farm, trade and manufacture, carrying out all the responsibilities of their Mothers. The boys were able to care for the land, hunt, care for animals, raise them and sell them and offer them as sacrifice. They could protect the home in the absence of the Father.

COMMENTS

The findings showed that an age appropriate comprehensive education system was in place. Children's achievable expectations across districts were held within each age category. Moral values underpinned each development stage. Each skill was linked to producing a necessary social skill for family and community development. The educational process was a type of apprenticeship. Family and community members played an essential role in the development of the children and determined the quality of the social accomplishments as well as the necessary behaviors and practices. Through the educational process the children learned to:

- Care for and raise their younger siblings (exhibit Mothering skills).
- Farm—gained environmental conservation skills, ecosystem management.
- Become gifted in creative works like singing, dancing and produce forms of artistry like fishing nets, baskets, weaving, carving, iron shaping etc.
- Be spiritually knowledgeable.
- Understand herbal use for medicinal purposes.
- Carry out the sciences used in small-scale manufacturing as well as day-to-day life.
- Work with, care for, and raise animals.
- Hunt and fish.
- Care for their personal hygiene.
- Carry out domestic duties in cooking, cleaning and washing clothes.
- Petty trade.
- Make major adult decisions and carry out adult roles and responsibilities at the ages of between 8–9 years old.
- Comprehend the disciplines necessary to be spiritually aware good persons.

Throughout their development the children were taught to concentrate, be observant, patient, and obedient. These attributes are fundamental to the accomplishment of their tasks and the maintenance of their social order. In all societies, these attributes are a prerequisite for attaining the higher disciplines. These findings showed that despite deprived circumstances these children were precocious by western standards.

LITERACY AS DOMINATION

Children are considered a blessing Africa-wide and their survival for these rural Traditional people is considered paramount to:

- Extending the family lineage
- The development of rural activities, farming, weaving, hunting, trading, manufacturing etc.
- Becoming prosperous

- Having a good name
- Receiving a good burial
- Developing family, community and Nation

Children born into these non-literacy environments were already disadvantaged in the main through abject poverty and marginalization when they attended schools to become literate. A study (2003) *Listening to the Children,* evaluated some schools in remote areas where some of the Mothers in the study lived. Two hundred and seven pupils 104 girls and 103 boys and 95 teachers, 22 women and 73 men were interviewed. Thirty-seven schools were visited and 207 children, 104 girls and 103 boys were interviewed from 33 schools.

As the hope of the future, the children's literacy attainment placed great responsibility on the Teachers. While no interviews were carried out with parents and community members, in many cases particularly in the north, PTA members and Chiefs came to ascertain the reason for the study. It was evident based on the punctuality and attendance of many girls and boys at the schools visited that the communities and families put a great deal of trust into the advantages of schools to their families. In most of the schools in the north, the availability of food rations for lunch and the liter of oil and bag of grain for girls attending for 28 days encouraged attendance.

Many schools visited had no textbooks, exercise books or writing tools. In Yendi and Builsa more girls attended schools than boys. Toilet facilities were inadequate in most schools and drinking water was not available at most schools, children were sent out to get water when school started. In some schools in Yendi and Tolon/Kumbungu children were drinking unfit water, the dregs of dam water where animals defecate and drink to also survive. The children's health was poor. This condition was mirrored in the communities in which the schools were built. In some schools in Builsa, Tolon/Kumbungu and Yendi, pupils were found sitting in their classrooms on time without teachers present. Some teachers had been absent for days and weeks. A substantial number of children attended with their sibling infants. All the children waited silently in many cases sitting at broken desks or on the floors in dark classrooms. While these examples were the worst-case scenarios they were too frequent to be ignored.

Most teachers did not come from the areas they taught in. Children were only allowed to speak the language of the teachers and in a significant number of cases that meant children could not speak their own languages in order to become literate in English or Arabic. For example, in Yendi, at predominately Konkomba schools only 3 teachers spoke Likpakpaln, the Konkomba language, so the children had to speak Dagbanli, the Dagomba language, to make the transition to English thus delaying the acquisition of literacy. In this way literacy hierarchies were established that commensurate with Nation people hierarchies cultivated within Nation states from enslavement and colonial times. Overall only 45 of the 95 teachers believed the children came to school with any skills. One Head Teacher believed the children had no skills. Conversely one Head Teacher who grew up in the same community he taught in believed the children came to school with Mothering, leadership, scientific and mathematical skills.

When the children were asked what would they do to help their families, they saw the most important needs as: food, water and electricity, healthcare, financial support for family business expansion, transport and literacy for their siblings. In terms of community needs the children wanted: Health facilities, water, electricity, school/literacy for all children, development money and commercial transportation. The order of needs changed for each district e.g., the children of Afram Plains did not need water or food.

It was evident that children who would otherwise be in their communities developing their intelligence, psychomotor, psychosocial and societal skills were severely debilitated by attending western style schools. While there were some teachers who loved the children too many disrespected the children and their families—one teacher is too many. A lack of historical and cultural knowledge probably confirmed some teachers' views that the children were members of inferior Nations. Certainly practitioners of Traditional religion were considered lesser beings who had never contributed to anything worthwhile. Only 6 teachers were aware of pre-colonial informal education and no teachers were aware of the African origin of formal education. Knowledge of local history was negligible, and those who knew any, knew little.

This lack of historical knowledge mirrors the background of the majority of teachers trained in the UK and the US. Without information to counteract the general debasement of certain groups, African descended girls and boys in the west and practitioners of Traditional religion in Africa, discriminatory practices take place to undermine these children, whether it is to punish them unjustly, exclude them, not help them and so on. Children are unable to perform well in these circumstances and may behave in ways to challenge injustices against them, either to become placid and withdrawn or aggressive and challenging. Tormentors who have the power to conceal their manipulation outlaw behaviors that challenge them. These were the same conditions that led Mothers in the UK and US to create schools that could respect their children and their ancestors.

Reports on academic achievements showed that rural children who attain mathematical and scientific skills as farmers and traders years earlier than western or westernized children failed dismally to achieve good results.

Based on observation and admissions from meetings with literate persons who came from Traditional families; as children become literate in English and Arabic they begin to lose touch with their Traditional background, learn to devalue Indigenous Knowledge and disrespect their ancestors and families. Some of those who attested to being guilty felt ashamed, and recounted instances where valuable knowledge had been lost because they had chosen not to inherit it.

For the Traditional child the ancestor world is integral to her self-identity and her destiny. Kemetic formal education, like the non-literacy education used in child development, was based on Traditional pedagogy featuring the intra-disciplinary aspects of learning so that for example there was no separation between religion, philosophy, spirituality, healing, mathematics, music and science. Western style schools undermine Traditional girls and boys, their ways of learning and their beliefs. Based on the numbers of successful African people worldwide it is clearly not impossible for children to excel academically in western schools. The point is, why go through this circuitous route with the heightened possibility of abandoning family and community?

Lack of basic needs and western style schools have contributed to the exodus of impoverished children seeking sustenance in urban areas turning them into street children and potential "rebel soldiers." A small amount of literacy and little hope of employment can create alienated girls and boys who can be easily abused, used, enslaved and financed by unscrupulous politicians desirous of war and conflict inside and outside the countries and the continent. The migration of children is a loss to communities that could prosper from their ingenuity if their communities could be redeveloped.

No one is listening, the Mothers are crying for the loss of their children. They ask: Who will save them? Who will care for them? Who will bring them forth children? Who will build the new societies? Who will bring them wealth? Who will bury them? The answer is Africa must respect its ancestors and deliver the people from the mire of foreign occupancy.

Cultural Redemption

Some issues

As Africa moves into the 21st Century, westernized politicians are more unified in becoming aware of the need for Africa to take back control of resources and the people's destiny, the potential of which is substantiated in the creations of New Partnership for Africa's Development NEPAD and African Union AU. The reality is that among the new thinkers are unscrupulous individuals whose primary interests are to carry out the wishes of their financiers in order to look after their families and to promote their

Nation people's (not Nation state) interests. Any realistic move towards Africa's renaissance cannot ignore the significance of indigenous knowledge and the need to respect African ancestors. Traditional religion, the most reviled and yet the most practiced religion in Africa embodies indigenous knowledge, love for the ancestors and the process of becoming an ancestor. It holds the source of power that most unifies all people.

The western and Arab worlds are supremely aware of this, that is why for centuries they have worked so diligently to establish their cultural identity as that which is divine. As Ekwe Ekwe (1993) has cogently argued, western models of governance can never sustain African life, as evidenced by the countless millions of African women, men and children who have died and continue to die daily since so-called independence. Therefore new leadership must turn inward to the continent for resolutions. Daily, indigenous knowledge is being lost as those who preserve it are dying. Their humanity is devalued and their death is viewed as natural, normal and necessary. They have no representation in government. So-called development is working against their best interests. How can African leaders support development policies that invite western experts to come and:

- Teach people how to be hygienic when they may carry contaminated, precious water daily for miles on their heads in order to cook and drink what little they have?
- Teach people what is good for them to eat, suggesting that the malnutrition they suffer from is due to their ignorance when in reality for several months of the year there is no food?
- Teach that Traditional Medicine is inferior when no medicine can heal diseases caused by contaminated water and inadequate food and constant disrespect?
- Teach that Mothers do not take care of themselves when they are pregnant when they are so deprived and their resources to survive are minimal?
- Teach Mothers to exclusively breastfeed their infants when they have been doing it for thousands of years, while western Mothers get their breasts implanted and use them to entice men and employment opportunities?
- Teach that too many children are being born because women and men need contraceptives and lessons on how to produce fewer babies?
- Teach that the infant mortality rate is too high because Mothers have bad caring practices when the babies are dying of malnutrition?

- Teach that the children are uneducated and ignorant and must become literate?
- Teach that the children are too ignorant to become literate?
- Teach that only western medication can treat AIDS?
- Teach that girls are prevented from going to school (oppressed) because boys are favored when boys are expected to take care of their families and communities so, if literacy can bring help, then they should go first?

Why is money spent on bringing ill-equipped schools into communities that do not have their basic needs met? Why is it that people charged with bringing help to impoverished communities live so well? Why do Aid people have such different standards for themselves than for those they are helping? Why are expectations for the needs of Traditional people so low? How many NGOs and Aid workers are in each Nation state in Africa? Are African people too ignorant to use the money appropriately? If money is available why can it not provide communities with the opportunity to Re-Develop and for example:

- Have clean piped water to every home
- Farm abundantly (no subsistence)
- Supply and Exchange as great traders (no petty trading)
- Supply Traditional medical doctors with state of-the-art equipment
- Develop a pharmacopoeia
- Learn literacy in Traditional pedagogic schools
- Build great Temples and learning centers
- Build sun driven generators for electricity
- Build wind generators for energy
- Give advice on environmental conservation skills
- Use computers to enhance Teaching and Learning
- Have vibrant Traditional active Governance and political bodies

These are the questions that need to be answered and the problems that have to be solved. Clearly, the West has proved it is incapable of providing for the needs of African people.

RESOLUTIONS

No serious changes can begin to take place unless discussions with Traditional governments representing the interests of their nations' peoples are held. In this way the work can begin to uncover and rectify injustices that have occurred through invasion and conquest and the installation of western governments.

Peace and Resolution meetings will have to be extended to resolve land issues in ways that are conducive to improving the lives of people who have been disenfranchised and forced into wars and extreme poverty and chaos in the interests of foreign controllers.

Nation state boundaries will have to be renegotiated in the interests of all people. If not, African leadership will continue to reify the chaos that Europeans and Arabs brought by using the same logic to analyze internal dynamics and the same means of violence to quell the voices of people who cry for justice. To carry out such fundamental work would need the values of great Traditional social democracies like Kemet that were founded on female and male reciprocity the basis of order.

The study on African Mothers in the UK and US asked how in the face of the debasement of African people can these Mothers perceive African culture to be of any relevance to their children's lives? There is no African Mother on the continent or off who believes her child is inferior to any other. The ancestors cannot allow that. This belief is the source of the revolutionary fire that burns in the heart of all African people.

The 21st century predicts the time when women, men and children of African descent are learning to revere and spiritually connect to their ancestors. The women and men who fought against oppression and sacrificed their lives over millennia to this end inspired them. The study on Traditional Mothers showed how western policies of development are undermining the people who hold the secrets of the ancients. The current situation is that Traditional families are under threat of death. Their children are being trained to move away from their cultural Traditions while the children of some diasporan Mothers are reconnecting with their ancestors creating schools more conducive to the appropriate development of the children. Both sets of Mothers are integrally bound to each other's salvation, and need knowledge and communication from each other to fully activate these schools to help the following generations to rise to develop the future of Africa. They need support to carry out this work beyond their borders, can leaders see beyond the confines of their westernized minds, do they have the Afrocentric vision to communicate with and unite the people and provide the means for true Development?

NOTES

1. Dove, N. (2002). "Defining a Mother-Centered Matrix to Analyse the Status of Women." This chapter argues that the level of a civilization's development can be ascertained by the status of women.
2. See Dove, (2003). "Defining African Womanism." This article develops an understanding of the historical and cultural construction of male supremacy and the significance of female power.

3. See Dove, (1978) *Afrikan Mothers,* p. 239. Deculturalization is a violent, brutal and dehumanising process that includes taking control of lands, controlling or destroying Traditional institutions, removing real leadership, torturing and abusing, children, women and men physically, mentally, economically and spiritually, denying people their humanity, withdrawing access to cultural knowledge, imposing ideas hostile to the continuity of a people, and destabilizing the family institution for the purpose of destroying the process of cultural continuity supported by a belief in the morality and righteousness of this procedure.

REFERENCES

Ainsworth, M. D. S. (1977) Infant Development and Mother-Infant Interactions among Ganda and American Families. In P. H. Leiderman, S. R. & A. Rosenfeld, (eds.), *Culture and Infancy.* New York: Academic Press.

Akbar, N. (1994). *Light from Ancient Africa.* Tallahassee, Florida: Mind Productions & Associates.

Awumbila, M & Nang-beifubah, A & Abugri, J. *Promoting Exclusive Breastfeeding of Children Aged 0–6 months in the Bawku East District of Ghana.* A paper delivered at the XV International Conference on Social Science and Medicine, Eindhoven Netherlands. 16–20 Oct, 2000.

Bynum, E. (1994). *Transcending Psychoneurotic Disturbances.* U.S.: Harrington Park Press, Imprint of the Hayworth Press Inc.

Diop, C.A. (1990) *The Cultural Unity of Black Africa.* Chicago: Third World Press (Published originally in 1959 as *L'Unite culturelle de L'Afrique noir).*

Dove, N. (1998). *Afrikan Mothers: Bearers of Culture, Makers of Social Change.* Albany, N.Y.: SUNY Press.

Dove, N. (2002). "Defining a Mother-Centered Matrix to Analyse the Status of Women." *Journal of Black Studies.* Vol 33 (1) 3–24 September.

Ekwe Ekwe, H. (1993) *Africa 2001: The State, Human Rights and the People.* Reading, U.K.: International Institute of African Research.

Hilliard, A. (1995). *The Maroon Within Us.* Baltimore, MD: Black Classic Press.

James, G. G. M. (1980). *Stolen Legacy,* N.Y: The African Publication Society. (Published originally in 1954 by Philosophical Library, N.Y.).

Kagitcibasi, C. (1996). *Family and Human Development Across Cultures.* N.J., U.S.: Lawrence Erlbaum Associates, Publishers.

LeVine, R. (1996). *Child Care and Culture.* U.K.: Cambridge University Press.

Karenga, M. & Carruthers, J. (1986). *Kemet and the African Worldview.* Los Angeles: University of Sankore Press.

Mararike, C. G. (1999). *Survival Strategies in Rural Zimbabwe: The Role of Assets, Indigenous Knowledge & Organisations.* Harare, Zimbabwe: Mond Books.

Serpell, R. (1992). *Afrocentrism: What Contribution to the Science of Development Psychology?* Paper presented at the Yaounde International Workshop on Child Development and National Development in Africa. Yaounde, Cameroon: April. University of Zambia & University of Maryland, Baltimore, U.S.

Stewart, N. A. (1996). Melanin, The Melanin Hypothesis, and the Development and Assessment of American Infants. In D. A. ya Azibo (ed.), *African Psychology*. Trenton, N.J.: Africa World Press.

Wilson, A. (1978). *The Developmental Psychology of the Black Child*. New York: Africana.

Yankah, K. (1998). Free Speech In Traditional Society: The Cultural Foundations of Communication in Contemporary Society. Accra, Ghana: Ghana University Press.

Political and Economic Future of the African World

Chapter Ten

Stuffing Old Wine in New Bottles: The Case of the Africa Union

Kwame Akonor, Seton Hall University

A bunch of broomsticks is not easily broken as a single stick.

—*African proverb*

The African Union (AU) was formally inaugurated on July 9, 2002, at Durban, South Africa, replacing the Organization of African Unity (OAU). African leaders, and supporters of the AU, generally argue that the new institution would enhance the economic, political and social integration and development of African people. Others are not so optimistic: they perceive the AU as a mere continuation of the OAU under a different name. This essay investigates what the AU is about and what is "new," if anything, about it. Presenting a pan Africanist critique of the AU, this essay argues that the AU, as presently constituted, does not offer much hope for the transformation of the continent: it will not lead to a greater political economic and ideological autonomy and development of African peoples. The humanitarian crisis in Darfur, Sudan, is discussed as a specific test to the AU's conflict management capacity and to the new organization's overall viability and authority.

A LOOK AT AU'S PRECURSOR: THE OAU

Representatives of 32 African governments established the OAU on 25 May 1963, in Addis Ababa, on signature of the OAU Charter. The OAU was born out of two factions in Africa that had competing ideological goals on African unity: The Casablanca Group (which consisted of Algeria, Egypt, Ghana, Guinea, Libya, Mali, and Morocco), and The Monrovia Group (championed primarily by Nigeria and Liberia). The Casablanca Group sought to transcend the balkanized political systems created on the continent through colonialism by ceding fundamental aspects of sovereignty for an *immediate* united Africa with a common currency, foreign policy, defense structure and economic platform. The Monrovia Group on the other hand, shared a concept of African unity that was intent on retaining the colonial demarcations and the newly won political independence: its intentions were to create an alliance of African states rather than a "United States of Africa." In the end, the Monrovia Group's idea of an *Africa of States* triumphed over the Casablanca Group's idea of an *African superstate*. To stamp out the prevailing vision, the OAU, in its Charter, specifically called for the respect of prevailing borders and non-interference in the internal affairs of member states (Mbuyinga, 1982; Naldi, 2000).

Thirty-nine years later, the OAU was dismantled to make way for the African Union. The rationale for this, the founding leaders (Mbeki, 2002) argue, is that the OAU having succeeded in its mission of decolonization and liberation was fitting for replacement by an institutional structure more attune to the current needs of the continent. But supporters of this logic, who tout the "the historic achievements of the OAU," are either in denial or are simply not telling the whole truth about the OAU's record. The fact is that the AU was born not out of OAU's success but rather its failures. A quick examination of OAU's performance (at the time of its transition to AU) vis-à-vis its stated objectives (at the time of its formation) makes this point convincingly clear.

First, the OAU aimed to "promote the unity and solidarity of the African States" (Article II (a) of the OAU Charter). Yet, Africa was far from united in 2001. The continent, often labeled "conflict ridden," accounted for half of all armed conflicts in the world at the time. Moreover, African states became pawns during the Cold War, thus allowing superpower manipulation during that period to stand in the way of genuine advocacy of African interests in international forums and the exercise of effective collective diplomacy.

Second, the OAU aimed to "achieve a better life for the peoples of Africa" (Article II (b) of the OAU Charter). Yet, by most measures, the African at the dawn of the twenty first century was poorer than s/he was at the time of the founding of OAU, in 1963 (World Bank, 2000). The pervasive and endemic nature of its development crisis prompted *The Economist* (cover essay, May 13, 2000) to declare Africa "the hopeless continent."

Third, the OAU aimed to respect the "Universal Declaration of Human Rights" (Article II (e) of the OAU Charter). Yet, in 2001, unarmed Africans in Angola, Burundi, Central Africa Republic (CAR), Chad, Democratic Republic of Congo (DRC), Guinea, Liberia, Sierra Leone, Somalia, Sudan and Uganda experienced some of the most egregious human rights violations by both government forces and armed opposition groups (Amnesty International, 2002). The Rwandan genocide of 1994 was a collective shame for the continental body. In 1975, the moribund OAU (out of tradition) even honored Uganda's Idi Amin with the organization's chairmanship, although the atrocities he was committing on his own people were hardly a secret.

Lastly, the OAU aimed to "eradicate *all* forms of colonialism from Africa" (Article II (d) of the OAU Charter). Though some African territories are still under foreign occupation,[1] all the mainland states in Africa are politically liberated. While the OAU can be credited for its sustained solidarity and commitment to decolonization, it must be quickly added that it failed miserably in addressing neo-colonialism.[2] As Nkrumah (1970) reminded us, political liberation is meaningful only when it is accompanied with economic autonomy. Today political independence, notwithstanding, the structure of African economies today (in terms of production and consumption) is highly dependent on one or more external power. Africa's excessive reliance on imported inputs; her continued production and export of single commodities (be it agricultural or mineral); and her powerlessness in determining the prices for her goods on world markets, make Africa's victory over colonialism pyrrhic.

One can make the case that the new continental organization, the AU, was needed due to the changes in the international environment, such as the demise of the Cold War, and the end of apartheid. But to laud the old organization's achievements when almost none existed or to pay the OAU tribute by granting it "a permanent place of honor in the history of the formation of modern Africa" (Mbeki, 2002) is a rewriting of history. Succinctly summarized, the OAU was a failure and hence the need to try again, with the AU. The AU can only do better than the OAU if it admits the OAU's failures and learns lessons from it.

THE MAKING OF AU

At the 35th OAU summit in July 1999 at Algiers, the Libyan leader, Col. Muammar Al Qathafi, extended an invitation for African leaders to attend an extraordinary summit in September of that year in Sirte, Libya. The theme of this 4th extraordinary summit was "Strengthening OAU capacity to enable it to meet the challenges of the new millennium."

The Summit, which was preceded as usual by a meeting of the OAU Council of Foreign Ministers, ended on September 9, 1999 with *The Sirte Declaration* (OAU, 1999), which aimed at:

"Effectively addressing the new social, political and economic realities in Africa and the world; fulfilling the peoples' aspirations for greater unity in conforming with the objectives of the OAU Charter and the Treaty Establishing the African Economic Community; revitalizing the [OAU] to play a more active role in addressing the needs of the people; eliminating the scourge of conflicts; Meeting global challenges; and harnessing the human and natural resources of the continent to improve living conditions." (OAU, 1999)

To achieve these aims, the Sirte Summit, *inter alia,* decided to:

"Establish an African Union in conformity with the ultimate objectives of the [OAU] charter and the provisions of the Treaty establishing the African Economic Community. Accelerate the process of implementing the Treaty establishing the African Economic Community, in particular: shorten the implementation periods of the Abuja Treaty, and ensure the speedy establishment of all the institutions provided for in the Abuja Treaty; such as the African Central Bank, the African Monetary Union, the African Court of Justice and in particular, the Pan-African Parliament." (OAU, 1999).

Following the Sirte Declaration, member states began working on a Constitutive Act for the AU. The inspiration for the AU Constitutive Act was drawn from the Treaty establishing the African Economic Community (AEC Treaty) since most of the text of the AU Constitutive Act appears verbatim in the AEC Treaty.[3] The AU Constitutive Act was adopted at the 36th OAU Summit, July 2000, in Lome, Togo. On March 2, 2001, African leaders met, again in Sirte, Libya, for a 5th Extraordinary OAU Summit. There, they declared the establishment of the AU, to be completed upon the deposit of the 36th instrument of ratification of the Constitutive Act of the AU. On 26 April 2001, Nigeria became the 36th member state to deposit its instrument of ratification, satisfying the two third member requirement. The AU Constitutive Act entered into force the following month, on May 26, 2001. At its 37th annual meeting in July 2001 at Lusaka, Zambia, the OAU charged its newly elected secretary-general, Amara Essy, Ivory Coast's former foreign minister, with the task of leading the year long transition of the OAU to the AU.

WHAT IS "NEW" WITH THE AU?

A structural comparison of OAU and AU reveals that the AU is more inclusive and diversified than the OAU it supplanted. First, the official languages of the AU now include Kiswahili, thanks to a last minute resolution adopted at the inaugural summit. The other working languages are all non-African: Arabic, English, French, and Portuguese.

Second, the AU's Constitutive Act has 14 objectives; nine more than the OAU Charter. It includes all of the objectives of the OAU (aside from the eradication of colonialism), and amongst other things, seeks to promote good governance and democracy.

Third, the AU's Constitutive Act is enshrined in 16 principles; nine more than the OAU Charter. Aside from the principles of non alignment and the dedication to the total emancipation of the continent found in the OAU Charter, the AU adopts all the principles of the OAU, including the principles of territorial sovereignty, non interference, and the inviolability of colonial boundaries. The reaffirmation of the national sovereignty of states as well as the reverence for the artificial colonial borders reveals the intent of the AU's founders to retain, rather than transform, Africa's political configuration. To be sure, AU's Constitutive Act, unlike the OAU Charter, while respecting the authority of member states, does have a principle that allows intervention in grave circumstances, such as war crimes, genocide and crimes against humanity. But it has neither clear guidelines on the modalities for intervention nor an enforcement mechanism to give its decisions binding force. The implication of this omission is examined, in the section on the Darfur crisis, at the end of this essay.

Lastly, the AU's Constitutive Act calls for the creation of 11 organs; seven more than the OAU. The new organs (many of which do not exist or are in the process of establishment) are a Permanent Representatives Committee (composed of Permanent Representatives and other Plenipotentiaries to the Union), Specialized Technical Committees (to provide expertise across a broad spectrum of development issues), a Pan-African Parliament, an Economic, Social and Cultural Council, a Court of Justice (whose jurisdiction and functions are yet to be determined), an African Bank, an African Monetary Fund, and an African Investment Bank. Two additional new organs, a consultative Council of the Wise (comprising highly respected African personalities) and a Peace and Security Council have since been established. The AU organs are certainly ambitious and some, such as the Pan African Parliament, are particularly important because if properly institutionalized would be a participatory process directly involving the African masses whose lives need significant transformation, rather than an African elite driven process. But the burning question is this: can a larger and more complex AU avoid the fate of its much smaller precursor, the OAU? If so, how? To answer this question effectively we need to examine why the OAU failed and infer some lessons from it, for the AU.

THE IDEOLOGICAL VACUUM

At the heart of the OAU's failings was not so much a structural shortcoming than it was ideological. The OAU lacked a cohesive ideology that could provide the *proper* situational interpretation of the African context. The essence of an ideology, as Zartman (1966) wrote, is not only to rationalize and explain the reasons for the present situation; "it also points the way to future goals" (Zartman, 1966, p.38). What the OAU lacked then was an ideology capable of rationalizing and explaining Africa's balkanization, dependency and underdevelopment, and an ideology capable of providing strategies that would guarantee and enhance Africa's power, prestige and progress in the post colonial era. Which ideology is capable of filling this vacuum? Pan-Africanism. Ofuatey-Kodjoe (1986) defines Pan-Africanism as an ideology with a cognitive component that recognizes all African peoples, both in Africa and the Diaspora, as being of one folk or nation, as a result of a shared cultural identity, a shared historical experience, and an indivisible future destiny (p.391). Thus, he goes on to argue, that the most fundamental goal of Pan-Africanism is the collective empowerment of African peoples wherever they are (p.391). It must be quickly added that calling oneself Pan-Africanist does not make one so, and being of African descent does not automatically make one a Pan-Africanist. Indeed, most of the OAU founders of yesteryear, and the AU founders of today, label themselves Pan-Africanist, without any appreciably clarity and commitment to the ideology of Pan-Africanism. They have neither bought into Pan African-ism nor Afrocentricity, its substantive counterpart, as ideological direction (Asante, 1998; Asante, 2001). By rejecting the brand of Pan-Africanism advocated by the Casablanca group, the OAU at its birth, consciously or not, gave its blessings to the colonial political and economic formation - together with its ideological and cultural systems. Indeed, the final curse of African independence, and the OAU's ascendancy, was that it solidified the balkanization and dependence inherited from colonialism. The problem was compounded when the Casablanca group rather than opting out of the OAU decided to remain in it, perhaps for fear of isolation. Ghana's Nkrumah, a staunch advocate of the Casablanca thinking, on arrival from the OAU's inaugural summit even remarked triumphantly that "the political unification of the African continent, my lifelong dream, is finally here."

(cited in Rooney, 1988, p.223). But of course, this was not the case; his Pan African ideal of a continental African government had been soundly rejected. And it also did not help much that none of the 22 newly independent countries since the OAU's founding refused to join.[4] Some newly independent countries joined the OAU merely for geographic reasons, well aware of the organization's impotence. Eritrea, OAU's last but one newest member, when joining the OAU in 1993 declared: "we are joining the OAU not because of your achievement, but because you are our African brothers." (Afeworki, 1993). According to Eritrea's Issaias Afeworki, membership of the OAU was "not spiritually gratifying or politically challenging [because] the OAU has become a nominal organization that has failed to deliver on its pronounced goals and objectives." (Afeworki, 1993). (Never mind that the OAU had failed to support Eritrea's bloody 30-year struggle for independence [the continent's longest civil war!] from Ethiopia, incidentally the seat of the OAU headquarters.)

Not surprisingly, the OAU became a geographical entity with no geopolitical weight. It forged a unity that further deepened the political marginalization, economic dependence, and cultural doubt of the continent; the very antithesis of Pan-Africanism. The lesson here is that a union cannot be effective without ideological uniformity or unity of purpose. For while it is necessary for all Africa and Africans to unite, there is no point to this project if the result is a united Africa with divergent and confusing perspectives on the goals of unity, or a united Africa where consensus on a shared African worldview is elusive. From a Pan-Africanist perspective therefore, it is better to have a united, empowered and independent Africa, comprising *some* African States, rather than to have a united, but weak and dependent Africa, comprising of *all* African states.

THE OLD PATTERNS PERSIST

Unfortunately, like the OAU before it, an overwhelming majority of AU's founding members, their good intention notwithstanding, eschew any genuine commitment and seriousness to the Pan-African ideal of an empowered African superstate that would increase the capacity of Africans to take direct control of their destinies. The preference for the status quo was made apparent during the Sirte Summit in September 1999 when African leaders, once again, retreated from the continental government thesis. While Libya's Qathafi (1999) argued passionately for a transformative entity, in the form of a confederation of African states, as a "historical solution" to the continent's numerous problems, an overwhelming number of his fellow African leaders remained deeply skeptical about his "United States of

Africa" vision. Qathafi's plea that African leaders "give up a little bit of their sovereignty in the interests of the whole of Africa" was not even entertained as a realizable goal (Pompey, 2000; Rosine, 1999). The leaders of Egypt, Kenya and Uganda spoke for many when they said publicly that the idea of an African superstate was premature (Kipkoech, 1999; Rosine, 1999). Granted, Qathafi's Arabic persuasion may predispose him to use non African cultural perspectives, rather than an African centered paradigm, as a basis for defining a better world vision. Be that as it may, his call for an African superstate, like that of the Casablanca bloc of the 1960's, is a central pan-africanist strategy to achieving collective power in the contemporary international system. Needless to say, the AU that was created has limited authority and coercive powers capable of changing the behavior of member states. Furthermore, since its ideological underpinnings do not promise the eventual collective acquisition of power, the AU cannot be expected to significantly transform the lives of Africans for the better. When we take a look at the AU's current efforts in the areas of security, economics, and politics, it becomes obvious, but not surprising, that they are contrary to the fundamental goal of Pan-Africanism.

In the area of security and the preservation of peace, the formation of a single African High Command is considered central to the fundamental Pan-Africanist objective of collective empowerment. First, it is logical from a Pan-Africanist perspective to have one army to manage conflicts on the continent and to maximize the power of Africa, relative to other actors, in the international system. Africa has a combined 3.5 million men and women in its armed forces, a number that any power bloc would be forced to reckon with. Second, an African High Command would help to reduce the military expenditures of individual African countries and divert such expenditures to much needed social services. Taken together, African countries spend in excess of $20 billion annually on the military. A significant reduction in such spending would result if Africa had an efficient joint force and a central command. However, Muammar Al Qathafi's call, since 1975, for abolishing national armies to create a single African army has been constantly rebuffed by his counterparts. The last time his idea was rebuffed was at the AU's extraordinary Summit in March 2004. At this summit, a watered down version of Qathafi's single army proposal, based on the maintenance of each African state's independence and sovereignty, was created instead. The creation of the African Standby Force (as this force is known) represents a marked departure from the OAU days, however there are numerous problems with its structures Important amongst these problems are, the lack of mechanisms to counter unilateral action of strong member countries; the non veto power decision-making structure; and the selection and inclusion of conflict prone countries as force members. Egyptian Foreign Minister, Ahmed Maher, later told reporters after the AU Summit that delegates rejected the Qathafi's proposal because "Africa is not ready yet for this [single African army] idea." (Quoted in Pitman, T. (2004)).

Regarding economics, the strategies and programs pursued by the AU and its member states indicate continued reliance on international capital and the uncoordinated development of individual national economies. No real attempt has been made to achieve continental African economic unity despite the obvious economic wisdom of such an approach. The observation by Green and Seidman (1968), almost four decades ago, is still true today:

> "Africa as a whole could provide markets able to support large-scale efficient industrial complexes; no single African state nor existing sub-regional economic union can do so. African states cannot establish large-scale productive complexes stimulating demand throughout the economy as poles of rapid economic growth because their markets are far too small. Instead the separate tiny economies willy-nilly plan on lines leading to the dead ends of excessive dependence on raw material exports and small scale inefficient 'national factories' at high costs per unit of output. Inevitably, therefore, they fail to reduce substantially their basic dependence on foreign markets, complex manufactures and capital." (Green and Seidman, 1968, p.22)

It should be noted that the specific economic policies pursued by the majority of African states are determined largely by the International Monetary Fund and other International Financial Institutions (IFIs), who demand explicit commitments from governments to implement remedial policies that they (IFIs) deem essential to the continued disbursement of loans. The impact of these structural adjustment conditionalities, while mostly negative, comprises the economic autonomy of African countries.

The AU's economic blueprint, the New Partnership for Africa's Development (NEPAD, 2001) does not veer off the path traveled by the individual African member states: it too sees international capital and the separate development of national economies as a panacea. NEPAD has serious flaws, too many to list here (For a concise critique, see Taylor and Nel, 2002). From a Pan-Africanist viewpoint though, NEPAD's biggest failing is that it does not sufficiently recognize African peoples as partners for, and of, development. As it stands now, NEPAD is an appeal to the goodwill and benevolence of the industrialized countries for aid and investment. Even so, NEPAD is an elite driven process that provides no means for mobilizing the African masses for real development. The AU's interest in securing international capital and maintaining neocolonial relationship with the West, (rather than pursuing genuine inter-African cooperation), led the authors of NEPAD to consult first with the Group of Eight industrialized countries, before African governments had had a chance to discuss it amongst themselves and with their own people. There is even talk of constructing a tunnel linking Africa with Europe. Senegalese President Abdoulaye Wade (2002), one of the authors and spokesperson for NEPAD, said: "NEPAD plans to construct a tunnel linking Africa to Europe under the Mediterranean Sea from the northern tip of Algeria through to Gibraltar." What about a much needed railroad or highway linking the continent, from Algiers to Antananarivo? The fact that NEPAD was conceived by a small group of African leaders, without any input from the masses, coupled with the rush to the G8 (G8, 2002) for the programs' endorsement made several AU leaders question the wisdom of the entire enterprise. One such critic was Gambia's president, Yahya Jammeh, who said: "People are sick and tired of African beggars. Nobody will ever develop your country for you. I am not criticizing NEPAD, but the way it was conceived to be dependent on begging" (Lokongo, 2002, p.18). Needless to say, NEPAD, as presently constituted, has the potential of dividing, not unifying, Africa: The G8, on which the AU relies for the programs' major funding, has already made it clear that it would only help African *countries* "whose performance reflects the NEPAD commitments"(G8, 2002). Western nations can thus pick and choose which AU member states are deserving of assistance, and those that are not. The overall effect would not be a stronger Africa. At best, it would reward *individual* African countries for good behavior. Thus one cannot expect NEPAD to transform Africa from its disarticulated, dependent and underdeveloped status.

When it comes to politics, it has been established that the AU's founding majority have no desire for a supernational political entity that would lead to a full and complete African unity. Africa today therefore does not have one state to represent it or a single voice to articulate its concerns in the international system; hence no power. Also, the political map of African remains a sacred cow despite the fact that Africa's 165 demarcated borders (the world's most fragmented region) have in of themselves become the basis of many African conflicts. Unfortunately Article 4(b) of the AU Constitutive Act, like Article 3(3) of the OAU charter before it, affirms these colonial demarcations. The AU should amend the principle of inviolability of these colonial borders and negotiate new boundaries that have more meaning for Africans. It must be borne in mind that the carving up of Africa in 1884 was not meant to unify but rather to divide the continent. These are by no means easy political choices but African leaders have to confront them before any real chance of optimizing Africa's power can be realized.

Politically, it seems what binds the AU is a professed commitment to democracy and good governance. Even on this score, the AU's efforts so far have, at best, been confused. This is because the AU has no established criteria on what constitutes "good governance" or "democracy" beyond the minimalist procedural requisites of free and fair elections. At its inaugural launch in July 2001, the AU barred Madagascar from the new organization and refused to recognize Ravalomanana as Madagascar's new president, citing the contentious nature of the elections and the unorthodox way Mr. Ravalomanana consolidated his "victory." The AU maintained that it would admit Madagascar only if fresh presidential elections were held. That the AU showed resolve early, on a key principle on which it was founded is noteworthy, but it appears, in this particular case, that the resolve shown was not carefully thought through. Madagascar's Supreme Court ruling that Ravalomanana's victory and government were legitimate, coupled with dissent among AU members on the issue, should have given the AU pause and deep reflection on its decision. Not long after AU's decision, several African countries (Senegal, Burkina Faso, Mauritius, Libya and the Comoros islands) broke ranks with the AU and endorsed Ravalomanana's government—so much for Africa speaking with a single voice! The AU did a face saving U-turn and recognized Ravalomanana the following year, a move which no doubt has cost AU to lose some credibility, especially since no new presidential elections were held.

In any case, the AU does not have much credibility on the democracy question to begin with: African leaders do not easily give up the reins of power, and Africa has some of the world's longest-serving Presidents. The following sample makes the case: Gnassingbe Eyadema has ruled Togo for 37 years. Gabon's Omar Bongo has been at the helm of his nation for 37 years. Libya has been under Muammar Al Qathafi for 35 years. Angola's Jose Eduardo dos Santos has 25 years under his belt. Zimbabwe's Robert Mugabe has been in power for 24 years. If the AU were serious about democratic values and good governance, membership to that body should not have been automatic, but rather granted on merit or a set of political criteria. For example, the basic membership prerequisites of the European Union (after which the AU is modeled) has three basic thematic criteria (political, economic and institutional, also known as the Copenhagen Criteria), where the political criteria directs the applicant country to achieve stability of its institutions guaranteeing democracy, the rule of law, human rights and respect for and protection of minorities. What the AU needs now are clear and consistent guidelines on what it considers to be the consent of the governed and enforcement mechanisms to ensure strict compliance. Ideally, the democratic principles advocated must be compatible with the values and practices of the African society.

MORE THAN PAN-AFRICANISM

Aside from the lack of, and/or commitment to, a transformative and empowering ideology based on Pan-Africanism, the OAU did not flourish due to operational failures caused by a lack of popular legitimacy, administrative bottlenecks, and financial stress. These issues will be briefly discussed in turn.

A major hurdle to the OAU's efficacy was that it was a state centric elite political organization that did little to involve the average African in its operations and decision making. Consequently, it had a flag and an anthem that no one saluted or recognized, and an Africa Day that was hardly celebrated. As indicated, the AU promises citizen involvement and participation, and especially the Pan African Parliament (PAP), holds promise of broadly representing the African citizenry. Though in its first five years of existence the Pan African Parliament is to have advisory and consultative powers only, a lot more can be done to make it an effective body by 2007, when it assumes legislative functions. First, the PAP representation should be broadened with respect to gender, the African Diaspora constituency and cross-national party coalitions. The seat currently allocated to women members in the PAP now stands at 20%. This can be said to be a good beginning, however, there is room for improvement as this 20% quota is 10% less than that which the Fourth UN Conference on Women urged as minimum for women parliamentarians. While it is true that representation of women in African national parliaments is scarce, it is not unreasonable to increase their quota, especially if we consider the fact that African women hold the keys to Africa's overall development. Next, is the issue of the Diaspora representation. Following a proposal by the Senegal government that Diaspora Africans be considered the "Sixth Region" of Africa, the AU has been working on the institutional development of the African Diaspora into its organs. This is a move in the right direction toward the pan-africanist goal of an empowered African collective at the global level.[5] The challenge the AU faces is to clearly define the criteria for membership of the African Diaspora, its rights, duties and privileges. The African Diaspora constituency must be accorded real and tangible (and not merely symbolic) membership. Their representation in the PAP will signal that the AU is serious in its efforts to integrate the continent and the diaspora. A final area where PAP representation can be made more inclusive is to provide mechanisms that allow the development of continent-wide political groupings, as opposed to national parties now envisaged for the PAP. Should this occur, the PAP members could form coalitions along ideological and tactical directions such as Workers, Pan-Africanists, Liberals, Socialists, Conservatives, etc.

Another bureaucratic hindrance to OAU's effectiveness had to do with the office of its Secretary General or permanent secretariat. Amara Essy (2002) who headed the OAU during its yearlong transition to AU remarked that the OAU was the most difficult organization he had ever seen. And it was indeed. This is because the Secretary General functioned at the whim of the OAU's heads of state and governments, with very little independence and flexibility (Meyers, 1976). Relating the efforts of Edem Kodjo, a past Secretary General, in the Western Sahara conflict, Sam Amoo (1993, p.248) noted that "he [Edem Kodjo] found himself performing a solitary tightrope walk . . . [with] no net to break his fall." Whereas the OAU had consisted of a secretary-general and five assistant secretaries-generals, the Commission of the AU has a chairperson, a deputy chairperson and eight commissioners. Unfortunately the AU Constitutive Act is silent on the duties and powers of the Chairperson of the AU. It is hoped that the head of AU would be endowed with powers that transcend administrative functions. To be effective, the AU head must be given greater political powers with the capacity to act independent of AU's decisions, and to influence policy making. Another area of difficulty relating to the permanent secretariat was that it lacked high level staff. To compound the situation, most of the OAU staff were political, rather than professional, appointees (Meyers, 1976). This situation promoted not only inertia and impotence; it also created a culture of despondency.

The final area in terms of material resources where the OAU was found wanting was its finances. The life-blood of any organization is money. And on this score the OAU was anemic. Its annual operating budget of $30 million, which came mainly from membership dues, was neither adequate nor forthcoming. At AU's launch in 2002, all but 9 members (Angola, Botswana, Cameroon, Ethiopia, Mauritius, Namibia, South Africa, Swaziland and Zambia) owed the OAU $54 million. As of June 2004, member states had paid up only $13 million of the AU's $43 million annual budget. Though financing of the AU and its organs is extremely critical to the AU's success and effectiveness, the AU Constitutive Act is virtually silent on how the AU will raise funds. When during the organization's third summit (July 2004) in Addis Ababa, AU Commission Chairman, Alpha Oumar Konare, unveiled a three-year strategic plan to launch Africa into the 21st century, member states endorsed texts on the "Vision and Mission" of the

AU, but failed to endorse the plan's $600 million annual operating budget, an amount more than ten times the $43 million currently budgeted for the organization. Unsurprisingly, they could not agree on how to fund the project either. The AU is said to be considering funding options besides member state contributions, including an AU trust fund to be financed by diasporan Africans, and a one-dollar levy on all international airlines to and from Africa. These are practicable proposals and others should be considered as well. The idea of Pan African Solidarity Visa (Tadadjeu, 2001) which would require non-Africans entering the continent to pay solidarity fee of $10 each, and which could potentially generate $200 million annually, must be given serious consideration. The AU cannot make any headway if members are not willing to pay the price for their collective vision. The AU, as a matter of principle, should not emulate OAU's bad habit of harboring profligate members: non paying members should be expelled outright.

LIMITATIONS OF THE AU: THE DARFUR CRISIS AS A TEST CASE

The ongoing humanitarian crisis in the Darfur region of Sudan exposes both the opportunities and constraints facing the AU. Already, the nearly two-year insurgency against the government of Sudan and the government's scorched-earth response to it have killed at least 50,000 people and forced more than one million Sudanese to leave their homes in Darfur (Johnson, 2004). While it is premature to predict the outcome of that crisis, it is not too early to assess the challenges that it poses for the AU's viability.

First, the Darfur crisis presents a litmus test for what constitutes a legitimate intervention by the African Union in the affairs of a member state. As noted above, the African Union does make provision for intervention in grave circumstances. Second, a successful intervention by the AU to stem this crisis would provide an opportunity for the AU to demonstrate to the world and to ordinary Africans that an African peace established, enforced and consolidated by Africans themselves is possible: a pax Africana (Mazrui, 1967).

The AU's approach to the crisis (to date) has been anything but swift and effective, and underlines the Pan-Africanist critique outlined in this paper. Despite the presence of AU peacekeepers (known as AMIS, or the African Union Mission in Sudan) and a cease-fire agreement between the Sudanese government and rebels, the situation in Darfur continues to deteriorate, with some 10,000 to 30,000 crisis related deaths per month.[6] Part of the problem has to do with the size, structure, and mandate of the AU force sent to Darfur. As of December 2004, there were only 800 AU soldiers in

Darfur, a region the size of France. The force is expected to grow to 3,320 by February 2005. One cannot help but wonder why the AU needed two years to send such a minimal force? To underscore the woefully undermanned size of the force, consider this: Liberia, a country one tenth the size of Darfur, currently has 15,000 U.N. peacekeepers–five times more than what is planned for Darfur.

Apart from the size of the force, there are other logistical problems facing AMIS, such as inadequate military equipment supplies and funding (estimated to cost $221 million), as well as language barriers. Even if the AU force had been more robust and swift in its response, it still would have been ineffective simply because it does not have the mandate to protect civilians. The current AU mission and mandate explicitly prohibit AMIS from using its weapons except in self defense (Wax, 2004, p.1). The AMIS is also prevented from taking any Sudanese into custody and from physically intervening in the conflict whatsoever. Citing the AU's sovereignty clause, the Sudanese government insists that it alone has the responsibility to protect the Sudanese people. The AU has not been able to get around Sudan's sovereignty claims because it failed earlier on to call the crisis by its rightful name: genocide. At its 3rd Summit in July 2004, the AU, not only failed to denounce Sudan for the Darfur atrocities, but went on to declare that the killings did not amount to genocide, although the killings clearly meet that definition. The U.N. Genocide Convention defines genocide as "killing" or "deliberately inflicting on the group conditions of life" intended "to destroy, in whole or in part, a national, ethnical, racial or religious group." It is noteworthy that independent findings had by this time established that the pro-Arab government-supported Janjaweed militia was systematically targeting the Bantu peoples of Fur, Masalit, and Zaghawa. One of the most thorough investigations on the Darfur crisis done during this period, by the Physicians for Human Rights, in June 2004, concluded that what was happening there was "completely commensurate with instances of past mass killing the world has only belatedly called genocide." (Physicians for Human Rights, 2004, p.11). The United States government and congress later labeled the conflict genocide. This is not an issue of mere semantics. Like Rwanda, lives are at stake in Darfur, and calling the crisis by its proper name would have given the AU the authority to define what constitutes legitimate intervention, and set the threshold for future interventions. The intervention that the current AU boasts of is merely cosmetic. Cosmetic interference is the decision to interfere in the internal affairs of a member state by another without any clear guidelines for such intervention and without an enforcement superstructure to effect desired change.

The accelerating genocide in Darfur and the AU's limited response thus far provides several interesting observations, and hopeful corrective action, for the AU. First, the crisis heightens the need for Africa to get serious about creating a supranational African High Command, with the capacity to enforce peace and security. Second, it also highlights the AU's need for a non-judicial mechanism for conflict resolution. Third, the crisis further shows the need for firm and prompt collective political will. Come July 2005, unless real substantial progress has been made, the AU should put tradition aside, and not allow Sudan to preside over the next AU summit meeting and to head the organization that year. Above all, the crisis in Sudan and the AU's agonizing snail's pace response shows that "Africa" today remains a geographical, rather than a political, reality: an Africa of states rather than an African superstate, where domestic sovereignty and nonintervention still constitutes the main principles guiding intra African relations. The desire for an effective and credible AU cannot be achieved if it lacks the political, economic and military muscle to safeguard and enforce the collective interests of its members.

CONCLUSION

The establishment of the AU is a monumental feat in the political history of Africa, and will continue, in the foreseeable future, to be an important vehicle for addressing the continent's numerous projects. But the AU cannot empower and develop Africa nor guarantee Africa's collective security and provide a common platform for Africa's collective diplomacy if the AU remains the way it is today: bereft of a genuine commitment to Pan-Africanism and an empowered African superstate.

To be sure, Africa can and must unite! But it would only succeed if the lessons of OAU's failures are mastered. This would require, amongst other things, leaders who share a pan Africanist commitment, and who are willing to engage the African citizenry in a search for solutions that preserve Africa's independence and dignity; strategies which reflect Africa's image and interests. It is a long way from 1963, but as we have seen, much work has to be done before the dream of the collective empowerment of all African peoples comes true. Till then the dream of African unity remains a mirage.

REFERENCES

Afeworki, I. (1993). OAU Summit Opens to Criticism from Newest Member Eritrea. *Agence France Presse—English*, June 28, 1993.
Akonor, K. (2002). Africa's Development. *New York Times*, June 26 2002. pp. A22.

Amate, C.O.C. (1986). *Inside the OAU: Pan-Africanism in Practice,* Basingstoke: Macmillan.

Amnesty International Annual Report (2002). *Africa Regional Update.* London: Amnesty International.

Amoo, S. (1993). Role of the OAU: Past, Present and Future. In D. Smock (ed.), *Making War and Waging Peace: Foreign Intervention in Africa,* Washington, DC: United States Institute of Peace Press.

Asante, M. K. (2001) *Afrocentricity.* Chicago: African American Images.

Asante, M. K. (1998) *The Afrocentric Idea.* Philadelphia: Temple University Press.

Davies, D. (2003). Jammeh: 'Why I Oppose NEPAD.' *West Africa* No.4364:14 February 24, 2003.

Emily W. (2004). A Peace Force With No Power; African Union Monitors in Sudan Face.

Frustrating Limits. *The Washington Post,* December 11, 2004. pp. A01.

Essy, A. (2002). Interview. In Ankomah, B. (2002). African Union in Danger of Being Stillborn. *New African,* June 1 2002. p.24.

Fabienne, P. (2002). African leaders downgrade Kadhafi plan for United States of Africa." *Agence France Presse*—English, July 12, 2000.

G-8 (2002). *G-8 Africa Action Plan.* Document from the G-8 Summit in Kananaskis, Canada, June 26–27. Also available online at http://www.state.gov/e/eb/rls/othr/11515.htm.

Green, R.H. & Seidman, A. (1968). *Unity or Poverty? The Economics of PanAfricanism* . . . Harmondsworth: African Penguin Library.

Hinich, M. J. and Munger, M. C. (1994). *Ideology and the Theory of Political Choice.* Ann Arbor, MI: The University of Michigan Press.

Johnson, D. H. (2004). *The Root Causes of Sudan's Civil Wars.* Bloomington, IN: Indiana University Press.

Kipkoech, T. (1999). African Political Union Is Premature. *The Nation (Nairobi).* September 13, 1999. Also online at: http://www.nationaudio.com/News/DailyNation/130999/.

Lokongo, B. (2002). Jammeh: 'NEPAD Will Never Work.' New African, September 2002: 18–19.

Mansour, K. (2004) War and Peace in Sudan: A Tale of Two Countries. London: Keegan Paul.

Mbuyinga, E. (1982) *Pan Africanism or neo-colonialism?: the bankruptcy of the O.A.U.;* translated by Michael Pallis. London : Zed Press.

Mazrui, Ali A. . (1967) Towards a Pax Africana: A study of Ideology and Ambition Chicago: University of Chicago Press.

Mbeki, T. (2003). Mbeki: African Union is the Mother, NEPAD is Her Baby. *New African* No.415:44–45 February 2003.

Mbeki, T. (2002). *Speech at the launch of the African Union.* Durban: South Africa. July 9. http://www.anc.org.za/ancdocs/history/mbeki/2002/tm0709.html

Meyers, D. (1976). The OAU's Administrative Secretary, *International Organization,* Summer 1976, 509–520.

Naldi, G. J. (2000). The Organization of African Unity: an Analysis of Its role. New York: Mansell.

NEPAD. (2001). *The New Partnership for Africa's Development.* October. Also available online at: http://www.nepad.org.

Nantambu, K. (1998). Pan-Africanism Versus Pan-African Nationalism: An Afrocentric Analysis. *Journal of Black Studies,* Vol. 28, No. 5. pp. 561–574.

Nkrumah, K. (1970). *Africa Must Unite.* New York: International Publishers.

OAU. (2000). *Constitutive Act of the African Union.* July 2000.

OAU. (1999). *Sirte Declaration .Fourth Extraordinary Session of the Assembly of Heads of State and Government.* Sirte, Libya. Also available online: http://www.au2002.gov.za/docs/key_oau/sirte.htm.

OAU (1991) *Treaty Establishing the African Economic Community,* June 3rd 1991, Abuja, Nigeria.

Ofuatey-Kodjoe, W. (1986) (ed). *Pan-Africanism: New Directions in Strategy.* Lanham, University Press of America.

Physicians for Human Rights (2004), *Calls for Intervention to Save Lives in Sudan: Field Team Compiles Indicators of Genocide.* Cambridge, MA Physicians for Human Rights June 23, 2004, p.11. Also available online at: http://www.phrusa.org/research/sudan/pdf/sudan_genocide_report.pdf.

Pitman, T. (2004), Gadhafi Calls For Unity At Start Of African Union Summit. The Associated Press, February 27, 2004.

Qathafi, M. (1999). Qadhafi tells OAU foreign ministers of 'United States of Africa' vision. *BBC Summary of World Broadcasts,* September 09, 1999.

Rooney, D. (1988). *Kwame Nkrumah, the Political Kingdom in the Third World.* New York. St. Martin's Press.

Rosine Ngangoue Nana (1999). "Little Support for the Proposed United States of Africa." *IPS-Inter Press Service/Global Information Network,* September 10, 1999.

Tadadjeu, M. (2001). L'argent fera defaut, *Le Messager,* Juillet 18, pp. 8.

Taylor, I; and P. Nel (2002). Getting the rhetoric right,' getting the strategy wrong: "New Africa," globalization and the confines of elite reformism, *Third World Quarterly,* 21, 1.

Wade, A. (2002). *NEPAD Plans to Build Tunnel to Europe.* July 15, 2002, http://allafrica.com/stories/200207150175.html.

World Bank (2000). *Can Africa Claim the 21st Century?* Washington, D.C: The World Bank.

Zartman W. (1966), National Interest and Ideology. In V. Mckay (ed), *African Diplomacy: Studies in the Determinants of Foreign Policy.* London, Pall Mall Press.

NOTES

1. The African territories still under foreign occupation are: Chagos Islands and St. Helena Island (United Kingdom); Canary Islands and Ceuta/Melilla (Spain); La Réunion and Mayotte (France); and The Azores and The Madeiras (Portugal).

2. Neocolonialism refers to a condition in which, despite political independence, a newly independent state remains vulnerable and sensitive to external

    manipulation due to the continuing control of its economy by colonial and imperial powers. (Nkrumah, 1977, p.174.)

3. Indeed, Qathafi told the African delegates that his call for a new continental body was inspired by the Treaty establishing the African Economic Community (also known as the Abuja Treaty). He said: "I went over the Abuja agreement many times and discovered that it contained everything, but none of it has been implemented." Speech transcript, "Qadhafi tells OAU foreign ministers of 'United States of Africa' vision." BBC Summary of World Broadcasts, September 09, 1999.

4. The only country to resign from the OAU was Morocco in November 1984 to protest the OAU's admission of the SADR which claims the independence of its southern provinces retrieved by Morocco in 1975 under a tripartite agreement with Spain, the former colonial power. In July 2001, Morocco again declined to join the AU for the same reason.

5. The AU's First Conference of Intellectuals of Africa and the Diaspora held in Dakar, Senegal on 6–9 October 2004 is an important step in this regard. In the future, non intellectuals must be given a role as well.

6. Source for 10,000 per month: BBC News, (2004) 70,000 Darfur Dead' Since March, http://news.bbc.co.uk/1/hi/world/africa/3747380.stm [Accessed 30 October 2004]. Source for 30,000 per month: Reeves, E. (2004) "The Meaning of AU Forces Deployment to Darfur," Sudan Tribune, http://www.sudantribune.com/article_impr.php3?id_article=6168 [Accessed 9 November 2004].

Chapter Eleven

Globalization, Development, and the Nation-State in Africa

Herbert W. Vilakazi, South Africa

I shall first deal with the issue of "globalization, development, and the nation-state," in historical context, and then focus upon the crisis of Africa, which is a crisis resulting from the failure of development in the continent as a whole, including in our own country, South Africa.

THE ISSUE OF AFRICA AND GLOBALIZATION

The issue of globalization is very relevant in a discussion of development policy imperatives for Africa. Does Africa not have a choice on this matter? In a sense, the Seattle demonstrations and riots, which resulted in the failure of the WTO meeting, have preempted the issue. It is a gross error to maintain that Africa has no choice on the matter of globalization.

We need to stress that every country in our time is part and parcel of global economic relationships. The uniqueness of capitalism in history is that it was the first economic system which operated as a global system. So, that is not the choice being put to nations, whether or not one's nation should have global economic ties. The burning issue is, what type of global economic relations do African countries want to enter into? That, of course, shall depend on the type of economic relations existing within each African country. We come to the issue of models of economic structure.

The Secretary-General of UNCTAD, Mr. Rubens Ricupero, has urged developing countries to approach globalization as follows: "Rather than reconcile themselves to the need to *adapt* themselves to a supposedly unmodifiable global system, they must strive to *shape* it according to their own development needs at their own pace and in line with their own strengths and weaknesses . . . In fact, contrary to what one frequently hears, it is not the amount and pace of international integration that counts but its quality. There is indeed such a thing as too much and too rapid integration of the wrong kind." (Report of the Secretary-General of UNCTAD to UNCTAD X, Thailand, 12–19 February 2000)

Principle number one, in my approach is the following:

The Development Paradigm Chosen by African Countries Must Determine the Policies They Adopt Towards "Globalization"

What is being suggested, by proponents of "globalization," is the opposite principle: Globalization must determine the development paradigm adopted by African countries.

So, the guiding principle is either

Globalization determines the development paradigm to be followed.

OR

The Development Paradigm followed determines or shapes policies towards "Globalization."

I think that African countries must adopt the latter path: the development paradigm they choose must determine their policies towards "globalization."

The very economic history of the presently industrially developed countries, at the time of their early industrialization, confirms the correctness of the principle that the development paradigm chosen must determine policies towards "globalization."

What is "globalization"? This controversial phenomenon called "globalization" is not the mere internationalization of economic, cultural, and socio-political relations now existing in the world. Few people in the world are opposed to closer, intimate and intricate relations among all the peoples of the world. Modern technology, modern science, modern means of communication, and the modern world market, have made the world truly one world, with all the nations and parts closely inter-linked. A classic document by Marx and Engels, *The Manifesto of the Communist Party,* announced and celebrated that phenomenon as long ago as 1847. That is not the present, controversial, "globalization."

The present "globalization," which has become very controversial, refers to specific regulations, rules, and recommendations, proposed by the IMF, The World Bank, and WTO, about how the international economic, social, intellectual, cultural, and political relations now existing in the world must occur and how they must be governed. For example, proposals and suggestions that the State must play a grossly diminishing role in economic matters; that there should be no discrimination exercised by any nation between national industry, on one hand, and foreign industry; that governments must divest themselves, as much as possible, of ownership of enterprises; that there should be free capital flows, allowing monies to move without State-imposed hindrances across national boundaries; that there should be free, unhindered trade among nations of the world; there is also the issue of specific rules relating to "intellectual property rights," etc., etc.

There is heavy controversy, among nations of the world, particular between the developed and developing countries, over these suggestions, rules, and regulations. It is these rules, regulations, and suggestions, which are being debated, argued over, critically questioned, or sometimes directly rejected. The controversy and conflicts over these rules, regulations, and suggestions, have been deceptively covered up by the term "globalization," giving the false impression that the controversy is over whether or not people want internationalization of economic, cultural, socio-political relations.

The issue of these rules, regulations, and suggestions, coming out of the Bretton Woods institutions, does affect possibilities and policies for development of different nations. The presently developed countries also went through the early stages of development.

Therefore, a very good model for developing countries is the very historical experience of the currently developed, industrial countries, themselves, in their response and attitude to globalization at a stage of development comparable to that of currently developing countries. In the 19th and early 20th centuries, the State in England, Germany, Italy, the United States, France, used its power to shelter young, developing national industries, and national agriculture, from open global economic competition, so as to give these national industries time and internal nourishment to grow, strengthen, and mature for a later stage of open competition with other national industries in the more open global economic competition.

Here are the words of a scholar: "It is, however, not only 'late development' that is crucially dependent on departures from doctrinal orthodoxy. The same was true of the 'early development' of England . . . The United States as well. High tariffs and other forms of state intervention may have raised costs to American consumers, but they allowed domestic industry to develop, from textiles, to steel to computers, barring cheaper

British products in earlier years, providing a state-guaranteed market and public subsidy for research and development in advanced sectors, creating and maintaining capital-intensive agribusiness, and so on. Elimination of tariffs in the 1830s would have bankrupted 'about half the industrial sector of New England'" (Chomsky, Noam, *Year 501*, Boston, South End Press, 1993, p. 103). The development economist, Lance Taylor has been more emphatic, as quoted by Professor Chomsky: "Import substitution [through state intervention] is about the only way anybody's ever figured out to industrialize . . . In the long-run, there are no laissez-faire transitions to modern economic growth. The state has always intervened to create a capitalist class, and then it has to regulate the capitalist class, and then the state has to worry about being taken over by the capitalist class, but the state has always been there." Chomsky adds: "Furthermore, state power has regularly been invoked by investors and entrepreneurs to protect them from destructive market forces, to secure resources, markets, and opportunities for investment, and in general to safeguard and extend their profits and power." (Ibid. 104.)

Another well-respected economic historian has written the following on the issue: "Direct subsidies and aids are only part of the story. The state's hand lay everywhere, even where not directly manifest. Even in Britain, government supported and protected overseas trade: the country as a whole paid the associated security costs of private venturers and adventurers in distant seas. Such indirect subsidy, easy to overlook, was crucial. In Britain again, as elsewhere, industrial promotion also took the form of defense against outside competition. The later record of British commitment to free trade (more or less mid-nineteenth century to 1930) has tended to obscure the earlier and much longer practice of economic nationalism, whether by tariff protection or discriminatory shipping rules (navigation acts). Economic theorists have argued forcibly, even passionately, that such interferences with the market hurt everyone. The fact remains that history's strongest advocates of free trade—Victorian Britain, post-World War II United States—were strongly protectionist during their own growing stage. Don't do as I did; do as I can afford to do now. The advice does not always sit well." (Landes, David, *The Wealth and Poverty of Nations*, New York, Little, Brown and Company, 1998, pp. 265–266)

What we need to grasp and understand clearly is that different economic stages require different supportive conditions. There is no clearer demonstration of that rule than the supportive environment which the US government, and European governments, created for the successful development of agriculture and agricultural business interests. For decades, the US government had government subsidies for US farmers, just as most

European governments have massive subsidies for European agribusiness interests. This served the needs of the agricultural business class interests of those countries, at that particular stage of economic development. Now, US agribusiness is in deadly competition with European agribusiness, for the world market. Now, the very same United States Government, which subsidized US agribusiness interests with massive subsidies, in past years, is agitating now for the dismantling of European government subsidies for Euro agribusiness, and the lowering of tariffs for agricultural products, so as to suit the new stage of market competition between US agri-business and the rest of the world, particularly between the US agri-business and European agri-business.

I must stress that Government subsidies for American and European agriculture, are still intact and in effect; and these subsidies are worth billions of dollars, pounds, and Euros.

African countries are not the equals of US, or European, agri-business. We cannot, therefore, be served to our success, by the same supportive environment which serves the interests of Euro, and US, agri-business now.

We must formulate our own position as Africans on this matter. The big, defining, question is: which development interests within our African societies should our policies support? We often forget what economics really is: "economics deals not with things but with relations between persons, and, in the last resort, between classes; these relations are, however, always *attached to things* and *appear as things.*" (Engels, Frederick, a review of Karl Marx's *The Critique of Political Economy*, 1859)

The overwhelming majority of African people, in all African countries, are peasants and workers and lumpen proletariat in cities. That should be the first concern, the primary target of development policy in all African countries. That is the primary market our policies should develop, and should have in mind, first and foremost, at this stage. African countries, as yet, have no African big Agri-business class interests. In South Africa, the big Agri-business class interest is the White capitalist farming class. The first requirement is to link this White agricultural class interest with the interest and imperative to serve the needs of the overwhelming majority of African people, who need food, and the need to develop agricultural business capacity within the African population. The first rule, in the agricultural history of the US, as well as of Europe, was, and has been to base agricultural policy on developing the capacity to meet the needs of the internal market. Developing African agriculture means, first and foremost, developing the African capacity to satisfy the consumption needs of the internal African population. Export and trade in agriculture, and in industry, too, must come after that policy imperative. That is healthy modernization and industrialization policy, and healthy national economics. That is what developed Europe, and developed America did, in their earlier development stages.

Let us suppose that there is an African country in which 90 percent of the people are subsistence farmers, living in the countryside, and only 10 percent live in urban areas. Of the 10 percent who live in urban areas, let us say that 50 percent are unemployed, living off their own individual talents for informal economic activities which may give them some money; 20 percent are government servants; 5 percent are shop owners, merchants, and business people; 5 percent are skilled industrial workers; and the rest of the 20 percent make their living, some as unskilled workers, and the rest through petty-criminal activity, prostitution, and God knows how else.

Let us make the picture even more interesting. Assume that the country has a nice sea-coast, with a recently upgraded harbor, and that this sea-coast has stimulated the development of some tourist industry and hotels.

Does this imaginary country not bring to your mind some real African country?

My point is that an effective development policy for such a country should focus, first and foremost, on the 90 percent of the population engaged in subsistence agriculture in rural areas.

A class issue then emerges when we consider the issue of globalization and foreign trade, with respect to this country.

Should the policy of globalization, as presented by the West, be decided on the basis primarily of the consideration of the interests of the 10 percent of the population which resides in urban areas? Or should the issue be looked at primarily from the point of view of the economic and life interests of the 90 percent of the population which lives off subsistence agriculture in rural areas?

I assert that the issue of globalization should be looked at primarily from the point of view of the economic and life needs of the 90 percent of the population which lives off subsistence agriculture in rural areas?

These people, engaged in subsistence agriculture in rural areas, are not likely to need many things from Japan, Europe, and the USA.

Therefore, a wise, mature leadership of such a country should approach the issue of globalization in the following manner: in deciding economic policies, and policies on globalization, we need to be guided by the particular stage of development at which the country is, at the time, and be aware of the fact that each stage of development has its own particular needs. At this stage of our country's development, we need to develop, first and foremost, rural areas and rural people. These people, and this type of development work, do not need that much from abroad. Therefore, free-trade with the developed Western countries is not top priority for us, at this particular first stage of development. We can pretty much for without intricate, many economic links with the countries of the West.

Our strategy of development shall be from the countryside to the urban areas. We shall urge members of urban, upper classes to tighten their belts, as far as items from abroad are concerned, such as Japanese or German or American automobiles, cameras, stereo-sets, etc. We shall impose a policy of strict economizing, as far as imported luxury goods are concerned. Not that we shall forbid all importation of goods made in foreign countries—we shall allow those which are absolutely necessary.

(Let me remind you, in parenthesis, that the very Western countries we have in mind, England, France, Germany, and USA, as well as Japan, in the East, adopted careful economic planning during World War I as well as during World War II. There was very precise, State-imposed prioritization of economic production and distribution. I am arguing that Africa is in a similar situation, a situation similar to War conditions: that is the seriousness of the crisis facing Africa in our time.)

As leaders in this imaginary-real African country, we shall encourage a policy of import substitution, i.e., developing our own capacity to produce what we need. We shall put top priority on making sure that each household has capacity for food security, as a general rule; the other wing of that policy shall be to empower those households and individuals who demonstrate a talent and inclination for commercial farming, knowing fully well that such households and individuals are a minority in any village; the State shall encourage households and NGOs to form cooperatives in rural areas, for purposes of increasing and diversifying agricultural productivity; the participation of youth in such economic activities shall be highly encouraged; the State shall also put high priority on education, health education, and skills development, in both rural areas and urban areas.

The development of infrastructure of roads, housing, communication, health, education, shall also receive high priority. Polytechnical education, skills development, for young as well as adults, shall also receive high priority, and this skills development and polytechnical education shall be planned to dovetail with the need to increase productivity, and increase diversification of the economy, as the next secondary stage, after securing food security for every household.

This emphatically does not mean closing down towns and cities, or neglecting their development; or neglecting the need to develop non-agricultural urban production. Non-agricultural, urban production shall also be encouraged; however, the policy shall be to rationalize it, to plan and reshape it in such a way that it dovetails with the great work of production and development taking place in rural areas, the site of the overwhelming majority of the population.

We shall encourage, in rural areas, the emergence of rural, non-agricultural industries, which shall be planned and oriented to dovetail with the needs of the urban population, and with the needs of urban industry.

I must also stress the point that we, in Africa, shall need to develop and conceptualize a new and different relationship between the city and the countryside, between urban and rural communities, than that which exists in the developed West, and which we inherited from the West. It is disastrous that we should see cities like New York City, London, Berlin, Mexico City, Delhi, Calcutta, Cairo, Athens, Paris, Brussels, emerging in Africa. The African ecology, the world ecology, and humankind as a whole, do not need such a development. We have a preciously rare opportunity in Africa, as the last continent to plan industrialization, to bring about a new, and healthier (not just physically, but also spiritually) relationship between the countryside and the city.

All this gigantic work, of course, shall call for a gigantic cultural revolution, in which we should attempt to imbue our people with a new humanism, the humanism of the African Renaissance, whose starting point shall not be the arrogance and air of superiority of today's city people. Whatever we may say in criticism of Mao Tse Tung, he was right and correct when he proclaimed: To the Countryside!

Even though he appears to have been discredited later, by the later Chinese generation and subsequent leadership, I argue that his positive legacy is obvious in today's China. By sending tens of thousands, hundreds of thousands, and millions of urban youth, and other city people to the countryside, to "learn from the peasants," as he put it, he made possible a fermentation of knowledge and skills development in rural China, a synthesis of the knowledge of city people with the knowledge of peasants, occurred. With what amazing results?

We are told that the major forward thrust in the development of the Chinese economy, in the 1980s and 1990s, was provided by the development of the rural economy of China, in which there were so many striking innovations. As Chinese scholars have put it in a recent publication: "It is unquestionable that the rural reform is playing a leading role in China's economic reform as a whole. There are many manifestations of this, and in a word, it is the growth leader of the new market economy system. This is by no means an accidental case, but has profound social and economic causes." (Gao Shangquan and Chi Fulin, Chief Editors, *The Reform and Development of China's Rural Economy*, Beijing, Foreign Languages Press, 1997, p. 21)

I must stress that every major turning point in the revolutionary transformation of China, from 1949 up to our time, began in the countryside. The reason is simple. As the same Chinese scholars put it: "About 80 percent of China's population of 1.2 billion is located in the countryside. Without rural development there can be no prosperity for the farmers, and no development and prosperity for China as a whole." (Ibid. p. 27)

In ending, let me use the experience of China, and the international politics on China, to make a point about a probable wise position of African leaders towards globalization and development policy.

From 1949 until US President Nixon's term, the Western governments, led by the US Government, imposed an economic embargo against so-called Communist China. The only economic relations China could have with a Big Power, was with the Soviet Union, and this relationship ended in 1960, when Russian Leader Khruschev severed economic relations with China. China then relied totally upon herself for development resources and skills.

In all that time, until the end of the beginning of the end of the embargo by President Nixon, the countryside was at the centre of the debate about correct economic or development policy within the Chinese leadership. The entire leadership never wavered, or differed, on the crucial nature of the Chinese countryside, of the rural economy, in formulating correct policy for the development of China.

This raises the absolutely crucial factor of theory in the leadership of society. May I paraphrase a historical political leader: without a correct development theory, or development paradigm, there cannot be effective and correct development of a society.

This, indeed, highlights the "subjective factor" in history. President Mbeki raised this issue in a remarkable speech he made, opening the debate in Parliament on "Reconciliation and Nationbuilding," on 29 May 1998, while he was still Deputy President. This is the speech in which he argued, in Disraeli's style, that "South Africa is a country of two nations."

In the speech, he had compared our own policy efforts to make the two nations "one," with Germany's policy efforts to weld the former East Germany together with the former West Germany. "Before we digressed to Germany, we were making the point that four or five years are not enough to weld the two nations which coexist in South Africa as a consequence of a long period of the existence of a society based on racism. To respond to all this, in conceptual terms we have to deal with two interrelated elements. The first of these is that we must accept that it will take time to create the material base for nation building and reconciliation. The second and related element is that we must therefore agree that it is the subjective factor . . .

which must take the lead in sustaining the hope and conviction among the people that the project of reconciliation and nation building will succeed."

The point I want to emphasize is that the whole of Africa, right now, is unable to move forward because of the failure of the African leadership at the "subjective level."

We have not grasped the fact that, as China could not move forward without basing herself and motion on changes and development in the Chinese countryside, we cannot move Africa forward without basing ourselves and our motion on changes and development in the African countryside.

Now that China has made tangible progress in rural development and agriculture, which has been a foundation for urban, industrial development, China has now reached a new stage of development in which the leadership can pose the question of globalization, and formulate a new policy from the previous one.

The same with the leadership of the imaginary-real African country we used as an example above, once we pass beyond the subsistence rural base of the African economy, we can raise the question of globalization again, as the developed Western nations did at a comparable stage of development, and we, Africans, can formulate a new policy on globalization.

Chapter Twelve

NEPAD and the Politics of Globalization: Redefining Local Space, Group Dynamics, and Economic Development

Emmanuel Ngwainmbi, Elizabeth City State University

As the 21st century dawns and multinational corporations increasingly turn to new technologies—satellite navigation systems, cybernetics, and telemetric—to enhance business relations and expand financial markets across tangible and cyber borders, wealthy and politically powerful nation-states have been handling diplomatic activities with considerable success. The same does not refer to regions with fragile democracies and weak economies, as they have been preoccupied with forming partnerships among local, regional and international organizations to address pressing socioeconomic problems. Any partnership that addresses strategies for the eradication poverty, the placement of nations in a network of sustainable growth and development, the reconstruction of a nation's global image and enhancement of its integration into the global economy deserves special attention in social science research. This is the sort of relationship recently conceived in Africa two years ago—the strategic framework of African government leaders, business executives and development experts. Following a mandate at the 37th summit of the Organization of African Unity (OAU) in July 2001, to the Heads of State of Algeria, Egypt, Nigeria, Senegal, and South Africa to develop an integrated socio-economic development framework for the New Partnership for Africa's Development (NEPAD), a program of action for the redevelopment of Africa was implemented in October 2001. This partnership is set up with institutions in developed countries whereby African countries will monitor standards of good government across the continent whilst respecting human rights and advancing democracy in return for increased aid flows, private investment, and a lowering of obstacles to trade by the West.

From a cursory glance, NEPAD's plan for the 21st century seems relevant if we were to consider contemporary local realities (widespread poverty, disease and incomparable wealth distribution) and socioeconomic correctives—the rapid expansion of economic relationships and integration of economic fortunes across national borders and inevitable continental competitions for markets. Realistically, however, the key promoting globalization forces in the 21st century are primarily concerned with amassing and maximizing profit at the expense of stifling 'young' democracies. Four inevitable conditions are responsible for this practice: (1) the increasing interconnectedness between nations with the help of fast-paced communication systems (internet, telephone, faxing, and videoconferencing) and meetings sponsored by regional and international organizations (UN, World Bank, NEPAD) restricts national sovereignty and democratic control over a country's political agenda; (2) increasing transactions across national borders are eroding the efficiency of national governing structures and the ability of democratic governments to manage economic and social affairs in the interests of the people, according to Beliaev (2003); (3) the mismanagement of local authority, wherein officials in decision-making positions lack the expertise to handle diplomatic and business matters with foreign negotiators, partially because of nepotistic practices, suffer an inferiority complex culled from the colonial experience, or have dubious reasons (often personal agendas) when negotiating business matters with representatives of foreign corporations. (4) Transnational financial and multilateral institutions like the International Monetary Fund (IMF) that provide 'young' democratic nations with short and long term loans as well as aid-giving nations are deeply involved in political decision making at national and multinational levels. Given these conditions, how would a regional political institution like NEPAD realize its objectives of take control of local markets, mobilize all sectors of society, eradicating poverty, place African countries on a path of sustainable growth and development, eliminate the marginalization of Africa in the globalization process and enhance Africa's integration into the global economy?

To properly address the question, we have to take a closer look at globalization, examine the path of globalization that nationalists have viewed with much skepticism and transnational or 'supra-national' have aggressively pursued corporations, drawing references from historico-economic and political experiences from African countries and the global view of NEPAD's agenda with reference to the politics of globalization in the 21st century.

THEORETICAL FRAMEWORK

Transnational relations, a liberal theory developed in the 1970s with complex interdependence as its central concept posits that states are the only important actors on the global stage (Kegley & Wittkopf, 2001, p. 41). This theory stresses the complex means by which growing relationships among transnational actors (partners) makes them vulnerable to each other's behavior and sensitive to each other's needs. Even multinational corporations and transnational financial institutions (banks) engage in interdependent activities not only because of their activities in pursuit of their own interests, but also because they act as transnational belts, making government policies in various countries more sensitive to one another (Keohane & Nye, 2001). This is the basis upon which the chapter will assess NEPAD's relationship with its action plans, internal and external partners.

GLOCALIZATION AND ETHNOGRAPHY

The sociocultural indicators of one developing region in one hemisphere—poverty, corruption and bad governing strategies—are not atypical to those of another hemisphere. In fact, Appadurai (1996) identified disjuncture between and across ethnos capes, ideoscapes, and mediascapes. The interlocking scapes, Murphy and Kraidy (2003b) affirmed, have intensified cross-cultural contact and spawned a dual process of cultural fusion and this ideocultural movement has led to what scholars increasingly call hybridization or hybridism (Garcia-Canclini, 1990). The concept of hybridism itself is the main debate concerning the cooptation of concepts of cultural specificity by global capitalism (Kraidy, 2002a).

The discussion into how globalization is received and experienced by the local community or by informed authorities within that community is warranted. First, we must examine the qualities of the informed local expertise and capacity of its resources in order to assess its ability to mitigate potential global influences on the local community. Next, we identify and assess the skills of the local expert vis-à-vis those of the development organization to determine the extent, if any, to which both entities can negotiate better working relations and achieve mutual benefits from the glocalization process.

The local authority is expected to possess five types of knowledge—cross-cultural, social, interpersonal, intrapersonal and group-specific, in order to effectively negotiate business relations with a transnational manager or company:

(1) Cross-cultural intelligence-In the context of translation, this refers to how much trust both culturally analogous parties have mustered in the interpreter, assuming negotiators need their services. To establish trust, the interpreter is expected to have a working knowledge of verbal and non-verbal attributes of another culture.

(2) Social intelligence is the ability to relate to people with similar or non-similar cultural traits and manipulate symbols to initiate clear understanding. One is more adaptable to a culture closer and valuable to him personally than to a distant culture.

(3) Interpersonal intelligence—how the local authority can understand and work with local people from all social backgrounds. The individual needs to have practical knowledge of local customs and of the foreign group's core values order to address the overall needs of both groups.

(4) Intrapersonal Intelligence—Ability for the individual to understand the self and manipulate different cultural themes that include verbal and non-verbal symbols and passions. Self-confidence is the key asset for interfacing with a cultural or ethnic other.

(5) Group specific intelligence. Here, the authority should have some knowledge of local customs and local administrative policies in order to manage culture shock—the disorientation experienced by persons suddenly subjected to unfamiliar situations.

The acknowledgement of one's vulnerability to control situations and one's willingness to learn and share ideas facilitates the management of cross-cultural intelligence. With a working knowledge of the mission of foreign organizations, the local authority can effectively negotiate the impact of services to be rendered by foreign entities—corporations, governing bodies, civic groups, and NGOs. Products and services intended for a global market have to be customized according to the nature of local culture and how the local resident conceptualizes glocalization.

THE AFRICAN CONDITION AND TRANSLOCAL POLITICS

In recent years, local political maneuvers have adversely affected the economy of most African countries with the exception of South Africa that has experienced increasing economic growth and stability since the end of apartheid in 1990 and subsequent democratic elections from Nelson Mandela, a political prisoner renown for his struggles against apartheid worldwide, became president. But the patronizing governing style of African leaders is engrained in the psyche of the African elite—a practice since tribes were ruled by monarchs, kings, and territories by colonial powers. In post-colonial regimes, it is almost impossible for Nepad heads-of-state to fulfill their promise to international partners to practice shared governance, become accountable to citizens or appropriate state funds without corruption when generations of Africans have been suppressed by autocratic regimes for centuries. For senior cabinet members to amass personal wealth with state funds while paying little attention to the socioeconomic needs facing their citizens (Obiakor, 2004; Museveni; 2000; Ayittey, 1992) is no longer an ethical problem, but a normalcy. Take the case of Equatorial Guinea (a NEPAD member-state) whose president and his family recently diverted millions of dollars from oil revenue into private bank accounts. According to the UN Office of Humanitarian Affairs and the US Senate Permanent Subcommittee on Investigation US oil companies and senior officials in Equatorial Guinean government engaged in clandestine operations resulting in land purchase, accommodation rental and security services in Guinea and financial transactions exceeding $200 million have made to the officials by Riggs Bank in Washington, DC since 1995. Riggs Bank has held US$750 million of accounts connected to Equatorial Guinea with too little evidence of the country's oil wealth used for public programs (www.irinnews.org, Accessed 7/17/04).

Reports published just one day after a CBS News report on "60 Minutes" (July 18, 2004) suggest US involvement in the corruptive practices in Equatorial Guinea and a cover-p between the US government, US oil moguls and the country. Though the Guinean president reportedly promised to use 12% of oil production (Guinea's share) ("60 Minutes," July 18, 2004), the public would not be served because senior government officials are a part of the president's family members who embezzle state funds. International human rights advocacy groups like Global Witness, have identified some African senior government officials among the most inept and corrupt in the world in post-independent era. West African public news media, allAfrica. com, and coverage by *BBC Africa News, Le Monde, La Figuera, Washington Post* or *New York Times* have consistently focused their reports on the reports of corruption. Since NEPAD published its action plan in 2002 (see mission statement at NEPAD.org) to address eradication of corruption, more high-ranking officials, ministers, program directors and persons in charge of large state accounts increasingly reportedly deposit state funds in foreign banks, particularly in Switzerland and US, for personal use. In some cases, embassy staff have put in their private accounts for interest accrual public funds earmarked for embassy operations, while pertinent government-related business like financial aid funds to compatriots enrolled in local universities and real estate bills (for embassy building rental, water and electricity use) are often delayed indefinitely. Though International Red Cross, Amnesty International, Doctors Without Borders, and other humanitarian groups normally provide assistance to "persecuted persons" in poor countries and dictatorial regimes those agencies lack military capabilities, a system of accountability or financial morsel to enforce justice in politically unstable regions.

These conditions conveyed to global societies via electronic media have generated external philanthropic assistance and enabled governments of wealthy nations to provide funding to economically challenged communities. To prevent conflict and wars between neighboring states from affecting diplomatic relations among their allies, nations have set up more peacekeeping forces and embassies and have established multinational agreements.

The Cross-Cultural Business Management Psychology

Any successful business relies on accountability and well-developed communication between parties—mutual trust. It takes time, working knowledge of each other's business values and planning to establish a business relationship with a foreign company. Fundamental differences between African and Euro-American cultures may not be a deterrent for Euro-American companies seeking a partnership with a NEPAD member country as many African urban managers in the public and private enterprise have been exposed to Euro-American management values through formal and informal experiences; education abroad and practical training in local institutions supervised by expatriates. The mélange of foreign knowledge (Germans talented in erecting infrastructures and American expertise in inventing products and forming new markets across borders) and local knowledge (Africans trained to think according to Eurasian, American and African customs) results in a wealth of ideas and skills that can be used during negotiation.

The Economic Malaise

I. Clandestine Business and Economic Growth

From a global corporate finance perspective, the fate of local NEPAD communities remains at the mercy of supranational institutions like the IMF, World Bank, rich governments and UN agencies which have used their influence to shape public policy with reference to import-export practice, financial regulations, employee hiring, taxation, banking, interest and currency exchange rate determination as well as spending decisions. Regulatory and policymaking changes in such institutions can open more markets to transnational firms, make existing transnational financial relationships more profitable and more stimulating on a global scale. Though workers in transnational corporations are paid in the local government's currency, which gives them greater purchasing power than non-expatriate workers, a government cannot control the banking location of or compel expatriates to bank locally or spend their salaries in local markets. As such, the local community harboring the foreign corporation may serve largely as a money-making "farm" or outsource—a form of foreign investment for expatriates.

Conversely, while the latter group may have a spending flexibility and can enhance the economy through direct spending in local markets, the "black" marketplace is a facilitator of trade and foreign direct investment—and arguably the best source for negotiating financial activities and increasing finance flows between NEPAD member nations and other trading partners. The U.S. dollar and euro are leading currencies for clandestine operations in Africa. With more than half of the approximately US $350 billion bills in circulation outside the US and a user-base of 300 million for the Euro, This is because they are well recognized globally and control large domestic markets, a high turnover and convertibility rate, and high value in world markets. Morris-Cotterill—an expert in money laundering research has foreseen increased laundering by nations that normally trade with European countries in a variety of currencies (2001, p. 20). This is the case because no African currency can match the euro or dollar in terms of value and buying power in Africa. Even if we were to consider international trade equation where the World Trade Organization (WTO) and other relevant world governing bodies emphasize farness and equitability between international trading partners and the volatility of the dollar, during the G.W. Bush administration, South Africa whose Rand is closest to euro and dollar in value (US$1 = 6.25 rand) than those of CFA markets (US$1 = 530 francs) main economically 'advanced' African countries like Nigeria (US$1 = 135. 929 naira) and Egypt (US$ 1 = 4.6 pounds) we may deduce that NEPAD would realize its programs in the countries with better exchange rates (S. Africa, Egypt and Botswana) than in those with weaker currencies (Nigeria, Cameroon and other CFA zones. Generally, companies from the EU (European Union) and US stand to make profits from African markets, (Nigeria, South Africa, CFA zones) despite the laundering of approximately US$3 million per year in African non-banking areas.

Consumer taste is another impediment to the strengthening of local markets and consequently the fear that local production may not sustain NEPAD's economic agenda. Ninety-eight percent of African consumers prefer foreign tertiary and technology products (clothes, cars, beverage, information technology) especially from Europe and America to African manufactures, so African traders who deal with such markets may be forced to launder. To remain competitive, African charter banks traditionally offer traders current published exchanged rates that are usually lower than the bargain rates in the 'black' marketplace. These banks as well as government institutions lack well-trained security personnel or advanced technology to eliminate money laundering. The corrupt nature of senior government officials and the increasing rate of bribery among citizens, all make it difficult for development minded experts and authorities to plan and develop a sustainable financial system within NEPAD regions, to fund their action plan. Through such laundering, the authority of local banks has diminished. Though more local banks are improving the amount of services, they are skeptical about giving out loans to potentially dependable lenders. Worse, more powerful business people deposit funds in banks abroad. Moreover, with new global electronic risk-free transaction channels like Western Union—a transnational financial corporation—has been facilitating the sending and receiving money to over one hundred nations, with 81 million transactions in 2003 alone, and Money Gram wherein $14 is charged for every $100–$200 (equivalent of 50,000–100,000 francs, CFA) sent to an African country, and with an average of 100 transactions per day from Africans abroad to their families, there is strong potential for grassroots economic change in Africa.

Eventually, money laundering may benefit the local economy in that funds from non-banking sources circulate twice as fast as those from banking sources, enabling citizens to engage in more petty commercial and business endeavors and sale of portable products. Even if NEPAD were to create its own banking system to give better investment access to local traders, the fact that these traders already receive better bargains for exchanges from local currency to Euro/dollar than vice versa and purchase and sale of foreign products may defeat NEPAD's intentions to grow the local economy. However, other finance transactions have been facilitating cash flow, creating a safe forum for the improvement of the local economy.

For the past ten years, approximately 100,000 or 98% of Africans living in Europe and America have sent approximately US$1 million to family members in Africa with only about 3–5 % transaction rate from Africa to Europe. The company has further undertaken philanthropic endeavors in Third World communities, building teacher housing in Tanzania, rebuilding a school in Benin donating construction equipment for primary school in Guinea, providing water supply systems to ten schools in Rwanda and one million pencils to schools in Senegal (www.westernunion.com/info/cd) and recently sponsoring earthquake relief in Algeria and financial assistance for orphans in Zimbabwe. According to the Media Relations Office, the corporation usually donates funds for community-oriented programs based on requests from agents in the foreign country. This people-oriented development approach is arguably better than the corporation-government approach widely criticized for promoting corruption among government representatives. However, the corporation has been accused of receiving more favorable rates for converting US dollars to all foreign currencies than otherwise. The Eastern District Court of New York (Master File No. CV 01 0335 (CPS) (VVP), filed a class action litigation charging that funds filed electronically between January 1, 1995–December 31, 2002 yielded a \$1 revenue gain per transaction yet Western Union and its agents (stockholders, subsidiaries, international agents, directors, accountants, and employees) and further alleged false advertisements and secret charges and fees misrepresentation, and inadequate disclosure to clients. With the money transaction woes and the steady increase of foreign nationals into Africa especially business cadres, due to relaxed visa regulations (see African government-managed websites), may relax the ability for African governments to control the local economy.

Through meaningful negotiation with foreign business partners and greater advertising of its objectives and achievements on NEPAD's website to target young consumers and proprietors, and other governmental sectors seeking connectivity, NEPAD could generate more funds in order to finance its programs.

II. PSYCHOLOGICAL FACTOIDS

Conflicts in national psychology and varying corporate cultures affect business operation at the executive decision-making level and corporate cultures (Lewis, 1996, pp. 2–3), when a capitalist company sets up business in a socialist country with a dictatorial regime. More conflicts are bound to exist when the foreign company installed locally and local partner have different investment interests. For example, in a US-Nigerian joint venture where the Americans are interested mainly in long-term investment-for-profit and the Nigerians in market share or short-term profit, the partnership is likely to stall or end in failure. And where joint ventures, planning and real-time transactions or prolonged negotiations are involved, two main cultural traits differentiating the local consumer and businessman from the

Euro-American counterpart—time and profit-making attitude—would pose problems.

Information & Communication Technology (ICT) and Cultural Hegemony

The triangular connection between culture, info technology and social change is not an obvious occurrence; it defines the parameters for community operation in the world. That political leaders massage mainstream media outlets in order to market their ideas and agendas is the reason for the huge investments in or marketing of info technology products all over the world. Info technology is a powerful decision-making mechanism for negotiating economic political and social authority. The economic value and identity of a place and its influence on the world today are determined by the quality and amount of its digital connections with other sites. To be relevant, space should have malleable weather and healthy conditions. Put more succinctly, the connection between sites (village, city, nation or globe) matter as much as and often more than, the sites of imagined closure (Couldry, 2003, p. 44) because entities identify and connect sites based on vested interest, especially economic potential. Hence, physically separated groups and engaged in negotiations for the connection of their sites must relinquish control of cultural space.

The local, national, regional or global are interconnected with worldwide economy and global financial markets (Melody, 1991) through info technology. With the power to transcend national boundaries, info technology can become the culture transmission agent and introducer of cultural traits to local residents (Ngwainmbi, 1997, 1999; 2001) and it can play a central role in the creation of global or international consciousness and in the reflexive processes of recreating human community (Monge, 1998, p. 145). In a similar way, knowledge about the world is increasingly preserved in repositories mainly accessible via communication networks (Monge, 1998a). However, the concern has been expressed that the culture of the institution exporting the technology has domineering effects on the societies that use it (Mowlana, 1996; Ngwainmbi, 1999), for the end-user must first learn the techniques in order to using it. In a sense, societies that increasingly create info technology sites make new connections with other societies but lose certain local privileges. Our citizenship status is no longer determined only through the neighborhood, township, village or country in which we were born and raised but through our manifestations of human rights, and our ability to negotiate meaning and understanding of the contexts of different cultures. Through globalization, a new deterritorialized system of centers and peripheries have been created on the levels of science, productivity, consumption and technology (Tehranian & Tehranian, 1997). It is with this new dynamic that some African nations formed a new partnership with an agenda to assess productivity, consumption, and governing policies. In its dialogues and debates, NEPAD leaders have tried to determine the role to be played by ICT in promoting collective regional development.

Media Outlets

AllAfrica Global Media, the largest distributor of African news and information worldwide which disseminates over 400 stories daily to financial, corporate, institutional and media clients and operates the leading Africa site on the Internet signed a strategic agreement with AFCOM International for collaborative efforts to help Africa bridge the digital divide with the developed nations. All Africa's Services utilizes its proprietary, interoperable technology platform to create reliable, accessible, and scalable application and collaborates with AllAfrica and AFCOM plan on a range of initiatives to increase the distribution of information for and about Africa.

Local newspapers have reported that some authorities with local knowledge, especially foreign diplomats, peace corps volunteers, missionaries, and expatriates serve as secret informants for foreign governments, human rights groups, or business entities with exploitative intentions. When there is putative sovereignty, yet foreign powers—governments and corporations—control the business of a country behind the scenes, as with France over central banks of Francophone Africa, there is evidence of neo-imperialism (Fredland 1999: Chapter 5). In addition, since it results in exploitation and unwarranted dominance, this sort of external interference complicates the rationale for recommending glocalization. However, the process of assimilation cannot be reversed, so local groups must be prepared to use foreign products, services and companies to their advantage. As they often fear an invasion of their space when foreign businesses and international organizations come to their communities seeking sites to set up structures, local residents need some form of assurance that their sites, artifacts and oral tradition will be preserved. To address this problem, they need to facilitate communication logistics with local residents and local authorities, the international organization by securing the services of local experts. Local technicians can in turn, produce the brand names of foreign companies, or pattern them according to local taste (social interests and commercial values) and, market them among their people at affordable prices. Such efforts would enhance duopoly and increase competitiveness in services and prices, an asset for the local consumer.

Grassroots Development

Research on grassroots development shows that advocates for global distribution and utilization of information and communication technology (ICT) products and services—powerful nations and companies—have undermined the problems faced by developing regions whose weak economy and low teledensity impede their ability to compete in the global marketplace have been raised among media practitioners and researchers (Kasoma, 1994, P. 77; Ngwainmbi 1997; 1999). That one-way flow of materials would only widen the information gap between rich and poor nations. Yet, the distribution of ICT remains disproportionate and fragmented, although media representatives of wealthy nations have cited ICT for more than fifteen years as the main tool for promoting international understanding and peaceful coexistence between nations. Third World communication practitioners and officials have been advocating the fair distribution of information between rich and poor nations by arguing that media moguls and major international corporations use ICT to secure new markets for their products and services in the postcolonial locale. Other practitioners have consistently argued that the terms of the New World Information Order (NWIO) implied the poor economic status and lack of sophisticated ICT in developing countries would prevent local political and business institutions from realizing key development plans asserting that the Western concept of a "free flow" of information globally, like free access to sites, trade and markets, in fact concealed the real nature of Western neo-imperial control (Mowlana, 1986; 1996; Ngwainmbi, 2001, 2004a; Kleinwachter, 1994, pp. 13–16). Equally embedded in the UNESCO-led round table with world information experts, was the charge that developing nations could not benefit from global communication because, unlike the progenitors of the global communication Third World nations, according to the MacBride report (1983) lacked the ideotechnical resources—sophisticated communication technology—that inevitably advance the societal and economic endeavors of the nation. But as of March 2004, ICT has not reached the nearly 60% of the world's population in remote areas due to its high cost of maintenance, and low market value of the local residents.

Though groups may share basic concepts and view them from different angles, and make decisions we may consider irrational or a direct contrast to our core values, they cannot implement strategies together without coming to grips with differences in their cultures. For the same reason, groups cannot cultivate mutual understanding through a sudden transformation of one group's values, but through gradual deliberate negotiations with the other group. Groups can make assumptions on the degree to which another group would approach it or accept its values by focusing on the cultural roots of the other group's national behavior.

Certainly, the new international economic order implied in the UN resolution adopted in 1973 requiring poor nations to benefit from the inventiveness of rich nations through better communication practices

(Fredland 1999: 196–197) did not succeed. Nevertheless, the ideotechnical gridlock can be overcome, by using local knowledge and on-ground personnel to address the effects of global pressures and ICT content on local conditions. To operate in a multi cultural environment, project managers have to be aware of the cultural differences and minimize cultural differences by determining the obstacles in national character or home country culture or redefining and resolving problems according to specific foreign market situation. Local authorities with strategic knowledge of the locale—government officials, NGO representatives, educators, healthcare, peace corps volunteers, expatriates and media practitioners—must bring their own knowledge to bear upon the products and services of the foreign entity (potential business partner, corporation, funding agency, expatriate, or political personality). Simply put, if a foreign organization is to implement a program to improve living standards, it must acquire the services of a local agency or expert and comply with local policies. However, the volatility of the political climate and local markets and the prevailing view business management as an at-will activity rather engage managers in the use of unscrupulous techniques for greater profit than involve local partners in long-term investment ventures. This practice, a demise of globalization, reflects the complex but frequently overlooked relationship between the local as a resource and the perception of the foreign entity as its progenitor. Therefore, through international trade and international programs, local urban communities, authorities, managers, employees and consumers stand a better of amassing greater economic benefits. By the same token, I posit that rather than impose their ideotechnical abilities on urban communities in developing regions, foreign entities should show respect for the people's culture and the right of each nation to share with the world knowledge about its interests, plans, social and cultural values.

There are different areas in which cross-cultural management and cross-cultural communication play a major role in the management of organizations employing people from different cultures (Gullestrup, 2002, p. 3). Organizations and local groups seeking short or long-term partnerships with any entity across real or imagined borders must engage in proper multi-cultural behavior by developing strategies. Any international profit-oriented business or non-government organization operating locally can negotiate the nuances and core customs of the locale to its advantage if it understands the latter. Among the foreign companies seeking business ventures, those of America and Europe have the greatest potential for making long-term investments because their currencies (Dollar and Euro) have the highest value and most consistent exchange rates in W. African markets, and their business management ethics are respected in local and urban communities.

NEPAD'S ACHIEVEMENTS AND STRATEGIC PLAN

NEPAD officials have argued that the "marginalization of Africa from the globalization process and the social exclusion of the vast majority of its peoples constitute a serious threat to global stability" (paragraph 2). Africans, they continue, "are appealing neither for further entrenchment of dependency through aid nor for marginal concessions" (paragraph 5) and Africa has been integrated into the world economy as supplier of cheap labor and raw materials draining Africa's resources rather than industrializing Africa partly because post colonial Africa "inherited weak states and dysfunctional economies that were further aggravated by poor leadership, corruption and bad governance" (paragraph 22). Additionally, colonialism "subverted hitherto traditional structures" and retarded the development of an entrepreneurial and middle class with managerial capability, or "made them subservient to the economic and political needs of the imperial class: (paragraph 21) and the "rate of accumulation" in the post-colonial period has not been sufficient "leading to patronage and corruption." (para. 25) The "vicious circle" of "economic decline and poor governance" has confirmed Africa's peripheral and diminishing role and "marginalization." (paragraph 26). Africans must not promote benevolence of foreign institutions; rather they must be the architects of their own sustained upliftment (paragraph 27).

Cognizant that globalization has coincided with the reshaping of international relations and is associated with new concepts of security and self-interest which include the right to development, and the redefinition of democracy and state legitimacy including accountable government, human rights recognition and popular participation in activities that produce collective, progressive national change (paragraph 43), African leaders developed a new framework of interaction with the world and promised joint responsibility in (1) Ensuring that NEPAD centers around African ownership and management (paragraph 47), (2) strengthening mechanisms for conflict prevention and resolution; promoting and protecting democracy and human rights in their respective countries by developing clear standards of accountability, transparency and participatory governance at the national and subnational levels; revitalizing and extending the provision of education with high priority to health services (HIV/AIDS), malaria and other communicable diseases; promoting women's role in socioeconomic development by reinforcing their capacity in education and training and by assuring their participation in the political and economic circles in African countries; and promoting the development of infrastructure (paragraph 49).

Generally, NEPAD's primary objective is to subscribe to an African-centered development agenda—one which would involve designing and implementing programs among members states—with the technical help of an evaluation system, the African Peer Review Mechanism wherein experts from different member states assess projects, processes and mechanisms set up by inviting state. This Afrocentric agenda for the establishment of business pertaining to Africa is not a new phenomenon as Africologists like Asante (1980, 1987, 1990), Nelson (1989), and a growing number of accomplished Africana social scientists (Conyers, 2004, pp.647–648; Obiakor, 2004) have successfully documented. African leaders at OAU (now African Union) meetings and world governing institutions including the UN and EU have consistently advocated the elf-reliant development approach for Africa. The agenda was strongly endorsed by international political and financial institutions partnering with Africa. Their locus for supporting NEPAD's "independent" position may be based then on two general underlying assumptions:

(1) These institutions have single-handedly managed almost all of Africa's economic and political problems by providing technical staff, food and other emergency relief and investing billions of dollars to support their development projects and using peace-keeping forces to curb the ever escalating violence on the continent, since the formation of the League of Nations in 1945. (2) In concert with the UN Charter's mandate against interference, non-alignment and protection of national integrity as any contrary operation would obstruct national sovereignty and ensure chaos among nations with fragile new democracies and lower economic output.

For NEPAD to begin realizing those objectives, on its own terms, the NEPAD Infrastructure Project Preparation Facility (IPPF) was set up in 2002–2003 with the African Development Bank to assist African countries, Regional Economic Communities, specialized infrastructure development agencies and related institutions to prepare viable regional infrastructure projects—particularly in energy, water, transport, and lCTs—for financing from public and private sources (see figures 1 & 2). According to *NEPAD Dialogue*, the Weekly Electronic Newsletter of the NEPAD Secretariat (May 3, 2004), the African Development Bank prepared a program for the rapid development of infrastructure projects needed to accelerate sub-regional and continental economic integration.

This plan has been lauded for its vision and African ownership approach in terms of design and implementation (Randriamaro, 2004) and NEPAD has been cited for having the potential to observe good governance—principles that resonate among the international financial and development institutions—like the UN, WB, WTO, IMF and other international creditors, and powerful western nations. NEPAD secretariat has designed protocols to facilitate the exchange of information and scientists across the African Laser facilities and has been promoting collaboration among laser researchers and mobilizing resources to upgrade laser facilities and design continental programs, (Electronic NEPAD Newsletter, July 9, 2004).

Other noteworthy successes include the establishment of the African Institute of Space Science (AISS), the Bioscience facility for Eastern and Central Africa and the African Laser Center. At the AISS, scientists shall group existing space science activities and facilities into a network for frontier science development. According to NEPAD Newsletter (Issue 54, July 9, 2004), this project is based on existing facilities with nodes across the continent involves active mobilization of local (state) resources and will enable Africa to exploit potential space applications including meteorology, remote sensing and satellite navigation systems to benefit tourism. The Bioscience center, a part of refurbished laboratories at the International Livestock Research Institute in Kenya is set up "to support countries in applying bioscience research expertise to produce technologies that will help poor farmers to improve agricultural productivity" and reduce the need to invest in new infrastructure.

The newsletter further documents that the African Laser Center, a network of large facilities that specialize in materials processing, atomic and molecular physics, agricultural and environmental sciences, medical applications of lasers and manufacturing, includes sites in South Africa, Senegal, Egypt, Ghana, Tunisia, and Algeria. According to NEPAD officials, the laser center will attract researchers from the continent to more scientifically and technologically advanced regions of the world by providing a competitive knowledge base and development facilities. NEPAD officials have successfully convinced member state to participate in the Africa Peer Review Mechanism (APRM). Not only have many states, including Mauritius (newest member, June 2004) embarked on the internal assessment, the review board itself has legitimized its image regionally and globally by its own composition—eminent scholars, representatives from strategic planning partner institutions, the African Development Bank staff (with a long history of promoting sponsoring socioeducational and economic stability), the UN Economic Commission for Africa and UNDP Africa Bureau

Table **4**. NEPAD Short-Term Action Plan Projects Financed by African Development Bank 2002/2003

Date of approval	Section	ADB Financing (US$ millions)	Total Project Cost US$m
17-Apr-02	GHANA—Tema Aflao Rehabilitation Road Project: Akatsi-Aflao	21.76	31.30
26-Jun-02	Tanzania/Kenya: Arusha-Bamanga-Athi River Road Study	1.39	1.47
18-Sep-02	ECOWAS: 'Interconnections of Railways Networks in ECOWAS Member Countries Study	3.70	3.90
13-Nov-02	MOROCCO/SPAIN—Strengthening of Electric Power Grid Interconnections Project	97.28	351.50
27-Nov-02	Nigeria-Benin: Power Interconnection Project	18.59	51.83
20-Dec-02	GHANA-TOGO—The Akatsi-Dodze-Noepe Road Upgrading Project	18.83	22.01
07-Sep-03	Burkina Faso/Niger Proposal to finance the Dori-Tera Road Study	1.04	1.10
21-Jul-03	ECCAS: 'Study on ECCAS Member Countries Electrical Networks Interconnection	3.70	3.98
22-Jul-03	Benin/Togo—Djougou-N'dali Road Improvement Project	22.36	34.25
05-Nov-03	Kenya-Burundi-Rwanda-DRC: Interconnection of Electricity Networks of Nile Lakes Countries Study	2.95	3.12
19-Nov-03	UEMOA/Ghana—Road Program 1—Mali-Burkina-Ghana	100.64	269.94
12-Aug-02	Mozambique-South Africa: SASOL Natural Gas Pipeline Project	80.00	1,189.92
		372.23	1,964.30

Source: *NEPAD Dialogue*, Number 44. Published May 3, 2004

Table 5. STAP Projects Currently under Preparation for Financing by ADB

Activity	(US$ millions)
Guinea-Côte d'Ivoire Road Study	1.18
Trans-Africaine Highway—Lagos-Mombasa: Nigeria-Cameroon (Abakaliki-Mamfe Section)	118.40
Dakar-Bamako: Kati-Kita-Saraya Road	37.00
Regional Power Trade Investment Program	3.98
OMVG-Sambangalou/Kaleta Hydroelectric Power and Transmission Study	4.44
OMVS: Gourbassy Power Transmission Study	3.70
Côte d'Ivoire-Mali- Electricity Interconnetion	37.00
Appui institutionnel de l'Autorité du Liptako-Gourma	3.70
Rwanda-Tanzania: Pre-Feasibility Study of Kigali-Isaka Railway	2.52
Guinea-Guinea Bissau: Boké-Quebo Road	31.08
Renforcement des capacités et développement de la micro-hydroélectricité	22.20
Ethiopia-Djibouti Interconnection Project	74.00
Mozambique- Malawi Interconnection	29.60
Tanzania /Kenya Road Study	1.48
SADC Shared Water Courses Support Project	17.76
Ethiopia-Sudan Interconnection Project	81.40
Zambia -Tanzania-Kenya Interconnection	111.00
	580.44

Source: *NEPAD Dialogue*, Number 44. Published May 3, 2004

resource persons. This non-political composition prevents a context for biased judgment and intimidation and fosters a climate for objective assessment and provision of candid results and recommendations on projects, which would enable the state to improve its development agenda.

NEPAD AND INTERNATIONAL RECOGNITION

When the UN General Assembly met on August 15, 2002 for its 57th session to conduct a final review and appraisal of its new agenda on Africa's development, South Africa's Permanent Representative to the UN formally presented the NEPAD document endorsed by the first Africa Union Summit held in Dublin, S. Africa from July 8–10, 2002. According to dominant UN media outlets (www.un.org/African Recovery) His Excellency, S. Kumalo requested that the document be translated into all UN languages and circulated for General Assembly and asked the world governing body to consider supporting the New Partnership for Development in Africa. Since then, most world governing bodies have expressed interest in NEPAD plans. The US International Relations Committee, Appropriations Committee and Subcommittee on Foreign Operations have been actively involved in promoting the economic stabilization and development programs of governmental organizations in Africa.

On May 18, 2000, US President, Bill Clinton passed into law the "Africa Trade and Development" bill (also dubbed the "NAFTA for Africa" Bill—House Report 434—or the "African Growth and Opportunity Act") authorizing a new trade and investment policy for sub-Saharan Africa and allowing cuts on tariffs for goods imported from Africa (www.house.gov; www.waysandmeans.house.gov. accessed 07/08/04). According to a press release (May 6, 2004) by the Millennium Challenge Corporation (MCC)—an independent agency of the US government, seven NEPAD countries (Benin, Ghana, Senegal, Lesotho, Madagascar, Mali, Mozambique) are among sixteen of the poorest countries eligible for US$1 billion aid the 2004–2005 fiscal year. The MCC Board selection criteria included the country ability to govern justly, invest in its own people, foster human rights, show trends in policy improvement, practice policies that produce sustainable economic growth and promote global security. Though MCC officials have verbally maintained that the US Congress does not deal with NEPAD as a governing body, the financial assistance could be tied to the NEPAD development framework of economic growth, e.g. infrastructure building—roads linking states. Given its existing policy on Africa, it is not clear whether Congress would formally establish a working relationship with NEPAD, however, as part of its duties for 2004–2005 sessions, the Appropriations Committee and Subcommittee on Foreign Operations plans to increase an undisclosed financial assistance package to Africa. EU and US governments plan to energize sustainable development. In 2002, the United States administration requested US$1.3 billion for FY04 from Congress, which would total US$5 billion in FY06—United States development assistance to Africa.

G8 development assistance to Africa may have reached US$10 billion in 2002 and in 2003, the EU and its member states made available €13.5 billion of additional grant resources to the European Development Fund (9th EDF), 80% of which was earmarked for development in Africa until 2008. As published in US State Department website, the EU and its member states made available €13.5 billion of additional grant resources to the European Development Fund (9th EDF), 80% of which will go to Africa over the next five years. In addition, despite a difficult budgetary background, EU member states are making progress towards achieving the commitments made in Monterrey. In particular, as far as G8 EU members are concerned. The Canada Africa Fund donated C$30 million to establish research laboratories for geonomics, proteomic, containment facilities for safe genetic plant manipulation, and research organisms for vaccine development.

France, whose direct bilateral assistance to Africa was estimated €2.340 billion in 2002, pledged to increase its ODA from 0.32% of its GDP in 2001 to 0.50% in 2007 and 0.70% in 2012 with 50% of additional aid targeting Africa; in that context ODA for Africa expected to reach €3 billion in 2003.

The United Kingdom announced to provide £1 billion per year direct bilateral assistance to Africa by 2006. Japan has already implemented ODA amounting to around US$700 million for basic human needs sector based on the commitment at the 2nd Tokyo International Conference on African Development (TICAD) in 1998. Japan will hold the TICAD III at the end of September 2003 to support NEPAD by mobilizing international resources and expanding global partnership (http://usinfo.state.gov/regional/af/trade).

To know whether these engagements and partnerships would last, we need to examine briefly the channels by which NEPAD negotiates understanding of its objectives and local partners with whom the organization must collaborate to sustain itself or collectively set up programs.

NEPAD INTERNAL COMMUNICATION AND LOCAL MEMBERSHIP

NEPAD publicizes its daily programs primarily through a listserv, weekly online newsletter, website, member-state broadcast and electronic media and occasional coverage in UN, WB, allafrica.com and other privately-owned websites. These outlets may also serve to promote the global campaign for NEPAD's programs by allowing companies, researchers, strategists, and students of African affairs to access news and information about daily engagements (heads of state, country program review results, meeting proceedings and working sessions of ministers of health, trade, infrastructure) and related sectors within NEPAD's strategic framework as part of its good governance policy. The deliberations of ministers and country representatives are reported on TV, radio stations and newspapers and internet across the region such transparent mediation allows citizens, decision-makers in powerful nations and institutions that provide material, knowledge and financial support not just free access to NEPAD operations but it enables those entities to appreciate the efforts of African governments to improve the social welfare of their citizens. This is not so new a phenomenon in the political and public circles of Africa, since the 1950s and 1960s when Africans took leadership positions in local government. Some African educators, scholars and political scientists have realized and acknowledged the milestones in African political economy and recovery. Obiakor (2004) found that an African-centered cultural and spiritual education flourished during pre-colonial and post-colonial, post-dictatorial communities, promoting reading, writing, and arithmetic, functional literacy and using education as a cornerstone for nationalistic, patriotic African (pp. 405–412). Fofunwa (1975) explained ways by which tradition African education (of mind, body, soul of African people) developed a positive relationship between the individual and her family, community and society. For Madu (1978) the African family represented the culture and connecting force of socioeconomic continuity as it provides childcare socialization, economic support and collective responsibility. Africans living abroad to support their families financially assist NGOs with funds and provide professional assistance for local endeavors (holding health care workshops). Ethnic groups in D.C. area helping build health centers in Mamfe, Cameroon, all in the spirit of "shared governance" and transparent development.

As new democracies and governments emerge with dismal experience on colonialism, it would be easier for the new partnership of nations to rethink transnational development on their own terms, strengthen existing programs that promote nationalism (as positive thoughts and helpful activities follow one's love for nation). Further, NEPAD should reorganize sectors that can promote the socioeconomic change like international trade, immigration and emigration policies and proper representation at international meetings on their own terms. After all, NEPAD countries are ipso facto members of powerful Western societies whose primary goal is to use media, military force, diplomacy and wealth power to install business structures in lucrative locales, amass profit control financial markets. Research by leading business scholars, political scientists and media practitioners and company executives major world corporations like Wal-Mart, Hilton Hotels, Siemens, and Toshiba as well as industrialized nations, all show a shift from global authority by military maneuvers to global control via politico-economic manifestations.

African countries have, historically, been on the receiving end of assistance. First, it was the intercontinental slave trade, with British, French and Spanish merchants shopping the sub-Saharan region for manpower. Then, it was the upsurge for markets for their raw materials. Iin the 20th century, it was African manpower supporting allied forces in the first and second World Wars, with African local leaders also participating or contributing to the events leading to the wars. Locales within Africa were used by Western Euroepan and American governments to monitor Soviet transnational interests, and since the early 1990s, following the dismantlement of apartheid and the erection of free elections, again monitored by the Federal Eletions Commission, Western involvment has grown. These movements, as we know from Eurocentric and Afrocentric scholarship, have created a more dependent environment, with Africans, including NEPAD think-tank (program reviewers and government officials) abroad, handling key posts in political, educational, and economic sectors in their respective countries, and using foreign management principles.

Is it realistic for NEPAD to advance an independent agenda and still be a part of a globalizing world? To what extent can NEPAD governors direct their respective plan toward a path globalization, and still maintain an 'independent' agenda, if they are to accept funds from abroad? To put this in perspective, we must review the roles of NEPAD partners and transnational corporations vis-à-vis a cyber mediated world.

NEPAD NON-GOVERNMENTAL PARTNERS AND ACCOMPLISHMENTS

NEPAD partnership is made of political, financial and private businesses institutions within Africa and abroad, each contributing to the ideological and technical management of the organization. Key local members include African countries, the African Union; Industrial Development Corporation of South Africa Ltd., that has financed 69 projects in 23 African countries, and has planned the financing of infrastructure building hotels in Angola & Madagascar, public telephone/Lesotho, alumina refinery/Guinea, gas and sugar project/Ethiopia, a copper-cobalt and export finance connected with infrastructure at Kinshasa airport/DR Congo, and development of oil fields in Cameroon); Cell C (a S. African cellular telephone service provider which supplied 3,700 postpaid contracts to Cape Town City in March 2004, rolled out 1,600 live base stations since its launching in Nov. 2001) and to delivered innovative products and tariff choices to consumers; and e-Africa (which planned to develop a broad NEPAD ICT strategy that would encompass legal, logistical, physical and socio-economic infrastructure, accelerate the development of African inter-country and global connectivity). The terms of the length of their membership is unclear, however, partners continue to release information on short-term action plans and financing strategies. For example, Cell-C has indicated it would provide and/or increase funding to NEPAD programs, possibly in exchange for advertising their products and services on NEPAD's official website.

Collectively, the socioeconomic development strategies of local private and state partners deserve measurable praise, so far. However, more skepticism surrounds NEPAD's capabilities in managing its action plans on its own terms and simultaneously coping with the inevitable on-going process of globalization.

GLOBALIZATION WITHOUT REPRESENTATION?: NEPAD'S PROBLEMS & VISIONS

Generally, however, the problems of globalization are perceived in terms of NEPAD's principles and strategic action plans involving foreign financial entities. On the one hand, most of its plans seem too ambitious and unrealistic, given a list of increasing internal problems that come along with globalization—urbanization, overpopulation, unprecedented exportation of human resources ("brain-drain").

The negative impact of globalization on Africa's internal operations has been identified by economists, political analysts and development practitioners, notably those working for international organizations. The massive corruptive practices of the leadership may result in the failure of the NEPAD itself, like other economic programs erected during the tenure of the OAU. Bisiriyu (2004) quotes a renowned Nigerian legal scholar as saying foreign aid in large quantities, and economic guidelines provided by the International Monetary Funds (IMF), World Bank and European Union to poor nations, make them permanently dependent on Western economies, and that aid from donor countries is defined by their foreign security interests and policies. The ineffectiveness of charity-led, or borrowing-led, development activities in Africa that NEPAD is advocating leads to the disengagement of grassroots citizens groups (village chiefs, action/focus groups, NGOs) in NEPAD's strategic planning. NEPAD's operational framework is based on foreign financial assistance; corruption perpetuated primarily by senior government officials still permeates the fabric of African society, obstructing accountability and efficiency in the management of business largely controlled by state institutions. Though NEPAD has emphasized the importance of having an African-centered initiative in mapping out Africa's future, the continent's leaders must address corruption as a precursor to effective development, then involve local representatives in the planning of development programs, generate their own capital to support development programs in their countries and minimize their dependence on foreign financial assistance.

Like any organization with transnational partners NEPAD finds itself a controversial situation because it must not interfere with the internal matters of member states or any nation, yet crises in other African countries have led to the inevitable immediate intervention of international forces. For example, such crises as civil wars in Sierra Leone, pro-democracy groups demonstration against the monarchy in Swaziland; the Aids pandemic, especially in Swaziland/Botswana with an infection rate of 40% among the adult population; massive corruption; food shortages from draught; poverty; low employment rates to name a few, required major resources and immediate international intervention. Although military and diplomatic assistance such as French hundred of soldiers monitoring border disputes between Cameroon and Nigeria; UN peacekeeping forces in Liberia, Burundi and Rwanda; the World Health Organization (WHO) and World Bank carrying out Aids prevention campaigns in urban areas, is consistent with international accord on emergency intervention such crises which could have been avoided through early intervention by local governments had there not been non-intervention treaties preventing foreign interference in internal matters of a nation.

INTERNATIONAL CONDITIONS AND IMPACT ON LOCAL POLITY

Fear of Terrorism (Terrorist Cells)

Theoretically, poverty and political instability—contiguous entities—might bring more terrorist groups to developing countries as idle and unemployed persons can be easily coerced into violent behavior for ransom to sustain their families. In reality, the formation of NEPAD coinciding with terrorist attacks against the US and its interests worldwide prompted a major shift in US foreign policy with the establishment of the international coalition against terrorism. After the attack on 09/11/01, US government categorized African states as "failing" states which could accommodate terrorists, as opposed to governments which can demonstrate control. The US Senate and the G8, as later explained in this chapter, have been providing a financial package to African countries (NEPAD members) that demonstrate the ability for political stability and civil rights—clearly principles that do not promote terrorist behavior. This is consistent with Taylor's (2004) revelation that developed nations set aside an extra US$64 million for NEPAD states that implement policies on good governance and economics. In hindsight, these governments could be seeking to ensure safe conditions for US and European interests (companies, diplomats and citizens) and not just to compensate governments preparing to build better working relations with their citizens. Such a relationship with Africa could become the platform for establishing new policies to fight international terrorism in Africa, instead of forming a partnership to tackle life-threatening issues like human rights, public safety, disease, poverty and conflict resolution. Any endorsement of the suggested tit-for-tat relationship by NEPAD officials may deepen the divide between Muslim communities (branded by Western media as anti-global and anti-democratic) and Christian communities around the world, and set a trend wherein only countries with anti-terrorist programs are eligible to receive special attention from rich countries and international financial institutions countries.

INSOURCING & IT PRODUCTS

Insourcing—the process of creating conditions for foreign companies to establish locally and boost the local economy by generating employment, creating new markets and income and improving the lifestyles of local residents and of providing a forum for expatriates and foreign nationals to improve interpersonal socialization skills—obviously has a multifaceted import to the African locale. After privatization of the telecom industry in most NEPAD countries in the 1990s, the information technology market especially capital and services provided, internet and phone, as I have stated (Ngwainmbi, 2001, 2004 a, b) has been growing, with scores of foreign providers and infotechnology companies outsourcing mainly to South, West and East Africa. This investment trend can bring greater freedom of expression—the much needed basic expression of human rights which has eluded African citizens earnings from the personal enterprise, e.g. internet café, cell phone and phone-card market most of which constitutes 85% of the previously unemployed college graduates—and could drop dramatically due to a cheap connectivity and supply of internet products.

Though the internet can jolt the inefficiencies in local firms and produce large savings in costs, the computer wage premium and income distribution will worsen when computer education spreads among the school-age population and workforce and more computer literate professionals would immigrate to the new markets (here African urban communities). According to Robert Litan (2001, p. 22), a Brookings Institution economist, it will take a US$300 billion investment on IT infrastructure for market in developing countries to experience any significant financial benefits. But as American and European countries continue to outsource factory and technology jobs to India ("60 Minutes" Report, August 1, 2004) and other emerging economies, minorities and blacks, including African immigrants working for such companies in the West, are likely to lose the incomes that enable them to subsidize living expenses for their families in Africa. Conversely, the increasing outsourcing to South Africa by American companies, according to US Chamber of Commerce and African American business websites, has enhanced job skills and raised the employment rate in the region.

CONCLUSION

Based on the arguments outlined in this chapter, a number of worrisome and tentative albeit strong conclusions can be drawn: (1) The race for globalization has created an international class solidarity and has increasingly supported corporate globalization at the expense of disintegrating local culture, marginalizing the development efforts of regional organs like Economic Community of West African States (ECOWAS)—a regional group of sixteen countries founded to promote economic integration in economic activities—and the Economic and Social Council (ECOSOC)—responsible for promoting higher standards of living, full employment, and economic and social progress; identifying solutions to international economic, social and health problems; facilitating international cultural and educational cooperation; and encouraging universal respect for human rights and fundamental freedoms. Globalization places 'integration' within the framework of a globalized economy for the liberalization of markets and free movement of capital. Put directly, the uneven nature of globalization has provoked a counter-hegemonic resistance and counter political movements that challenge its exclusionary practices and its silencing of African people's voices. To that end, the key alternative to integrating African locales into the new globalized system requires the practice of good governance, an open economy, greater access to markets abroad and locally, free and unfettered flow of capital. Contrary to its popular objective of gaining independence and managing its own affairs without allowing a significant international influence the African nation has been an ardent dependent to its partners and the international financial institutions, since the formation of League of Nations, receiving economic subvention regularly. In this capitalist era—the 20th and 21st centuries—financial assistance is normally accompanied by "hidden agenda." Overall, NEPAD's development objectives are reasonable, and with the increasing involvement of established local organizations, and NEPAD's continuous commitment to fostering that partnership it can realize most of its goals. After all, hope itself is a crucial resource for the construction of healthy relationships and communities (Barge, 2003, p. 63). In a practical sense hope can be used to explore the practice of creating positive communication frameworks (Craig, 1989; Craig & Tracy, 1995) and fostering nation-building efforts. When communities become hopeful about the future, their personal being improves as they perceive themselves as having the capacity to cope with adversity, achieve desirable goals and have increased self esteem (Irving, Snyder & Crowson, 1998; Peterson, 2000). As long as NEPAD officials and partners continue to demonstrate transparency by disseminating widely their action plans and applying available (technical, financial) resources and (2) make proper negotiations with partners for greater control of their institutions, African citizens, working partners and cynics would become more hopeful and more supportive of NEPAD's programs. The irony is that the principles of good governance so prescribed by NEPAD—transparency, independent judiciary, basically shared governance—would deprive such rulers of the means to maintain their patronage networks. As Taylor (2004) puts it, trying to undermine elites who benefit from the neo-patrimonial state or make them undermine their positions is naïve, and for this caste the system is based on privatized patronage. To begin implementing a rubric of good governance, would inevitably damage the elites' own personalized grip on the system and reduce their ability to service their clients, inevitably leading to their loss of power (*www.fpif.org* 02/04/04). Though member states have not been significantly active in implementing their development plan (www.africafiles.org 7/8/04) Africa's economic growth rates would improve from 4.2 percent to an average growth of 5.4 percent despite a slowness in development of assistance of $22.2 billion in 2002. Pledges for foreign intervention have been echoed by the UN Secretary General at an inaugural speech at the Aids Conference in Taiwan (on July 17, 2004). The Special Adviser to UN Secretary General, according to a report on NEPAD's newsletter (July 20, 2004) has urged African leaders to encourage donors, including the UN Millennium Project, World Food Program, FAO, IMF) to redouble efforts of official development assistance to civil society in the poorest areas.

But as NEPAD has pitted its self-reliance strategy with its plan to depend heavily on foreign capital and to support foreign direct investments (see paragraph 130 of the NEPAD document), it is impracticable to conceive a progressive African civil society guided by the so-called principles of good governance by NEPAD heads of state. The practical approach to good governance would be for African leaders to surrender the basic human rights of African people (rights to food, water, and energy), as Economist Yash Tandon (2002) has rightly stated. Because there will be both winners and losers from international trade relations, even if the net change is beneficial (Ebert, 2001), we should use failures to focus on factors that elevate hope and ensure success for the organization.

SUGGESTIONS/RECOMMENDATIONS

Globalization should be seen not necessarily as a political struggle confronting one nation or regions but the process whereby nations collectively confront problems and manage business now and in the future. Similarly, governmental organizations must continue to influence the process. When Mikhael Gorbachev (former Russian President), described the United Nations as a system of "unity in diversity" in a speech to UN delegates marking the end of the Cold War, he was alluding to globalization. Globalization should be a "united nations"—a source of world "unity" and celebration of "diversity." Government organizations must exist and foster a sense of peaceful coexistence and diversity among nations, as new communication and transportation technology have brought expectations of holistic participation. For its own part, NEPAD must bring together tribal and modern cultures as well as other sectors of the African society in the Diaspora in a spiritual and practical sense, in order to present a unified front amidst a changing global community. The African community abroad and home-based human resources, role of NEPAD secretariat in collecting and disseminating information, community banking systems and community/focus groups are among the appropriate practices needed for the sustenance of NEPAD programs and a benefit-oriented participation in globalization. Using the following specific elements, NEPAD can expand its strategic plan and implement programs to achieve some of its socioeconomic objectives:

1.   a. Apply African immigrants/International community factor

Over 400,000 Africans live abroad and about 95% of the employed ones send approximately $100,000 daily to their families via Western Union and international banks. Approximately 1,500 money transacting locations in NEPAD states and 91 locations in Cameroon, for example, serve approximately 200 persons receiving funds per day. Western Union charges $15 per $1–99 overseas transaction and both the sender (Western Union) and the disburser (Amity or other African banks) share the proceeds of exchange rates based on US stock market rate for that day. Since local banks have not used such proceeds to support development efforts, NEPAD could set up a task force of vocationally trained resource persons to give the recipient (family) tips on how to invest such funds toward starting and owning small scale businesses like tailoring, computer service, and cash crop farming.

b. Human Resources

NEPAD secretariat should manage a databank of African experts and a speaker's bureau drawing members speakers from individual countries and scheduling them to speak on healthcare prevention and disease management issues, financial management, sponsor seminars on how to generate and sustain personal income. African families abroad can help the local economy by sponsoring specific-NEPAD targeted projects (e.g. building hospitals).

c. Investment in technology

NEPAD officials should ensure that their investment in information technology products take into consideration market conditions that promote private enterprise, for the socioeconomic growth of nations depends largely on the commercial endeavors of the masses, especially the re-training and continuous employment of the educated elite who have historically caused political problems for the government.

2. NEPAD Secretariat should have an electronic databank of resumes of African academic and vocationally trained citizens accessible on the world wide web to enable hiring institutions and companies to reach the over 500,000 students who graduate from African universities and 2,000 in universities abroad per year. Graduates from African institutions could qualify for jobs requiring knowledge of the African environment while jobs requiring intercontinental expertise may be suitable for Africans in the Diaspora. This would curb the unemployment rate of skilled persons and the violence and burglaries in the cities.

3. The NEPAD communication sector should maintain a databank of accredited African media organizations and communication officers at the NEPAD secretariat and both African and international media should be given unfettered access to NEPAD meetings and program activity sites, to cover pertinent matters affecting the public like education, the economy and healthcare. NEPAD should follow the International Press Institute's recommendation by asking member states to remove legislative restrictions on the media, for the free press has the ability to assess and monitor NEPAD's programs and offer advice for improvement than government controlled press. NEPAD could retrieve proceeds from advertisements on member state broadcast, electronic and print media outlets in order to fund the activities of existing communication centers, like the African Council for Communication Education (a researcher/practitioner run organization) the Advanced School of Mass Communication (Yaoundé-Cameroon) and the West African News media & Development Center (WANAD).

4. Women who constitute 65% the labor force in rural areas, numerically dominate men by a ratio three to one, and many of whom are well educated should play a greater role in national

decision making. Randriamaro's (2001) recommendation that more women be included in the strategic planning decision-making process makes sense, as they contribute greater resources toward grassroots development than men. African leaders who support NEPAD must pay special attention to the demand that wealthy nations must not use aid as a bargaining tool in pursuing their economic, political and military interests.

NEPAD leaders must not cave in to pressures to accept aid, trade and investment in exchange for political and military compliance. Rather, foreign companies installed in Africa should prove their worth to civil society and become accountable to public needs by sponsoring training programs in the communities and creating more wage jobs, following all local and international environmental and labor regulations, and executing policies that enable local businesses and persons to become shareholders.

a. Community mobilization strategies

Without their input the programs involving the young people aged 14–35 who constitute 80% of human resources, would fail. Two types of campaigns are necessary to ensure full community involvement in regional development—corporal input and mobilization or utilization of popular local persons. Multilateral institutions must receive input from grassroots community group heads in the formulation, implementation and evaluation of global socioeconomic policies of the multilateral institutions. NEPAD needs to garner support from focus groups for business and trade policies that protect workers rights and basic human rights. To achieve this, they should carry out media campaigns in the marketplace, use drums or loud speakers at social gatherings (Riley, 1993, p. 253–254) and other successful methods in mobilizing communities and in promoting a positive nationalistic spirit among members of civil society (Ngwainmbi, 1994, 1996; Starosta, (1974b); Montgomery & Duck's (1991) performance-oriented pattern of group-information sharing.

NEPAD community action groups can use local sports heroes and popular artists in promoting better understanding and support for its development agenda. Gratefully, each region on the continent has a stronghold on a particular sport.

As highly successful athletes are revered by this population group, they should be used during soccer, marathon or rugby events or national celebrations (like Independence Day) to give public speeches on disease prevention methods, primary education, environmental protection and other socially relevant issues.

Though UN agencies have applied some of these methods, a cumulative technique has not been tested. The 2010 World Cup Soccer Tournament to be hosted in Southern Africa will be a tangible source of economic empowerment in Africa, as over ten NEPAD member states will provide training facilities, accommodation, and match sites for country representatives, soccer fans, players and FIFA officials (the soccer world governing body). NEPAD officials can coordinate efforts between FIFA and the local organizers in the supply of technical resources, including construction crews. A report on CNN Saturday Morning, (broadcast on 07/31/04) projected that $US 3.2 billion will be pumped into the local economy and 160,000 jobs will be created during the tournament. Though this may result in an increase in employment, there is great potential for long term-self sustenance, if NEPAD officials set up a task force to address post-World Cup plans for local and international trade between local sponsors, technicians & economists/experts in the World Cup activity countries and CEOs of foreign companies involved with the event. South African World Cup Soccer organizers and NEPAD CEOs can apply a business plan similar to that which turned Atlanta-Georgia into a leading global business center following their hosting of the 1996 Olympic Games.

c. Community banking

Because local businesses have traditionally spent their capital on non-profitable purchases and have struggled with indigenous trade, and because local bank loan policies have not favored the economic aspirations of lower and mid-scale business—farmers, traders, restaurant managers—(Ngwainmbi, 2004c), I propose that NEPAD's economic sector should (1) promote non-traditional banking methods like 'njangi' houses (in Cameroon where persons contribute an amount of money for one person per month and each contributor is entitled to receiving a lump sum from the group, per month); (2) establish farmer's banks—the credit unions and local barter currency) with policies that promote local investment in the village, city, church, or focus group and enable borrowers to pay back with affordable interests, in a timely fashion, (3) if NEPAD can agree on a common currency for similar business transactions, member countries would eventually become less reliant on foreign assistance and would take control of the development of community capital and the designing of programs that suit local needs.

These goals can be realized only if NEPAD states demonstrate respect for human rights. Also, any civil society to effectively implement those recommendations there should be input from civic groups abroad (notably Africans), as the patronistic behavior of many leaders and policy makers may obstruct the effective management of local banks. Local banking sectors and transnational corporations should also reaffirm the values and principles contained in *Article 19* of the *Universal Declaration of Human Rights*, as the prerequisite for conducting business locally, and the UN Office for Humanitarian Affairs should make sure trade rules comply with international laws on human rights in order to promote fair trade, debt cancellation, micro-credit issuance and local control over regional development policies and practices.

As the 21st century progresses, Africa's image abroad would be based on the positive achievements of the organization and the historical circumstances (slavery, government ineptness, massive corruption, famine, poverty and life-taking diseases) that have marginalized the continent's reputation in local and global business and political decision-making sectors would be suppressed and widespread accountability, matured democracies and strong economies would dictate the pace of life in Africa and its influence in the world. Already, with the increasing education rate on all levels, locally improved communication networks, the educated African elite abroad positioned in major corporations and more African athletes in excelling in professional world sports (Olympics, Soccer and Rugby clubs), Africa's image is not only changing but through those results, NEPAD's strategic objectives and development programs stand a good chance of being received in a positive way internally and globally. While NEPAD may take some of the credit for such successes, officials must remain consistent in the pursuit of an African-centered development agenda.

REFERENCES

Appadurai, A. (1996). *Modernity at large: Cultural dimensions of globalization.* Minneapolis, MN: University of Minnesota Press.

Asante, K. M. (1980) *Afrocentricity: The theory of social change.* Buffalo, NY: Amulefi Publishing Company.

Asante, K. M. (1987). *The Afrocentric idea.* Philadelphia, PA: Temple University Press.

Asante, K. M. (1990) *Kemet, Afrocentricity and knowledge.* Trenton, NJ: Africa World Press.

Ayittey, B. G. (1992) *Africa Betrayed.* New York: St. Martin's Press.

Barge, J. K. (2003) Hope, Communication and Community Building. In *Southern Communication Journal,* 69, 1, pp. 63–81.

Beliaev, M. (2003). *Democracy and Globalization: Sources of Discontent.* Department of Cultural Studies, Saratov State University, Russia. http:/globalization.icaap.org 07/15/04

Bisiriyu, R. (June 21, 2004) Nepad May Fail Africa. In www.allafrica.com/stories/20040621.

Conyers, L.J. (2004) The Evolution of Africology: An Afrocentric Appraisal. In *Journal of Black Studies, 34,* 5 pp. 640–652.

Couldry, N. (2003). Passing ethnographies: Rethinking the sites of agency and reflexivity in a mediated world. In P. Murphy & M. Kraidy (Eds.), *Global media studies: Ethnographic perspectives* (pp. 40–56). New York: Routledge.

Craig, R.T. (1989). Communication as a Practical Discipline. In B. Dervin, L. Grossberg, B. J. O'Keefe, & E. Wartella (Eds.) *Rethinking communication, Volume 1: Paradigm issues* (pp. 97–122). Newbury Park, CA: Sage.

Craig, R.T. & Tracy, K. (1995). Grounded Practical Theory: The Case of Intellectual Discussion. In *Communication Theory, 5,* pp. 248–272.

Ebert, T. L. (2001) Globalization, Internationalism, and the Class Politics of Cynical Reason, In *Nature, Society, and Thought, 12,* 4 pp. 389–410.

Fredland, A. R. (1999). *Understanding Africa: A political economy perspective.* Chicago: Burnham Publishers, Inc.

Fofunwa, A. B. (1975) *History of education in Nigeria.* London: George Allen & Co.

Garcia-Canclini, N. (1990). *Culturas hybridas.* Mexico City, Mexico: Grijalbo.

Gullestrup, H. (2002). The complexity of intercultural communication in cross-cultural management. *Intercultural Communication, 6.*

Irving, L. M., Snyder, C. R. & Crowson, J.J. (1998). Hope and coping with cancer by college women. In *Journal of Personality, 66,* pp. 195–214.

Kleinwachter, W. (1994). Three waves of the debate. In. G. Gerbner, H. Mowlana & K. Nordenstreeng (Eds.), *The global media debate: Its rise, fall and renewal* (pp. 13–20). Norwood, NJ: Ablex.

Kraidy, M. (2002a). Hybridity in cultural globalization. *Communication Theory,* 12, 316–339.

Lewis, D. R. (1996). *When cultures collide: Managing successfully across cultures.* London: Nicholas Brealey Publishing.

Litan, E. Robert (2001, March/April) The Internet Economy. In *Foreign Policy: Global Politics, Economics & Ideas.* pp. 16–24.

MacBride, S. (1983). *Final report of the international commission for the study of communication problems.* Paris: UNESCO.

Melody, W.H. (1991). The information society: The transnational economic context and its implications. In G. Sussman & J.A. Lent (eds.), *Transnational communications: Writing for the third world* (pp. 27–41). Thousand Oaks, CA: Sage Publications.

Monge, P. (1998a). Communication theory for a globalizing world. In J.S. Trent (ed.), *Communication: Views from the helm for the 21st century* (pp.3–7). Boston: Allyn & Bacon.

Monge, P. (1998b, Autumn). Communication structures & processes in globalization. *Journal of Communication.* pp. 142–153.

Mowlana, H. (1986). *Global information and world communication: New frontiers in international relations.* White Plains, NY: Longman.

Mowlana, H. (1996). *Global communication in transition.* Thousand Oaks, CA: Sage.

Madu, O. W. (1978). Kinship & Social Organization. In C.C. Mojekwu, V. Uchendu & L V. Hoey (Eds.) *African society, culture and politics: An introduction to African studies* (pp. 76–90). Washington, D.C.; University Press of America.

Montgomery, B. & Duck, S. (1991) *Studying interpersonal interaction.* New York: Guilford.

Morris-Cotterill, Nigel (2001, May/June) Money Laundering. In *Foreign Policy: Global Politics, Economics & Ideas.* pp. 16–22.

Murphy, D. P. & Kraidy, M. (2003b). International communication ethnography and the challenge of globalization. *Communication Theory, (13)* 3, 304–323.

Museveni, Y.K. (2000). *What is Africa's problem?* Minneapolis, MN: University of Minnesota Press.

Nelson, W. E. (1989) *Africology: From Social Movement to Academic Discipline.* Columbus, OH: Center for Research and Public Policy of the Ohio State University, Black Studies Extension Center.

Ngwainmbi, K. E. (1994). *Communication efficiency and rural development if Africa.* Lanham, MD: University Press of America.

Ngwainmbi, K. E. (1996). Information Sources in a Traditional African Society. In C. Okigbo (Ed.) *Media and sustainable development* (pp. 389–408). Nairobi, Kenya: African Council on Communication Education and Kenya Litho Press.

Ngwainmbi, K E. (1999) *Exporting communication technology to developing countries.* Lanham, MD: University of America Press.

Ngwainmbi, K. E. (2001) Black Connections and Disconnections in the Global Information Supermarket. In J. T. Barber & A. A. Tait (Eds.) *The information society and the Black community.* Connecticut: Greenwood Press.

Ngwainmbi, K E. (2004a) Globalization and NEPAD's Development Strategic Plan *Columbia University International Affairs Online.*

Ngwainmbi, K E. (2004b) Bridging the Digital Divide in Developing Regions, *Columbia University International Affairs Online.*

Ngwainmbi, K. E. (2005a) NEPAD's Development Perspective: Bridging the Digital Divide with Good Governance. In *Journal of Black Studies,* 2005, Vol. 35, No. 3, pp. 284–309.

Ngwainmbi, K. E. (2005b) The Black Media Entrepreneur and Economic Implications for the 21st Century. In *Journal of Black Studies.* 36, 1 pp. 3–33.

Ngwainmbi, K E. (2006) Glocalization, Local Culture and Change in West Africa: A Template for Negotiating Socioeconomic Understanding with Foreign Companies and international Organizations. In *Communication for Development and Social Change: A Global Journal* (forthcoming).

Ngwainmbi, K. E. (1997) Information Flow in Africa. In *EDI Forum,* The World Bank Group, 3, 1.

Obiakor, E. F. (2004) Building Patriotic African Leadership through African-Centered Education. In *The Journal of Black Studies,* 34, 3, pp. 402–420.

Peterson, C. (2000). The future of optimism. *American Psychologist, 55,* pp. 44–55.

Prempeh, E.O. k (2004). Anti-Globalization Forces, the Politics of Resistance, and Africa: Promises and Perils. In *Journal of Black Studies,* 34, 4 pp. 580–598.

Randriamaro, Z. (2004) The NEPAD, Gender and the Poverty Trap: The NEPAD and the Challenges of Financing for Development in Africa from a Gender Perspective. Published in www.net.web/iccaf 7/25/04 (ICCAF—Inter-Church Coalition on Africa).

Randriamaro, Z. (2001), Financing for the Poor and Women: A Policy Critique in Financing for Development. Proposals from Business and Civil Society, Barry Herman and al. (Eds.), *UNU Policy Perspectives 6*, United Nations University Press, New York.

Riley, M. (1993). Indigenous Resources in a Ghanaian Town: Potential for Health Education. In *Howard Journal of Communication, 4, 3*.

Starosta, W. (1974b) The Use of Traditional Entertainment Forms to Stimulate Change. In *Quarterly Journal Speech, 60*.

Stromquist, P. N. (2002). *Education in a globalized world: The connectivity of economic power, technology, and knowledge.* Lanham, MD: Roman & Littlefield.

Tandon, Y. (2002) NEPAD and FDIS: Symmetries and Contradictions. Paper presented at the African Scholars' Forum on the New Partnership for African Development (NEPAD), Nairobi, 26–29 April, 2002.

Tehranian, M. & Tehranian, K. (1997). Taming modernity: Towards a new paradigm. In A. Mohammed (ed.), *International communication and globalization* (pp. 119–167). Thousand Oaks, CA: Sage.

Taylor, I. (2004, Feb. 16) Why NEPAD and African Politics Don't Mix. In *Foreign Policy in Focus*.

Chapter Thirteen

On Governance, Personal and Military Power in Post-Independent Africa

Peta Ikambana, Director, Justice Program, American Friends Society

Hundreds of millions of Africans throughout the continent are trapped in poverty and paying the price for their countries' government mismanagement. These people are not the primary beneficiaries of many promises made by their governors when they seize the power. On the contrary, these governors quickly become their worst nightmare, unable to fulfill their legitimate dream of better lives, in a rich continent. These governments are well known for cutting health, education, social spending, and decreasing labor protections in order to boost their military power. Africans are obliged by their own governors to live in a constant and profound economic and social misery, while those in power are increasingly concentrating their wealth. African poverty is an outcome of the unjust acquisition of national resources by the powerful. The disproportionate movement of wealth from the people to these powerful governors is a distinguishing feature of African politics. I believe that these inequities are a necessary component of the African political system, based on the concentration of military and personal power in the hands of dictatorial regimes.

With a goal of contributing to a more humane standard of living for every African (including but not limited to basic economic right to livelihood, food security, shelter, sanitation, health care, education, healthy environment, etc.), this presentation is intended to explain the structural consequences of personal and military power in Africa.

1.   Personal Power

Personal power is a phenomenon in which the personality of a chief is the only foundation of institutions, and the chief attributes the legitimacy of his power to himself. Personal power is also the power of a statesman who, without legitimacy, but because of his personal ascendancy or exceptional circumstances, is capable of demonstrating superior power than any existing authority in the country. Personal power is characterized by the concentration of power in the hands of one individual and the personification of power in that individual. It often becomes political power when the state is confronted with seemingly overwhelming challenges. The concentration of power in one individual often leads to his becoming the personification of power. Individualization allows the person to substitute himself for the primary sovereign. Generally, the individual initiates his ascent to power through a coup d'etat, which often negates his legitimacy in the eyes of the people. However, the person/chief becomes the basis of institutions and their leaders, who therefore receive their own legitimacy and raison d'etre from him. Moreover, given that there will always be a Busiris for any dictators, the exercise of power can easily create a legal framework for justify itself. This is compared to Machiavelli's providence man sent by destiny to establish enduring institutions. In fact, without endurance, instability could destroy the institutions. The Machiavellian vision endows this unique, lonely, and genius individual with a mission to provide the state with institutions and laws intended to survive through his drive and life, even after the individual's death.

The consolidation of power is necessary to enforce order and maintain the peace of a state. People need unity and, therefore, one person must have all the power: no sovereignty without unity. Only singular decision-making can guarantee the harmony among the parts of the political body. From an ideological standpoint, scholars of the 18th century enlightened absolutism justified this type of power, arguing that it was necessary to achieve much needed social reforms. In practice, the individual that incarnates personal power does not act alone. On the contrary, he governs with the support of numerous, faithful followers who make sure that his orders are respected, reinforced, and executed. This group of people can neither disagree with the chief nor survive without him. All orders come from the chief who is made to believe he is the incarnation of national interest. Loyalty to the chief is reinforced through punishment and financial incentives.

2. The Culture of Militarism

Traditionally, Africans were not used to military institutions. The only known standing armies in the history of Africa were found in the Asante, Dahomey, Zulu, and Muslim states. In modern Africa, the involvement of the military in the political arena was gradual. No military presence was to be found in the first decade of independence both in public and in politics. However, reality will change quickly and the military factor will become a major factor in the history of African politics. George B.N. Ayittey (1992) pointed out four possible reasons to explain this dramatic and unfortunate shift:

a. Increasing **recognition of the role of the military** in Pan-Africanism: led by Kwame Nkhrumah of Ghana, this way of thinking was based on the assumption that Africa needed to establish an all-African Command Guard to liberate African colonies and to stop the European imperialism and racism throughout the continent.

b. **Self-preservation** of the elite in power: postcolonial African government leaders utilized military power to claim legitimacy, gain recognition and credibility, and worse, intimidate and deter political malcontents.

Three out of five African leaders come to power thanks to a military coup. When social and national conflicts arise, military solutions are often favored by the political elite. For example, the Democratic Republic of Congo has never elected a President since its independence from the Kingdom of Belgium. The only legitimate and democratic elections held in the country were in 1960, leading Patrice Emery Lumumba and his ANC to power. What happened to that elected leader and his government has been the topics of hundreds of books, and movies. From 1965 to the present, the country has known three auto-proclaimed presidents: Mobutu SeseSeko Kuku Ngbendu Waza Banga (1965–1997), Laurent-Desire Kabila (1997–2000), and Joseph Kabila (2000–2006).

As an institution, the military has been presented as a modernizing factor for countries in transition from traditional to modern stages of political and economic development. Unfortunately, in Africa, militarization has become a door of opportunity for political elites to seize and maintain their power, therefore advance economically. The preponderance of militarism is evident in the way national and social priorities are defined: defense and military spending usually receives the largest chunk of a nation's budget.

c.   **Mediocre political and economic performance** of African nationalist leaders: Most African nationalists who led their countries to independence from colonial power became heads of states. But their performance was below average. They led their countries to economic and political disaster. Therefore, military elite reacted to the situation with a real sense of patriotism and presented themselves as alternative to national leaders' incompetence (Mobutu, Eyadema, Sassou Nguesso, Augustino Neto, Thomas Sankara, etc.)

d.   Personal ambitions: the takeover of the political power by African military power by African military turned to be negative factor for the development of the continent. In fact, self greed turned to be the only justification for their presence in power.

A recent study of the same phenomenon in the 90s does not show significant improvement. In fact, Chazan and Cie (1992) affirmed that the militarization of politics in Africa may be explained by reference to a configuration of several variables, including:

a.   Economic stagnation and rapid decreases in standards of living: this combination creates political uncertainty and intensifies popular demand for change.

b.   Loss of political legitimacy of the incumbent government.

c.   Low levels of institutionalization and relatively high levels of factional competition.

d.   Non inclusive system of government.

e.   Military charisma to articulate his political ambitions (Sankara, Mobutu).

f.   Personal ambitions.

g.   Examples of successful military coup d'etats in neighboring countries.

CONCLUSION

The least we can say about African military regimes is that they have not promoted the dignity and well-being of the African people as they initially pretended. No economic, social, political, or cultural developments were promoted under these regimes. The only right most African people got from their military leaders has been the right to worship the dictator's personality. In exchange, African people have been de-humanized, again, but this time, by their own leaders.

Any political power must be rooted in and justified by a real popular legitimacy. There are three types of legitimacy which correspond to three principles of social obedience: a human being obeys the leaders established by social customs, validated by reasons, and elevated by human enthusiasm above any other human beings. Based on these three principles, we can distinguish three types of legitimacy: traditional, charismatic, and legal. Modern political systems are based on the assumption that a written constitution is the source of the exercise of political power.

Only full democratization will allow the disappearance of military intervention in African politics. By democratization we mean a process which recognizes a complete expression of political and civil right, and the acceptance of social organizations of interest, including unions. A real democratization process is complete when the major democratic structures are in place, including:

1. Realization and consolidation of democratic compromise by all political and civilian actors involved.
2. Respect of the legal system by the governing elite and its allies.
3. Neutralization of the military forces.
4. Guarantee of the rights of economic groups.
5. Role of political parties and unions.

Chapter Fourteen

African Reparations: Dealing with a Unique and Unprecedented Moral Debt

Ronald Walters, University of Maryland

INTRODUCTION

Global racism is a social, economic and political process of human subordination, characterized by slavery, colonialism and modern racial discrimination, visited extensively upon African peoples among other peoples in the world for centuries. As a crime against humanity, the impact of these processes has promoted multiple forms of oppression which have prevented African peoples from achieving their rightful place in the global system with material equality and cultural dignity, within states and between African states and the Western system. In short, it has created a substantial distance between the racial groups who benefited from these global processes and those who were its victims. Second, fair restitution has never been made in a manner that has matched the depth and scope of this crime and in particular, states have not done enough to replace the economic infrastructure which was lost, without which the project of mass racial equality will never be achieved. The primary consequence of human suffering will persist and prevail and most important, the construction of true democratic society will continue to be abated as these states maintain dominance over African peoples through an ideology and a social practice of white racial supremacy.

THEORY

Slavery Practiced Under Writ of Law

The system of global slavery emerged in the Mercantile system as a profitable scheme involving the sale of human beings, their socialization to service for free labor and the attendant physical brutalization and inferiorization of their humanity. As such the participants in the slave trade, slavery and colonialism were states who at every point in the process provided the legal authority for citizens to participate in this commerce. By authorizing their citizens to practice slavery as a legitimate form of economic activity, those states acquired many of the elements characteristic of the impact of slavery.

The Asiento of March 26, 1713 between the King of Spain and Government of Great Britain allowed the British to import Africans into Spanish territories in America by the British (who paid a duty of 33 pieces of eight per head to the Spanish crown). Similarly, the Asiento of July 13, 1713 between Great Britain, France and Ireland with Spain, made possible the introduction of Africans into other Spanish territories in the Americas. In 1808, the United States government legally abolished the slave trade and in 1807 the British took similar action as well. Afterward the United States and Britain, at the Treaty of Ghent in 1814, agreed to work to eliminate the slave trade in a context that strongly indicated they were aware of the crime against African humanity and the basic norms of human rights. In fact, in Article X of that Treaty, they held that, "the traffic in slaves is irreconcilable with the principles of humanity and justice . . ."[1]

The Slave State and Pauperization

Nevertheless, Slavery had an indelible impact upon the states which authorized this practice. Writing in 1857, George Weston, a Washington, DC author, described in precise detail the manner in which slavery impoverished white by their inability to compete with free labor.[2] Weston offered that whites needed labor, and as such were either forced to work for less than standard wages in order to compete with Africans, or had to leave the area altogether. The impact of white migration and the lack of skills of those who remained, led to the general lowering of the wage base, making it necessary for those whites to supplement their livelihood by living off of the land, a pursuit which was also complicated by their inability to compete with the planters agricultural products produced with slave labor. Therefore, as slavery expanded, poverty in the region expanded, fostering a great divide in the distribution of wealth not only between whites as a whole and blacks, but between the rich white planting class and the vast majority of poorer whites. In an 1862 work, Elliot Cairnes put it succinctly, "the tendency of things therefore, in slave countries is to a very unequal distribution of wealth."[3] Poor whites in the South, then, were ripe for racial manipulation of the planter class for a considerable time to come. For, as Frank Tannenbaum observed about slavery in Argentina, there was not a white "however miserable" who would not put on "a wig and a sword," joining the reality of membership in the racial class of whites, pretending to share their class interests as well.[4]

At the same time, Africa came under the yoke of Colonialism through its exploitation by Europeans in the slave trade and, as such, an internal process of slavery emerged to support the European exploitation of the mineral, agricultural and animal wealth of the Continent after the slave trade was stopped. The point one makes about the development of Colonialism is consistent with the paradigm described by Weston as an internal process of regional pauperization within the United States. If one substitutes the rich planter class for the European powers, the African slaves in America for African slaves under European colonialism in Africa, and the whites in the Southern part of the United States for the white settlers in Africa, all of the ingredients exists that explain the way in which slavery and colonialism resulted in the maintenance and deepening of poverty and the arrested development in Africa.

This integrated system of racial oppression managed by Western European states, with the tacit support of relatively powerless African chiefs, led to the modern divide between the life circumstances and the opportunity structure that provides the environment within which African peoples live today. In fact, the legacy of victimization from the triple crimes of slavery, colonialism, is that they have entered modern global system experiencing multiple aspects of oppression.

RESTITUTION

There is a fundamental reality that the ending of official slavery did not insure black freedom in any quarter of the African diaspora and that, thus, what was regarded as "freedom" did not either bring about the kind of security that would permit African descent people to mount a proper course to development or to have the resources with which to seriously engage in significant development projects. Whatever they did was largely the result of self development through personal and collective thrift or large-scale social movements, such at that promoted by Marcus Garvey, or the early black churches in Africa and the United States. Even in Latin America, although most African descendant peoples were socialized into the Catholic religion of their colonial masters, they practiced African religions in the Macumba and Candomblé, which provided the basis of collective social life.

Therefore, some Western states which have had a substantial, largely dependent population of peoples of African descent and those which have inherited such populations since World War II, have attempted to make restitution to peoples living within their state through various targeted public policies as a response to the agitation of African descendant people themselves.

Also, many of the states of Africa came into existence through the agitation of the African independence movement and have received development assistance from various European powers since that point, administered on terms and in such modest amounts that, in most cases, resembles the former official colonial relationship.

The question that must be addressed to the global community is whether, in either case, of Africans living in European, American and Latin American states or on the African Continent, the magnitude of the economic, social, and political assistance has been sufficient to close the divide between Africans and African descent peoples with Europeans or European descendant peoples.

Modest Amelioration Regimes in America

In America, the regime of laws that were passed in the 1960s, such as the Civil Rights Act of 1964, the Voting Rights Act of 1965, the Fair Housing Act of 1968 and the Affirmative Action law of 1971 were not designed to provide blacks with anything that did not exist for other American citizens. In other words, the focus was on assisting blacks to enjoy normal citizen access to the public accommodations and services on the basis of equality with other American citizens in education, employment, and public treatment, business development, housing and in the many areas where public funds are utilized to assist citizens. These measures were designed to achieve "paycheck equality" and it should be noted that in August of 2001, nearly 60% of blacks do not make the national average family income and nearly 30% are defined officially as poor. Thus, even "paycheck equality" has not been realized.[5]

Moreover, the relatively modest regime of law which includes Affirmative Action, the only measure which might arguably have arguably designed to make up for the past, has largely benefited white females and, in any event, has been under serious attack for the past two decades and severely weakened a conservative Supreme Court.[6] Similarly, the adoption of Affirmative Action in Europe, Latin America and South Africa has been fought by the European descendant ruling classes in the same terms as elaborated by neoconservative intellectuals and politicians in the United States. They have manufactured a perverse doctrine which has made them the victims and the powerless black masses the oppressors with the assistance of the state. In all of these areas, the emergence of conservative political movements have arisen to block the further attempt by the government, at both the state and local levels, to implement public policies which make up for the past. The have fought and largely won the struggle against universal integration of the schools, a valued goal of the Civil Rights movement.[7]

Thus, equality on any measure has not been achieved as serious distortions, disparities and subordination of African Americans continue to exist in areas such as: perversion of the black media image, serious diseases, health care coverage, treatment for illnesses, access to adequate school facilities and teachers, the availability of funds to finance higher education, high incarceration rates and application of the death penalty, inferior housing and access to affordable housing, access to employment and underemployment, persistent disrespect in public facilities and, of course, poverty.[8]

Modest Ameliorative Regimes in Africa

On an international level, the financial and development assistance strategies and operation of former colonial states have had a minimal impact on the economic distance between Africa and the Western state system. Their policies have not resulted in the achievement of genuine economic independence by any existing African state. In fact, the legalization of such dependence is achieved through the development of the World Trade Organization and through investment treaties which give the competitive advantage to Western corporation, rather than to Africans.

Such an example is the African Growth and Opportunity Act, passed in 2000 by the Clinton Administration with strong bi-partisan support and the support of the African states. This legislation intervenes unnecessarily in African affairs, urges the elimination of protective features of African economies—in contravention to studies by the United Nations Trade and Development agency, and, in any case, does not contain the financial strength to support serious levels of African trade and investment with the United States.

What Is Missing

Nevertheless, even if the modest regimes designed to achieve "paycheck" equality were reached on all of these measures, blacks would still face a situation of *dependence* for lack of wealth comparable to whites, since census data show that a 10–1 gap exists, a fact that is the direct successor of economic and social subordination. In addition, the most recent census data also illustrates the truncation in the business sector within the black community where, with over 800,000 black businesses, 90% are single proprietorships, that to say, having only one employee.[9]

What is missing in Africa and the Diaspora is that which was taken away from Africans through the centuries of oppression. One direction of the damage was that free labor made possible the enormous sums that were contributed to the development of the West, as indicated above. However, the other direction of the damage was that the resources that would have been used to develop institutional infrastructure for social development, the resources with which to mount a serious campaign of self development in several fields, the resources with which to seriously compete in the global system economically, and a consequence—politically, were displaced.

The consequence of Racism, both in the Americas and in Europe, as Pierre Jallee[10] said, placed Africans "outside of history" and prevented them from amassing the kind of resources that would have made it possible for them to become captains of industry, builders of national and international institutions, masters of their own individual destiny on par with other peoples. In short, what was taken away was the ability to create new personal situations, even new worlds consistent with their imagination, something which cannot be quantified.

RECOMMENDATIONS

The global system is managed by an entente of European powers with the recent entrance of Japan and China, but for the most part, a racial hegemony has existed which has been responsible for the much of the lack of human rights experienced by people of color, especially African peoples. Yet the international institutions have failed to adequately address the implications of the racial problem, largely because of the dominance of this racial group in their affairs. As we have seen recently in Kosovo and Rwanda and in other places, Racism is more lethal than the concentration of international leaders on weapons systems, or fluctuations in GDP, or even some natural disasters, because more people have been killed historically as a result of bigotry, even though the weapons of the day were the instrument. In fact, more African people have been butchered and are still being oppressed today by the racism of exploitation, a rank disinterest which helps to perpetuate poverty and disease, or through the kind of inaction as noted by the failure to intervene in the massacres in Rwanda. As a consequence, modern racism continues because of the lack of vigorous human rights intervention by the individual state, or by the international institutions to design and foster public policies which truly make up for slavery, colonialism and racism.

This author supports the existing set of laws that have been developed in the United States, Britain and in other countries to fight against racism and to protect human rights and would ask the assistance of the global community to see that they are vigorously enforced where they exist and adopted by an ever expanding set of nations. We have made some racial progress through the moderate regime. Slavery among African Americans has been all but eliminated, except for its deployment in migrant labor where blacks and Hispanics are often affected. An internal colonialism exists in the inner cities of America where poverty, crime and disease are rampant and where the police exercise social control and government has all but ignored the urgency of development.

African states face a dilemma which is that their underdevelopment is compounded by the recent trends toward economic globalization which finds that the competitive environment has intensified through the regional consolidation of states. North and South America are consolidating trade relations through the promulgation of the North Atlantic Treat Organization and the US/Canada Trade Zone; the European states have achieved a single currency in the Euro and promoted trade and investment consolidation in their competition with external powers; and the Asian states are pursuing more intense trade and investment opportunities in their region than externally. In this atmosphere, African states cannot compete as individual entities. This realization has stimulated the recent decision of African leaders to form the African Union. However, they must also be more aware of the extent to which decisions that appear to be economic or diplomatic are actually racial and seek to enhance and use the collective power of the African continent to oppose them. Moreover, utilizing their membership in international agencies, they must more vigorously assist Africans in the Diaspora in the fight against racism in their various locations.

Given the reality that the moderate regime of human rights has failed to promote equality and is under attack, it would be disingenuous for delegates to the World Conference Against Racism to tinker with the virulent oppression that faces peoples of African descent, only to ask the global community to approve of the moderate regime of laws and practices now in place. Rather, delegates should demand that vigorous action against racism of the highest order be employed.

Reparations for Slavery and Racism

Thus, Reparations for slavery and post-slavery racism are warranted as an approach which reflects the degree of distance and disparity between the black and white communities and which possesses the possibility of helping to close the distances referred to. Here, I will not seek to formulate a program, since

several groups in America and Europe are working in this area. It is imperative that the World Conference Against Racism legitimizes the claim of people
of African descent that a crime against their humanity occurred,

- because one of the last court cases of Black American slavery
  brought about a prosecution as late as 1954;[11]
- because of the precedent set by the recognition of the claims of
  other people who have received Reparations, such as the American Indians, Japanese Americans, and Jewish Americans;
- because the results have lingered into the 21st century, such that
  the measures to designed to achieve "paycheck equality" have
  brought about only modest results and that a new solution is
  urgently in need of consideration;
- because the Organization of African Unity has supported
  Reparations:
- because official "freedom" from slavery did not make African
  peoples whole;
- And because, even the elimination of racism could merely lock in
  the structures of Social distance created by the damage done by
  racism, if nothing else is done.

Here, I would refer to the Declaration of the International Conference
on Reparations held in Abuja, Nigeria, April 27–29, 1993, which: "Calls
upon the international community to recognize that there is a unique and
unprecedented moral debt owed to the African peoples which has yet to be
paid—the debt of compensation to the Africans as the most humiliated and
exploited people of the last four centuries of modern history."

In the context of the precedents established and in the context of the
demand contained in the Abuja Declaration, which represents the senti-
ment of all people of African descent, not to legitimize the claim of African
peoples to Reparations would be a new act of global racism.

Debt Relief

Also in this context, the notion of an African debt to Europe and America
is fatuous and ahistorical, and only represents the fact that African countries came into independence at a time when the services they needed had
been monetized by the international financial system. In any case, the missing part of the Independence movement was a commitment to heal the land
by programs which rebuilt infrastructure, re-educated people, and provided
capital for large scale business education and development. So, the entire
so-called African Debt should be eliminated.

African slavery was Europe's first Marshall Plan and now there needs to be a reverse gift back to those who originally provided the labor power, free of charge to lift the minerals out of the ground which went to Europe, America and Latin America to fuel the economic development of those regions.

Change Must Come

If nothing changes, "the color line" as Dr. W. E. B. Du Bois observed, will continue to be the most intractable problem of the 21st century.[12] However, even with some significant changes—the elimination of racism—it still may not bring about the entry of formerly dependent and oppressed people into the global social system on the basis of equality and dignity. In fact, if racism were ended, and nothing else is done, the assumption that is popular is that people would then be free to pursue their destiny with equal competence as others. However, the elimination of racism, without the infusion of resources, could only sustain the structural features of racism in the form of the social distances which have been created because of the damage it has historically done. That is why restorative justice in the form of Reparations must accompany the attempt to eliminate racism. The damage produced by the structural features of racism may be seem most vividly in South Africa, where the erection of an apartheid state was administered by the construction of physical residential patterns of separation. From this structure, oppression could be administered more efficiently. However, now that the new dispensation has come and non-racial behavior has lessened because of the changing equation of political power, if the structures are not eliminated, very little will change, since only resources can overcome the structures and allow the kind of freedom of mobility for people to overcome them—even to build upon them and change their nature into positive projects.

Nevertheless, the global contradiction is building which finds rising levels of education and mobility, and an increasing awareness that people of color contributed to grandeur of the civilization and yet cannot enjoy it themselves. This is the contradiction which will increasingly make peace in the world system untenable unless the international community acts now to foster change.

NOTES

1. W. E. B. Du Bois, *Suppression of the African Slave Trade to the United States of America, 1638–1870*, Mineola, New York: Dover Publications, 1970, Appendix, p. 247.
2. George M. Weston, *The Progress of Slavery in the United States*, New York: Negro Universities Press, 1969.

3. John Elliott Cairnes, *The Slave Power*, New York: Harper TorchBooks, 1969, p. 76.
4. Frank Tannenbaum, *Slave and Citizen*, Boston: Beacon Press, 1992, p. 10.
5. "Economic Inequality Seen as Rising, Boom Bypasses Poor," News, The Pew Research Center For The People & The Press, June 2001.
6. Charles Babington, "Court Leaves Intact Ban on Blacks-Only Scholarships at U-MD," *The Washington Post*, May 23, 1995, p. 1. Adarand constructors, Inc. V. Federico Pena, No. 93–1841, June 12, 1995. Maryanne George and Erik Lords, "U-M School's Race Policy Rejected," *Detroit Free Press*, March 28, 2001, p. 1A.
7. Christina Ling, "Census: Black-White Integration Remains Elusive: African American Population Concentrated in South, Urban Areas," *Reuters*, August 13, 2001.
8. Robin Estrin, "Study: Race Has Powerful Role in US," *Associated Press*, October 1, 1999.
9. "Minority Businesses Grow," Census Bureau, U. S. Department of Commerce, 2001.
10. Pierre Jallee, *The Pillage of the Third World*. New York: Monthly Review Press, 1968.
11. Len Cooper, "The Damned: Slavery Did Not End with the Civil War," *The Washington Post*, June 16, 1996, p. F1. Also, Pete Daniel, *The Shadow of Slavery: Peonage in the South, 1901–1969*, Urbana: University of Illinois Press, 1972.
12. John Hope Franklin, *The Color Line: Legacy for the 21st Century*, Columbia: University of Missouri Press, 1993.

Contributors

THE EDITOR

Ama Mazama is associate professor of African American Studies at Temple University. She holds a Ph.D. from La Sorbonne in Paris where she graduated with highest distinction. She is a leading theorist on African issues and has written several important books and scores of articles. Her co-edited work, *The Encyclopedia of Black Studies,* is the definitive work of the field.

CONTRIBUTORS

Adisa Alkebulan is assistant professor of Africana Studies at San Diego State University. He received the B.A. in Pan-African Studies from Kent State University and the M.A. and Ph.D. from Temple University. His main interest is the relationship language plays in the transformation of African societies.

Kwame Akonor is assistant professor at Seton Hall. He was formerly at Brooklyn College of the City University of New York (CUNY). Dr. Akonor is founding director of the New York-based African Development Institute, a non-governmental "think-tank" devoted to critical analyses of—and solutions to—the problems of development in Africa. He earned his Ph.D. from The Graduate Center (CUNY).

Molefi Kete Asante is professor of African American Studies at Temple University. Dr. Asante is the author of sixty five books on various African topics. He is among the most cited African scholars and is known widely for the theory of Afrocentricity. He earned his Ph.D. from the University of California, Los Angeles.

George Sefa Dei is professor and chair of the Department of Equity at the Ontario Institute for Studies in Education at the University of Toronto.

Nah Dove is formerly professor of African American Studies at Temple University. She has been conducting research in Ghana for the past three years.

Minabere Ibelema is professor at the University of Alabama at Birmingham.

Peta Ikambana is the director of the Justice Program for the American Friends Service. He is the author of a major work on Mobutu's totalitarian government. Dr. Ikambana has studied the styles African leaders choose to govern in an effort to suggest new democratic ways of ruling.

John Marah is professor of African American Studies at SUNY Brockport.

Daryl Zizwe Poe is associate professor of history at Lincoln University. His book on Nkrumah is widely read and quoted.

Filomina Steady is professor of Africana Studies at Wellesley College. She has been the leading interpreter of the African woman's condition and prospects for many years. Without the critique of Professor Steady the women's movement would not be able to speak with authority.

Herbert W. Vilakazi is an independent scholar and researcher in African civilizations. His work has been cited by numerous scholars.

Emmanuel Ngwainmbi is professor and chair, Department of English at the Elizabeth City State University.

Ronald Walters is professor of political science and international studies at the University of Maryland. Considered to be one of the most distinguished African American political philosophers, Dr. Walters is the author of many books and articles on African politics.

Index